Epistemology

Classic Problems and Contemporary Responses

Laurence BonJour

ROWMAN & LITTLEFIELD PUBLISHERS, INC.
Lanham • Boulder • New York • Oxford

ROWMAN & LITTLEFIELD PUBLISHERS, INC.

Published in the United States of America
by Rowman & Littlefield Publishers, Inc.
A wholly owned subsidary of The Rowman & Littlefield Publishing Group, Inc.
4501 Forbes Boulevard, Suite 200, Lanham, Maryland 20706
www.rowmanlittlefield.com

PO Box 317
Oxford
OX2 9RU, UK

British Library Cataloguing in Publication Information Available

Library of Congress Cataloging-in-Publication Data

BonJour, Laurence, 1943–
   Epistemology : classic problems and contemporary responses / Laurence
BonJour.
      p. cm — (Elements of philosophy)
Includes bibliographical references and index.
   ISBN 0-7425-1371-8 (alk. paper) — ISBN 0-7425-1372-6 (pbk. : alk.
paper)
   1. Knowledge, Theory of. I. Title. II. Series.
   BD161 .B585 2002
   121—dc21

                                                          2002002372
Printed in the United States of America

∞™ The paper usedin this publication meets the minimum requirements of
American National Standard for Information Sciences—Permanence of Paper for
Printed Library Materials, ANSI/NISO Z39.48-1992.

Contents

~

Preface

This book offers an introduction to epistemology, intended for readers who have some general background and/or aptitude in philosophy, but little if any previous knowledge of epistemology proper. It reflects material that I use in a junior-level introductory epistemology course, one that is populated largely but not exclusively by philosophy majors. In my department, there is also a more advanced senior-graduate-level course in epistemology that covers more advanced issues and material, but it is my belief that this book, supplemented by suitable additional readings, would also be suitable as a text for the single upper-division epistemology course that is offered by many departments. The book is in any case not intended, at least not mainly, as a stand-alone text, but should be supplemented with readings that are appropriate to the level of the course and students. Many of the works that are discussed in the book would make good choices, but there are lots of other possibilities as well. I also hope that the book will be accessible and valuable to those who are not enrolled in formal courses, but who want to gain some idea of what epistemology is all about.

The book reflects two deep-seated convictions of mine, one about epistemology in particular and one about philosophy in general. The first and more important of these is that the place to start in epistemology is with the classical problems approached from the traditional, essentially Cartesian perspective. Much epistemological discussion and argument in the past century and especially the past three decades or so has in fact consisted in revolutions or attempted revolutions against this traditional approach, and an account of what I regard the most important of these is offered in part two of the book. But it seems to me a fundamental mistake to start, as is often done, with the revolutions, offering only a brief and frequently strawmanish indication of what is being revolted against. To do so often has the result of making the whole subject seem rather pointless to the student, since it seems to consist so largely of tearing down views that he or she has not yet developed any inclination to take seriously in the first place. It is primarily for this reason that much more than half of the book is devoted to the traditional problems and dialectic—though I should add that, having once played at least a modest role in one of the anti-Cartesian revolts, I have since come to believe also that the Cartesian approach is to be preferred to the more revolutionary alternatives, and that the prospects for its success are much more hopeful than is usually thought.

The second, less problematic conviction is that philosophy is essentially *dialectical* in character, consisting of arguments and responses and further arguments and further responses back and forth among the different positions on a given issue. It is this dialectic that I have tried to exhibit, though obviously not completely. It is important for a student who wants to understand this dialectical development to become, to some extent at least, a participant rather than a mere observer. To aid in this, I have tried to indicate points in the discussion where a view or issue has been presented fully enough to make it reasonable for a student to attempt to think about it on his or her own, trying to form some independent reaction or assessment *before* seeing what else I may have to say. (This is why such questions and challenges to the reader are placed in the text rather than at the ends of the chapters.) Students who take seriously these repeated opportunities for independent reflection will get substantially more from the book—in part because they will be in a much better position to critically evaluate my own conclusions and suggested assessments. I have also sometimes indicated further issues, not treated in the book, that are valuable to think independently about, and following up some of these will also lead to a richer engagement with the subject.

I am grateful to Robert Audi, the editor of the series in which this book appears, for giving me the opportunity to write it and for very helpful comments on the penultimate draft of the manuscript; to students in several editions of the introductory epistemology course, whose reactions and puzzlement and comments helped me to clarify my presentation of these ideas; and to my wife, Ann Baker, for many valuable comments and suggestions, unstinting encouragement, and much, much more besides.

CHAPTER ONE

~

Introduction

The book you are reading is an introduction to the philosophical subject of *epistemology*. As a first stab, epistemology is the philosophical study of *knowledge*: its nature, its requirements, and its limitations. The best way to begin our inquiry into this area is to try to get some idea, in an initial and tentative way, of why and in what way knowledge seems to deserve or even require philosophical investigation and scrutiny—so much so, as it turns out, that epistemology is often regarded as the most central area of philosophy in the period since the Renaissance. And to do that, it will be useful to say just a little about the general character of philosophy itself.

Philosophy has been described in many different ways, not all of them consistent with each other. But perhaps the most helpful characterization at a general level is that philosophy is the search for *reflective understanding*: in the words of a prominent recent philosopher, the effort "to see how things in the broadest possible sense of the term hang together in the broadest possible sense of the term."[1] As this might already suggest, the philosopher is particularly concerned with broad and general topics or areas: the nature and makeup of human beings, the basic ingredients and structure of reality, the nature and basis of value. Most of the general topics that the philosopher investigates can also be studied from other points of view, especially from the perspective of empirical science. But while the philosopher may make use of the results of these other investigations, his or her focus is different: more general, more abstract, and focused in a distinctive way on intellectual *problems* that arise in the effort to understand, places where our thinking seems

1

to get tied into knots or tangles that are difficult to unravel, hard to make clear sense of. It is the presence of problems of this sort that makes a subject of particular concern to philosophers. And it turns out that that knowledge is a subject area in which the problems are especially difficult, pervasive, and troubling in their implications.

The most central and important of these problems will constitute the main subject matter of this book, and specific accounts of them will come later. But our goal for now is to get some initial idea of how and why such problems arise, of why knowledge, perhaps contrary to your first impressions, is puzzling or problematic in ways that make it difficult to achieve an intellectually satisfying understanding of it. One place to start is with a rough list of the various sorts of things that *seem* from a commonsense standpoint to be reasonably clear cases or instances of knowledge. To keep the project manageable, I will relativize the list to my own case, but such lists could obviously be similarly constructed for others or for whole groups of people. (Indeed, all of you who are reading this should try to construct a parallel list for yourselves.)

Here are some plausible general categories and specific examples of things that I know or at least confidently seem to myself to know:

1. Facts about my present subjective experiences or states of consciousness: that I feel an itch in my left thigh; that I am thinking about how to explain the problems pertaining to knowledge; that there is a large and variegated patch of green in the middle of my visual field.
2. Facts about my presently perceived physical environment, including my own body: that I have two hands; that there is a computer screen before me; that music is playing in the background; that there are large evergreen trees outside my window.
3. Facts about the larger perceptible and social world beyond my present experience: that there is a large lake a few blocks from my house; that my wife is presently teaching her class at the University of Washington; that there is a large range of mountains called "the Rocky Mountains" several hundred miles east of here; that there are several million people in New York City; that there are two main governments in the British Isles, one centered in London and the other in Dublin.
4. Facts about my personal past, the past that I actually experienced: that I had Grape-Nuts for breakfast this morning; that I used to live in Texas; that I took my dogs to an off-leash park last Sunday; that I have had various specific physical injuries at different times; that I taught various specific courses in the past (though here many details are fuzzy

or altogether lacking); that there was a black-capped chickadee on my bird-feeder this morning; that I had dinner last week with several of my colleagues and a visiting speaker.

5. Facts about the historical past that were not part of my personal experience, though they were experienced at least in part by others: that my wife grew up in Spokane; that Bill Clinton was elected president in 1992 and again in 1996; that there was a worldwide Depression in the 1930s; that the United States was first a British possession and then achieved independence under the leadership of George Washington; that the Roman Empire once controlled most of the known world.

6. Facts about the experiences and mental states of other people and at least some animals, in the past and sometimes in the present: that my wife was anxious this morning about her first class of the term; that many of the people at the concert last week enjoyed and were enthusiastic about the performance; that a certain student in one of my classes was puzzled during a certain lecture; that one of my colleagues is often angry at the administration; that an injured protester (observed on television) was in pain; that my dogs are excited by the prospect of a walk.

7. Facts about the dispositional and character traits of both myself and others (both people and some animals), again in both the past and present and extending into the future: that I am a cautious person; that most of my colleagues are very responsible; that one of my dogs is easily frightened; that some people are afraid of water.

8. General and causal facts concerning observable objects and processes: that small amounts of sugar will always dissolve in large quantities of water; that green apples (of varieties that turn red or yellow when ripe) taste very sour; that indoor plants will eventually die if they don't receive water; that a thrown baseball will bounce off a cement wall.

9. Facts about future events: that the pane of glass I am holding will break when I drop it onto the paved driveway; that it will rain again in Seattle; that my research quarter will come to an end; that the 2004 presidential election will take place; that I will eventually die.

10. Facts that were or are outside the range of anyone's direct observation or that could not in principle be observed: that it is very hot in the center of the sun; that gases consist of tiny molecules; that the pinpoints of light in the sky are in reality large stars; that evolution occurred; that the picture in my television set is produced by electrons striking the back of the screen; that computers store information via magnetic coding.

11. Facts the knowledge of which does not seem to depend on sensory experience at all[2]: that $2 + 5 = 7$; that triangles have three sides; that anyone who is a bachelor must be unmarried; that when a certain container A is larger in volume than a certain other container B, and container B is in turn larger in volume than a third container C, then container A must be larger than container C; that if the surface of a ball is uniformly red at a certain time, then it is not also uniformly green at that time; that either today is Wednesday or today is not Wednesday.

And this list is almost certainly quite incomplete. Each of the lists of specific examples could be extended in various directions (try doing some of this for yourself). And there are also further general categories that many people would want to include, though almost all would agree that these are more questionable: especially those facts supposedly corresponding to moral and religious beliefs.

As we will see, there are problems and issues that can be raised about each of these apparent categories of knowledge. Perhaps the most obvious questions to ask right now are: First, what does it *mean* to say that I *know* each of these various things? What conditions or criteria must be satisfied for such a claim of knowledge to be true or correct? Second, supposing that I do in fact know these things, *how* do I know them? What is the *source* or *basis* of my knowledge? In some cases, the rough answer to this second question seems fairly obvious: I know about my immediate perceived environment via *sensory experience*, about my past history via *memory*, about the mental states of other people via observations of their bodily *behavior* (including especially their verbal behavior: what they say or seem to say). But further questions can be raised about how each of these alleged sources of knowledge works and about whether it is genuinely dependable. And for many of the other general categories of apparent knowledge, even the rough answer to the question about its source or basis is less clear. How can we know facts about the future? How can we know facts about unobservable entities? How can we know facts like those in category (11), where sensory experience seems not to be involved at all? (Note also the important assumption being made throughout the list, one which is both natural and will turn out to be correct but must still eventually be discussed, that it is only *facts*, that is, roughly, things that are *true*, that can be known, that are even candidates for knowledge.)

A further, though still closely related question arises from the reflection that there are also obviously even larger numbers of facts in each of the indicated categories that I do *not* know. Some of these I could come to know with varying degrees of effort, but many of them would be difficult or impossible for me to know. So what then is the difference between the two sets of items, the known and the unknown? Again rough answers suggest themselves for many of the categories, but elaborating these in detail presents problems.

One more important question that can be asked right now is whether I really do know all of the things that I think I do (or that common sense would say that I do)—or, much more radically, whether I really know any of them at all. What initially gives force to this question (along with uncertainties about how the various sorts of knowledge are obtained) is the familiar fact that sometimes I turn out not in fact to know something that I thought that I knew: that my dog is outside (the door was ajar and he slipped back in); that there are only three books on the table (there is another one hidden under one of the ones that I see); that there is a drugstore on a certain corner (it has burned down or closed); that there is a robin in the yard (it is really a varied thrush); that a certain student is following my lecture (she has just learned to judge when to nod or smile, but actually, as will be revealed when she tries to answer a question, has no idea what I am saying); that a certain person is honest (he is really just a good liar); that vitamin C prevents colds (it really has no effect of this sort). As these examples reveal, it is easiest to find clear examples of apparent but nongenuine knowledge in categories (3), (7), (8), and (9), but there is no obvious reason to think that mistakes are confined to these categories, as opposed to just being harder to discern in the others. (Whether mistakes of this sort are possible in *all* of the categories, most particularly (1) and (11), is a more difficult issue, one that will be considered to some extent later.) Another point suggested by the examples is that the clearest examples of seeming knowledge that turns out not to be genuine are those in which the claim in question turns out to be false (again reflecting the idea that only facts or truths can be known). But it should not be assumed, and will in fact turn out not to be true, that this is the only way in which a claim of knowledge can be mistaken.

The concern raised by cases of apparent knowledge that turns out not to be genuine, of what we might call "failed knowledge," may seem relatively minor, unthreatening, and easily dealt with. From a commonsense standpoint, such cases are relatively infrequent and seemingly easy, at least in principle, to identify. Thus it remains unclear that they should be taken as symptoms of a serious problem. But there are two reasons why such a response seems too easy, not really intellectually satisfying. One is the point already noted that merely the fact that easily noticeable cases of failed knowledge are rare provides no clear reason for thinking that less easily discernible ones are not much more common, perhaps even quite pervasive. If our efforts at knowledge can sometimes seem to be successful when they actually are not, why could this not occur much more commonly than we think without our being able to tell—to know—that it does? Real confidence on this point seems to demand at the very least a much clearer understanding of how knowledge works, of what determines whether apparent instances of knowledge are genuine. And the second point is that such an understanding would be intellectually valuable in any case, even if the commonsense reaction to the problem of failed knowledge is basically correct.

It is this concern that apparent knowledge might not be genuine which motivates the French philosopher René Descartes, often described as both the father of modern philosophy and the father of epistemology, at the beginning of his famous *Meditations on First Philosophy* (1641):

> Several years have now passed since I first realized how numerous were the false opinions that in my youth I had taken to be true, and thus how doubtful were all those that I had subsequently built upon them. And thus I realized that once in my life I had to raze everything to the ground and *begin again from the original foundations*, if I wanted to establish anything firm and lasting in the sciences. [13][3]

The problem in question was certainly much more obvious in Descartes's time, when modern science was in its infancy and the cross-currents of conflicting opinion and doctrine were much harder to sort out and evaluate. But the problem for us is essentially the same, and it is at least not obvious that there is any easy and unproblematic solution to it to be found. The central risk, of course, is that in trying to decide whether we really know one thing we will inadvertently appeal to other things that we think we know, but about which we are in fact mistaken. And this is probably the basic reason for the very radical character of Descartes's proposed solution, suggested in the second of the quoted sentences, which we will examine in the next chapter.

One last question of a preliminary sort: How much does it *matter* whether we know what we think we know? Why do we *care* about knowledge—in particular, what is it about knowledge that really matters for our lives? My eventual suggestion will be that it is in fact not so much knowledge itself but rather certain of its key ingredients that are our main concern. But this is getting ahead of ourselves and must await later discussion.[4]

We turn then, in the next chapter, to a discussion of Descartes's historically seminal epistemological program and of the basic principles that underlie it.

Notes

1. Wilfrid Sellars, *Science, Perception and Reality* (London: Routledge & Kegan Paul, 1963), p. 1.

2. At least insofar as our reasons or evidence for the claims in question are in question; there might still be some sort of causal or genetic dependence.

3. Italics added (think about what the italicized phrase might mean). All quotations from Descartes's *Mediations* are from the translation by Donald A. Cress (Indianapolis, Ind.: Hackett, 1993). References to the pages of this translation will be placed in the text.

4. In chapter 3.

PART ONE

~

The Classical Problems
of Epistemology

~

CHAPTER TWO

Descartes's Epistemology

As already noticed briefly in the first chapter, the work that is arguably the starting point of modern epistemology is Descartes's *Meditations on First Philosophy* (first published in 1641). It is likely that many readers of the present book are already familiar with the *Meditations* and with the engaging though perhaps also somewhat overly picturesque scenario that Descartes offers there. The main aim of the present chapter is not to offer yet another discussion and evaluation of that scenario and of the specific arguments and conclusions that Descartes offers in connection with it. Though we will have to pay some attention to the specific details of the *Mediations*, our main concern in this chapter is to discern and extract the underlying epistemological principles or assumptions that Descartes is relying on and, to some extent, defending there—which I will refer to as the principles of Cartesian Epistemology.[1] It will turn out that these Cartesian principles provide a surprisingly good guide to the central issues that have been the focus of epistemological discussion from Descartes's time all the way to our own.

The Method of Doubt

We have already taken note, in the previous chapter, of Descartes's starting point. He has come to realize that very many of the things he has previously believed are false, and the question is what he should do about this. This is a question worth thinking about with some care. What would *you* do if you realized that many of your beliefs were mistaken, but had no very firm idea of which ones or how many? One obvious alternative would be to continue to examine and scrutinize your various beliefs and opinions individually, looking for mistakes and trying to correct them. But the problem with this, also briefly noticed earlier, is that such an examination of a particular belief would inevitably rely in large part on your other beliefs and convictions, particularly on the underlying principles that you accept, explicitly or implicitly, concerning how to identify beliefs that are false and how to arrive at beliefs that are true.[2] And if some or all of these other beliefs and principles should turn out themselves to be mistaken, then the whole project of identifying and eliminating mistaken beliefs would very likely be doomed to failure, since you would be as likely to retain old errors and even introduce new ones as to weed them out.

At least in part for this reason, Descartes proposes something much more radical: he will tentatively reject any view or opinion or principle that is not "completely certain and indubitable," any for which he can find "some reason for doubt," some possible way in which the claim in question might be false in spite of whatever apparent reasons or basis have led him to accept it so far [13]. Here it is important to understand that the possible way in which a particular belief might be false does not have to be probable or even very plausible—it is enough that it is merely *possible*, something that cannot be *conclusively* ruled out. Anything for which such a basis for doubt can be found is something that *might* conceivably be false and so is something that cannot be accepted or relied on if the goal is to conclusively eliminate all error.[3] (It might of course be questioned whether the complete elimination of error is a reasonable goal, one that we have any realistic chance of achieving.)

There are several stages to the resulting progression of doubt, as Descartes considers different kinds of beliefs and the ways in which they might be mistaken, but it will be enough for our purposes here to focus on the final and decisive one: the famous "evil genius" hypothesis.

> I will suppose . . . an evil genius, supremely powerful and clever, who has directed his entire effort at deceiving me. I will regard the heavens, the air, the earth, colors, shapes, sounds, and all external things as nothing but the bedeviling hoaxes of my dreams, with which he lays snares for my credulity. I will regard myself as not having hands, or eyes, or flesh, or blood, or any senses, but as nevertheless falsely believing all these things. [16–17]

According to Descartes, such an evil genius (in effect a being with God's alleged omnipotence, but differing from more standard versions of God in being bent on deception) would be capable not only of deceiving me about the material world (including the contents of such sciences as physics and astronomy) and about my own physical nature, but also even about such areas as arithmetic and geometry:

> May I not, in like fashion, be deceived every time I add two or three or count the sides of a square? [15]

To repeat, Descartes is not saying that it is probable or even especially plausible that such a being exists; indeed he would probably concede (though this too could obviously be doubted!) that the existence of the evil genius is extremely unlikely. But it is enough to provide a *possible* basis for doubt that its existence cannot be conclusively ruled out. Thus by the end of Meditation One, it might look as though Descartes has found a reason to doubt *every* belief he has, whether about the material world or about such abstract subjects as arithmetic and geometry. The reason is simply the *mere possibility* that such an evil genius exists.

The *Cogito*

Does anything at all survive this process of systematic doubt? Descartes initially takes seriously the possibility that it may be "not within [his] power to know anything true" or perhaps rather that he can only "know for certain that nothing is certain" [17]. But this turns out in the end not to be so. For as he famously argues, there is at least one thing that cannot be doubted on this basis, about which even the evil genius cannot deceive him, namely, his own existence:

> But doubtless I did exist, if I persuaded myself of something. But there is some deceiver or other who is supremely powerful and supremely sly and who is always deliberately deceiving me. Then too there is no doubt that I exist, if he is deceiving me. And let him do his best at deception, he will never bring it about that I am nothing so long as I shall think that I am something. Thus . . . "I am, I exist" is necessarily true every time I utter it or conceive it in my mind. [18]

Though he does not use exactly this wording here, the gist of this argument is captured in the famous Latin sentence "*Cogito ergo sum*," "I think, therefore I am," and it has come to be referred to simply as the *Cogito*.

While there are many questions that can and have been raised about the *Cogito*,[4] Descartes's basic claim that his belief in his own existence cannot be doubted, that this is something that he cannot be mistaken in believing or accepting, seems plainly correct. (Doesn't it? Think about this for yourself before proceeding.) What is not clear, however, at least initially, is that this result can contribute very much to Descartes's overall project of purging his supposed knowledge from error and restoring a substantial body of knowledge that is certified to be error-free. (The mere elimination of error could of course be achieved, in principle at least, by simply believing nothing at all.) Descartes is careful to make clear that that result yielded by the *Cogito* is not that the flesh-and-blood, biologically constituted, historically located person René Descartes exists, for the evil genius could still obviously deceive him about the physical and biological and historical aspects of his nature. The secure and indubitable conclusion, he says, is only that he exists as "a thinking thing; that is, a mind, or intellect, or understanding, or reason" [19]. And this, even if correct, seems to amount to very little. If the evil genius could still deceive him about everything else, then the Method of Doubt seems to have left Descartes in a situation of extreme, albeit not quite complete *skepticism*: a situation in which his knowledge is confined to this single, crucially important but still extremely limited fact.

Descartes does not, however, view the result of the *Cogito* as being limited to this extent:

> But what then am I? A thing that thinks. What is that? A thing that doubts, understands, affirms, denies, wills, refuses, and that also imagines and senses.
>
> . . . Is it not the very same "I" who now doubts almost everything, who nevertheless understands something, who affirms that this one thing is true, who denies other things, who desires to know more, who wishes not to be deceived, who imagines many things even against my will, who also notices many things that appear to come from the senses? What is there in all of this that is not every bit as true as the fact that I exist—even if I am always asleep or even if my creator makes every effort to mislead me? . . . For example, I now see a light, I hear a noise, I feel heat. These things are false since I am asleep. Yet I certainly do seem to see, hear, and feel warmth. This cannot be false. [20]

Descartes's claim in this passage, a claim that is absolutely crucial for his subsequent argument, is that the immunity from even possible doubt, the *indubitability* that is a feature of the claim about his own existence, is also in the same way a feature of his awareness of his specific conscious states of mind, his specific thoughts and desires and sensory experiences—that the evil genius could no more deceive him about the contents of those states of mind than about his own existence. And this in turn gives him an essential further starting point, over and above the bare fact of his own existence, for the project of reconstructing his knowledge.

But is Descartes right that the evil genius could not deceive him about the contents of his own mental states? The issue is difficult, and Descartes's claim here is certainly far less obvious than the analogous claim about his own existence. Consider as an example the awareness of a particular sensory content, such as my visual experience of a large green coniferous tree directly in front of me. Now the evil genius could surely deceive me about whether there is really a tree there, that is, could cause me to believe that there is a tree when there is not. It[5] could also seemingly, though somewhat less obviously, deceive me about the significance of the sensory experience I am having, for example, could cause me to believe mistakenly that my experience is of the sort that depicts or is usually caused by or associated with a large green coniferous tree.[6] But could it deceive me even about the existence or character of the specific sensory experience itself? (Think about this for yourself before proceeding, but don't leap too quickly to a conclusion.)

Well, why couldn't the evil genius deceive me about this? Couldn't it, being omnipotent, produce in me the *belief* that I was having such-and-such a specific sort of experience when actually I was not? Suppose that it can: it makes me believe that I am having a visual experience of a green square (to take a somewhat simpler case) when it is in fact false that I am having such an experience.[7] And wouldn't this amount to deceiving me about even the existence of the experience? But think carefully here: according to this supposition, I believe that I am having an experience that I am not in fact having. Do you think that this is really possible? Could I really believe that I am having an experience of a green square (or of pain or of the taste of fudge), when I am not really having such an experience? Wouldn't I at once notice the discrepancy between the belief and my actual experience and so cease to accept the belief?[8]

Though he never explicitly considers this issue, I think that Descartes would have responded to it in the way just suggested: As long as the evil genius produced only such a belief in me without also producing the actual conscious sensory experience itself, I would be deceived by such a belief, if at all, only for the briefest instant. The falsity of the momentary belief would be immediately apparent to me by comparing it with whatever conscious experience I actually was having.[9] (And, of course, if the evil genius also produced in me the relevant sort of conscious sensory experience, then I would no longer be being deceived about its existence.) There will be more to be said later about the issues in the vicinity of this question,[10] but for now I propose to grant Descartes this further claim, at least provisionally, and proceed to examine the use he makes of it.

So by using his Method of Doubt, Descartes has tentatively rejected the vast preponderance of his beliefs, but not quite all of them. Two important kinds of beliefs have survived the Method: (1) the belief that he exists as a thinking thing; and (2) the many specific beliefs that he has about the contents of his various specific experiences or states of mind.

The Existence of God

Descartes now has what he describes as his "first instance of knowledge" [24]: he knows that he exists and that he has states of mind of various specific sorts. But how is he to go beyond this still pretty meager beginning? The only very obvious way to get from such a purely subjective starting point to further conclusions of any sort about the world *outside* his mind is to find some sort of rationally cogent *inference* from the former to the latter, from the premise that he has such-and-such specific states of mind to the conclusion that something of such-and-such a specific sort exists in the mind-external world. If there is no rationally compelling inference of this sort to be found, then it seems that Descartes's knowledge will be confined forever to his own mind and its contents. This would still be a severe sort of skepticism, albeit less severe than the one that would limit his knowledge to the mere fact of his existence.

Is there any cogent inference of this general sort to be found, any rationally legitimate way of inferring from the contents of our subjective mental states to facts about the external, at least primarily material world? Perhaps the most prevalent view from Descartes's time to our own, and especially in the twentieth century, has been that there is not, that Descartes and the others who have followed his lead have backed themselves into a corner from which there is no escape.[11] This is quite possibly the most difficult of all epistemological issues. We will return later to the question of whether this pessimistic assessment is correct[12] and still later to the issue of whether there are viable epistemological approaches that can somehow avoid the issue entirely.[13] For the moment, our task is to examine the general structure of Descartes's own approach.

Considered at an abstract level, Descartes's strategy is to argue that (1) the fact that the content of his mental states has a certain feature (or features) can only be *explained* by supposing that (2) that feature is caused by and correctly represents something existing outside of his mind. Since he already knows that his mental states have the specific content that they do, he can then infer that the external cause in question must exist. What is needed then is a defensible specific instance of this general pattern of argument.

Descartes considers briefly [26–27] the possibility that he might be able to infer from (1a) the fact that he has perceptual ideas of various kinds of material objects to (2a) the existence of actual external objects that those ideas resemble[14] and that produce them. But to be justified in claiming that facts of the sort indicated by (1a) can *only* be explained by facts of the sort indicated by (2a), he would need some background premise or principle of inference to this effect, one that he somehow *knows* to be true if he is to thereby know the resulting conclusion. According to Descartes, however, his reason for thinking (prior to the doubt) that facts of the sort indicated by (1a) must be explained by facts of the sort indicated by (2a) is only that he "has been so taught by nature," that is, that he is "driven by a spontaneous impulse to believe this," an impulse that he eventually characterizes dismissively as "blind." And this, he argues, is plainly not good enough. Such spontaneous impulses have often led him astray; and (a deeper point that is only suggested but not really stated explicitly) they involve no insight into how or why the claim in question must be true.

The specific argument that Descartes eventually endorses [28–34] is instead that (1b) he has an idea of God, understood as "a certain substance that is infinite, independent, supremely intelligent and supremely powerful, and that created [him] along with everything else that exists," and that the existence of this particular idea can only be explained by supposing that (2b) it is ultimately caused by a being actually having those characteristics, that is, by God himself (or herself), who therefore must exist. (And, as we will eventually see, it is by appeal to the supposed fact of God's existence that Descartes attempts to reconstruct his other knowledge of external reality in a way that is allegedly free from error.)

This argument also obviously requires some sort of background premise or principle that establishes that (1b) can only be explained by supposing that (2b) is true. Unfortunately, the principle that Descartes actually suggests is notoriously implausible, indeed difficult to really make very clear sense of. It is the principle that "there must be at least as much reality in the efficient and total cause as there is in the effect of that same cause" [28]. Here "reality" means something like *perfection*; and the sorts of reality to which the principle applies are supposed to include both "formal reality," that is, the reality (or perfection) that a thing has by virtue of its actual existence and qualities, and "objective reality," that is, the reality (or perfection) that an *idea* supposedly has by virtue of the formal reality that what it represents would have, if it existed.[15] The suggestion is then that these two seemingly very different sorts of "reality" (or perfection) are nonetheless on a par from the standpoint of causation, that is, that what causes an idea of something must have as much reality (formal or objective) as the object represented by that idea would have; and hence that the objective reality (or perfection) of Descartes's idea of God can ultimately be explained (since an infinite chain of ideas is impossible) only by the existence of something having the same degree of *formal* reality (or perfection) as the idea has *objective* reality (or perfection), that is, by the actual existence of God.

The "Light of Nature"

There is no way, in my judgment, to make either the foregoing argument or the causal principle that underlies it at all plausible, the most obvious problem being that merely objective reality seems obviously easier, "cheaper" to produce than formal reality, thus allowing the idea of God to be produced by something much less exalted in its characteristics than God himself (or herself), for example, by human imagination. Our immediate concern, however, is to understand the epistemological status that this causal principle is supposed by Descartes to have—even though he is surely wrong that it actually has it. Descartes's claim is that the causal principle has a status that is different from and epistemologically superior to that of the principle discussed earlier concerning ideas of material objects and the objects that they supposedly resemble. Whereas his belief in the latter principle results merely from a spontaneous but "blind" impulse, the causal principle is revealed to him by what he refers to as the "light of nature," whose results "cannot in any way be doubtful" [26].

But what exactly is this "light of nature," and why are the beliefs or convictions that it produces supposed to have this status? Descartes refers to it as a cognitive "faculty" and says that "there can be no other faculty that [he] can trust as much as this light and which could teach that [the things revealed by the light of reason] are not true" [26–27]. Somewhat more helpfully, he describes the results produced by this faculty as "evident" and as "manifestly true" [28]. The underlying idea seems to be that the causal principle and other beliefs and convictions (if there are any) that result from the "light of nature" are *self-evidently* true, that is, are things that can be seen to be true simply by thinking about their content. It is this self-evidence that Descartes somewhat picturesquely describes as being revealed by the "light of nature." And in virtue of being self-evident, beliefs or convictions having the status that the causal principle is alleged to have can seemingly be known independently of any reliance on sensory and introspective experience: known *a priori*, as later philosophers would put it (though Descartes does not actually use this phrase).

To repeat, it is more than doubtful that Descartes's causal principle actually has this status. But even if this particular candidate for the status of self-evidence is unsuccessful, it seems pretty obvious on reflection that Descartes needs *something* having this general sort of status if he is going to infer successfully from the contingent fact that he has such-and-such specific mental states (especially states of sensory experience) to the existence of specific kinds of external, especially material reality. Such an inference will, as we have already seen, require a *known* connecting principle of some sort, a principle saying that if someone has mental states with those specific contents, then it follows (somehow) that a certain sort of external reality must exist. But how is any such principle to be known? To say that it too is inferred from the fact that Descartes has mental states with various specific contents would mean that the knowledge of this principle would have to depend on *another* known connecting principle, one saying this time that if certain specific mental contents occur then the first connecting principle must be true. And then how is this second principle itself to be known? To say that it is also known in this same way would then require a *third* known connecting principle, and so on, leading to an infinite and apparently vicious *regress* of such principles, each dependent on the next, none of which would ultimately be known, since the series could never be completed. And the only apparent way to avoid this regress is to say that *some* principle (and it may as well be the first one in the sequence) can be known without reliance on this sort of inference, that is, known independently of the fact that Descartes has certain specific mental, especially sensory states.[16] And the only way that this can apparently be so is if the principle is self-evident in the way just described.[17]

If Descartes is right that there are beliefs or principles having this status, then he has seemingly identified a *second* sort of possible knowledge that he can use as a starting point for further reconstruction, even if the specific instance he appeals to is highly dubious: if there are claims or principles that are genuinely self-evident, then they can be used to supplement his knowledge of the contents of his own mental states (and of his own existence), thus possibly providing a basis for inference to further knowledge, including knowledge of the material world. This idea of self-evidence also raises various problems and issues that will be taken up later.[18] But there is one specific difficulty, growing out of Descartes's own position, that needs to be mentioned now, in concluding the present section.

In developing the idea of self-evidence that seems to underlie Descartes's appeal to the "light of nature," we have temporarily lost sight of the specific problem that motivates his whole discussion, namely the concern that his various beliefs and convictions might result from the actions of the envisaged evil genius who uses all of his power to deceive. This is indeed pretty much the way that Descartes himself proceeds, but we must now ask the obvious question: Couldn't the evil genius deceive Descartes about the causal principle itself, making it *seem* to be self-evident, *seem* to be revealed by the "light of nature," even though it is actually false (and analogously for any other allegedly self-evident principle to which Descartes might appeal)? Indeed, at a point prior to the specific discussion of the causal principle and of the resulting argument for God's existence, Descartes himself lends force to this question by mentioning the truth of the proposition that two plus three equals five (or rather, equivalently, the falsehood of the proposition that two plus three does not equal five), surely an obvious example of a seemingly self-evident claim, as something of which he cannot be certain until the worry about the evil genius has somehow been laid to rest [25].[19]

Moreover, reflection on this point suggests an even deeper problem for Descartes's position: not only is it far from clear that self-evident claims can escape the doubt that results from the evil genius hypothesis, but even worse, Descartes's attempt to meet this doubt turns out to be a circular, question-begging argument (involving the so-called Cartesian circle). Descartes proposes to alleviate the doubt by proving the existence of a perfectly good God, who is therefore not a deceiver, and whose existence thus rules out the existence of an all-powerful evil genius. The proof relies, as we have seen, on the causal principle, which in turn depends on the underlying principle that self-evident claims revealed by the "light of nature" are true. But this last principle is not secure from doubt, according to Descartes himself, as long as the existence of the evil genius has not been ruled out. The resulting circular argument thus moves from the general principle that self-evident claims are true to the specific causal principle to the existence of a nondeceiving God to the nonexistence of the evil genius to the conclusion that self-evident claims are true and can be trusted. It thus establishes the nonexistence of the evil genius only by relying on a general principle that cannot be known to be trustworthy until that nonexistence has already been established, thus rendering the argument circular and so futile.

Though this fatal objection to Descartes's actual argument is quite clear, it is less clear what further conclusions we should draw from it. While it might seem at first to suggest that the practice of accepting claims and principles on the basis of their supposed self-evidence does not yield knowledge after all and accordingly should be rejected, it is unclear, as Descartes himself suggests in the passage quoted earlier, what the alternative to self-evidence might be, at least with regard to beliefs or principles warranting inferences that go beyond the contents of one's own mental states. Such beliefs or principles cannot be justified by appeal to the mental states that they attempt to go beyond, and self-evidence seems to be the only other possibility. Again the threat of skepticism looms.

But *perhaps* the right conclusion is that Descartes's implicit standard for knowledge is too demanding, that is, that knowledge does not after all require overcoming all *possible* doubt. We will return to this issue later.[20] For now, we turn to an examination of how Descartes, having (as he supposes) established the existence of a nondeceiving God (and so having eliminated the possibility of the evil genius), tries to reconstruct the rest of his knowledge, in particular knowledge of the material world.

Knowledge of the Material World

The account of knowledge of the material world that Descartes offers in the last of the six *Meditations* is in fact disappointingly thin. We have already taken brief note of the central theme: that the God whose existence has allegedly been established, being perfectly good, cannot be a deceiver. And since God "has given [him] a great inclination to believe" that his sensory ideas "issue from corporeal things," Descartes says that he cannot see "how God could be understood not to be a deceiver, if these ideas were to issue from a source other than corporeal things," which accordingly must exist [52].

Even this most minimal conclusion about the material world could hardly be more shaky, relying as it does on proofs of the existence of God that few other than Descartes would accept. But even if this problem is provisionally set aside, a further, more immediate question is how much he can know in this way about such "corporeal things" beyond the bare alleged fact of their existence. Descartes can hardly claim that God's not being a deceiver means that all of the specific beliefs about the material world that he or we arrive at via sensory experience are guaranteed to be correct, since it is too obvious, to him as to us, that these beliefs are often internally contradictory. But then which, if any, of his or our more specific beliefs about the material world, beliefs about the existence of specific sorts objects in particular places at particular times, can be salvaged from the doubt on this basis?

Descartes makes a number of remarks that bear on this question, but none that yield a very clear and definite answer. The main ones are the following: First, since our "sensory grasp" of material objects "is in many cases very obscure and confused," we have no reason to think that "all bodies exist exactly as I perceive them by sense" [52]. Second, we can know that material bodies have all of the features that are clearly and distinctly understood, "that is, everything, considered in a general sense, that is encompassed in the object of pure mathematics" [52]. This seems to mean only that we can know that material objects have the general kinds of qualities subsequently labeled "primary qualities" (by John Locke[21] and others), such qualities as size, shape, and motion, but not necessarily that we can know that specific instances of these qualities are present in a particular case ("for example, that the sun is of such and such a size or shape"). Third, for other kinds of perceived qualities, the ones that do not lend themselves to mathematical measurement ("colors, sounds, odors, tastes, levels of heat, . . . grades of roughness, and the like"), we can conclude only "that in the bodies from which these different perceptions proceed there are differences [of some sort] corresponding to the different perceptions—though perhaps the latter do not resemble [that is, are not accurately represented by] the former" [53]. Fourth, our perceptions are still adequate to the primary purpose of "signifying to the mind what things are useful or harmful" to the person, even though they tell use nothing about "the essence of bodies located outside us" (that is, nothing very specific about the true natures of material bodies) "except quite obscurely and confusedly" [55]. Descartes sums all of this up by saying that we should not doubt that there is "some truth" in our perceptions, adding that the fact that God is not a deceiver means that where there is falsity in our opinions, he must have also given us a faculty that allows us, at least in principle, to correct our mistakes [53].

Thus, despite the rather upbeat tone on which the *Meditations* ends, Descartes's attempted reconstruction of our knowledge actually salvages little that is very specific from the doubt induced by the evil genius hypothesis, and thus leaves us in a state of severe, albeit not total skepticism with regard to knowledge of the material world. We will have to consider in later chapters[22] whether it is possible to do any better on this regard.

It is worth noting in passing, however, that there are at least traces in Descartes's discussion of an argument that might prove more successful and that at least avoids Descartes's extremely dubious reliance on theology. At certain points in his discussion, Descartes notices two important facts about our sensory experiences of the material world: First, our sensory experience is involuntary, independent of our will [26, 49]. Second, our various sensory experiences are, in general, related to each other in such a way as to fit together into a cohesive whole, thus differing significantly from the fragmentary experiences characteristic of dreams [58–59]. Taken together, these two facts seem to demand *some* sort of explanation (think about why this is so), with the claim that the experiences in question are systematically caused by and are reflections of an independently existing world representing at least one obvious explanatory possibility.[23] We will consider later whether or not this general sort of argument has any real hope of success.[24]

The Principles of Cartesian Epistemology

On the basis of the foregoing discussion, we are now in a position to formulate the central principles or basic assumptions of Cartesian epistemology, principles that have largely shaped the subsequent 300-plus years of epistemological discussion (though often, especially in recent years, only by providing a target for criticism):

1. *The concept of knowledge.* The view that has been standardly ascribed to Descartes is that only beliefs that are *infallible*, beliefs that are *guaranteed* to be true, can really count as knowledge. Descartes never actually states such a view, but the way that he employs the idea of knowledge in relation to the doubt suggests it pretty clearly. (Notice that the propositions that are the objects of such beliefs need not be *necessary* truths, that is, need not be true in every possible world: my own existence is, alas, merely contingent, but I still cannot, as the *Cogito* argument shows, be mistaken about it.) Presumably the person who has knowledge must actually have the infallible belief in question; and Descartes seems to suggest that this belief must be very strong: he or she must be *incapable of reasonably doubting* that the proposition in question is true. And finally, it seems clear that for Descartes the person must realize that the belief is infallible, must see or grasp the *reason* why its truth is guaranteed (since a belief that is in fact infallible but not recognized as such could still be doubted). Thus we have the following three-part Cartesian account of knowledge: knowledge is a strong or certain *belief* for which the person has a *reason*[25] that guarantees *truth*.

2. *The rational or* a priori *basis of knowledge.* One initial basis for knowledge is provided by claims that are revealed by the "natural light," that is, that are self-evident. Claims that have this status are knowable *a priori*, without reliance on sensory or introspective experience. Things known in this way thus provide one starting point or *foundation* for knowledge, on the basis of which other kinds of knowledge, including most importantly knowledge of the material world, can perhaps be inferred.

3. *The empirical basis of knowledge.* According to Descartes, the specific contents of one's own conscious states of mind, including beliefs, desires, sensory states, and many others, are known with the same certainty as one's own existence. This knowledge resulting from *immediate experience* thus provides a second starting point or *foundation* for further knowledge.

4. *The inference to the external, material world.* Everything else that we know, especially knowledge of the material world, is known via inference from these two foundational elements. The general form of such an inference that Descartes's discussion suggests is an *explanatory* inference, in which the reason for accepting various claims about the material world is that they provide the best explanation for facts about the contents of our mental states, especially our sensory states, with this inference being governed by self-evident principles. Descartes's own version of this inference uses the existence of God as an intermediate step and is extremely dubious. But there is at least a hint of a different version, appealing to the involuntary and cohesive character of our sensory experience, that *might* prove more successful.

Whether it is possible to build a tenable epistemology around these principles, despite Descartes's own rather conspicuous failure to do so, is an issue that occupies us in various ways for most of the present book. The upshot of most recent philosophical opinion is that the answer to this question is "no," that an acceptable epistemology, if possible at all, will have to depart very substantially from these Cartesian principles. My own belief is that this conclusion has been too hastily drawn and in fact that the principles of Cartesian epistemology are, when appropriately generalized and supplemented and with only minor corrections, still quite defensible as the basis of a satisfactory epistemological account—though it takes most of the rest of the book to make even a preliminary case for this conclusion. Subsequent chapters in part one consider the issues raised by each of these principles in the order listed, though with a digression after the first to deal with an important issue that Descartes does not consider and a digression at the end to deal with some further questions. In part two, we then consider the most important of the contemporary criticisms of and alternatives to the Cartesian epistemological program.

Notes

1. "Cartesian" is just the adjective meaning "belonging to or pertaining to Descartes."

2. Try to decide for yourself whether this is right. Consider some specific examples of things you believe and try to figure out how you might decide whether they are mistaken (assuming that you can manage to take this possibility seriously).

3. Here again, try to see how this would apply to some of your own beliefs. Pick out some examples of things you believe, preferably ones that seem quite secure and unquestionable, and see if you can imagine possible ways in which they might still be false (remembering that these need not be plausible or reasonable, just *possible*).

4. Just what sort of an argument is it, if indeed it should be viewed as an argument at all? What is its premise? If it is "I think," as the "*Cogito ergo sum*" formulation suggests, then what entitles Descartes to this premise? And what is the status of the conclusion supposed to be, according to Descartes? He seems to suggest that it is *necessarily true*, but how can the fact that a particular person exists, even if restricted in the way that Descartes proceeds to restrict it (to his existence as a thinking thing only), be a necessary truth: something that has to be true and that couldn't be false, or, as it is most standardly put, something true in any possible world? (Can you think of examples of truths that *are* necessary in this way? Consider, for example, the proposition that 2 + 3 = 5. Could this have been false in some possible world or situation?)

5. It seems unnecessary to ascribe gender to the evil genius.

6. Exactly what the relevant relation here is will be considered in more detail later, in chapter 7.

7. Notice that this assumes that such a belief and such an experience are distinct mental states, that having the former is not just the very same thing as having the latter. Does this seem right to you?

8. I might of course misunderstand the *words* "green square" (maybe I think that "green" means the color of ripe apples) and believe a proposition that I mistakenly think can be expressed using these words, but which is really expressed correctly by saying that I am having an experience of a red square (suppose that this last claim is true). But then I don't really have the belief originally in question, the belief that I am experiencing a green square; instead I have the belief that I am experiencing a red square together with a mistaken belief about how to correctly express this latter belief in English.

9. But couldn't the evil genius, being all powerful, bring it about that I simply fail to notice the discrepancy between my belief and my experience—even though I am directly conscious of both? Can't it just be stipulated that it *somehow* does this? Maybe so, but it is hard to be sure that this is really possible if we have no idea at all of how it would work.

10. See chapters 6 and 9.

11. This has been thought to be so even without reliance on the problem of the "Cartesian circle" that afflicts Descartes's specific view (see below).

12. See chapter 7.

13. See chapters 9–12.

14. As Berkeley noticed later on, albeit without fully understanding its significance, talk of *resemblance* between ideas and objects cannot be taken literally, since ideas cannot literally have at least most of the features that they depict objects as having; for example, an *idea* could not be literally solid or hot. Thus such talk of resemblance must be taken as a somewhat misleading way of talking about the fact that an object actually has those features that an idea *represents* or *depicts* it as having.

15. Thus a specific kind of object or entity, for example, a pine tree, is supposed to have a certain degree of *formal* reality, corresponding to how perfect a kind of entity it is; and the corresponding idea, the idea of a pine tree, would then have the very same degree of *objective* reality. (Descartes has little to say about the specific degree of reality pertaining to entities other than God, and we will not worry about that question here.)

16. This is a bit misleading, in that he would apparently at least have to have the belief or conviction that the principle holds, in order to know it. The point is that his basis for knowledge, his reason for thinking that the principle is true, would not depend on the existence of such a belief or conviction: he would believe it because it is self-evident, rather than it somehow being self-evident just because he believes it.

17. The one way in which one might attempt to avoid the need for such a self-evident principle connecting the occurrence of specific mental states with external existence would be to hold that there is some sort of external thing whose existence is *itself* self-evident, without the need for any inference from the occurrence of specific mental states. It is interesting that Descartes also attempts an argument of this sort in the fifth of the six *Meditations*, where he presents a version of what is called the "Ontological Argument" for the existence of God, arguing that in virtue of the very conception of God, such a being must exist. Though many have found this argument fascinating, there is an overwhelming consensus that it does not work, and I will not consider it further here.

18. In chapter 5.

19. Indeed, Descartes seems to suggest in this passage that even the beliefs that seemed to survive the doubt, those pertaining to his own existence and the contents of his mental states, are uncertain until the nonexistence of the evil genius has been proved. If this suggestion were right (is it?), it would make the problem discussed next in the text even more serious than it already is.

20. In chapter 3.

21. In his *An Essay concerning Human Understanding* (1689), Book II, ch. 8.

22. Primarily chapter 7.

23. Something like this argument is present, much more explicitly, in Descartes's most important immediate epistemological successor, John Locke. See Locke, *An Essay concerning Human Understanding*, Book IV, ch. 11.

24. See chapter 7.

25. As the possibility of self-evidence makes clear, such a reason need not be independent of the known proposition itself.

CHAPTER THREE

~

The Concept of Knowledge

Having examined Descartes's epistemological view as a kind of prologue, we will now turn to a more detailed consideration of a variety of more specific epistemological issues, focusing mainly on those that naturally arise out of his discussion. Our first specific concern will be to achieve a deeper understanding of the concept of *knowledge* itself. What is it to *know* something? What, that is, are we saying of a person when we ascribe knowledge to him or her? A further set of questions, already briefly noticed in chapter 1, concerns the significance of the concept of knowledge. *Why* does it involve the specific conditions that it does? How do those conditions fit together or connect with each other in an intelligible way? And, most fundamentally, why do or should we *care* about knowledge? Why is having knowledge important and valuable in the way that we normally take it to be (if indeed it really is)?

We have already encountered one specific account of the concept of knowledge, the one that Descartes seems to have roughly in mind (though without formulating it very explicitly) in the *Meditations*. According to that account, for a person S to know some proposition[1] P at some time t, the following three conditions must be satisfied (with the subscripts indicating that these are the conditions of the *Cartesian* conception of knowledge):

1_C. S must *believe* or *accept* P at t without any possible doubt.
2_C. P must be *true*.
3_C. S must have at t a *reason* or *justification* that *guarantees* that P is true.[2]

It is obvious on reflection that condition (3_C) makes condition (2_C) redundant and so unnecessary: If S has a reason that *guarantees* P's truth, then it follows automatically that P is in fact true. But since there are other accounts of knowledge that we will consider and want to compare with this one in which the condition that is parallel to Descartes's condition (3_C) does not in this way entail that the condition parallel (and in fact usually identical) to (2_C) is satisfied, it will be clearer to list condition (2_C) separately in spite of its redundancy in this case.

The Cartesian account of knowledge is in fact one specific version of a more general account of knowledge that has come to be generally referred to as "the traditional conception of knowledge." According to this general account, knowledge requires the satisfaction of three conditions at least roughly parallel to Descartes's: (1) a belief or acceptance condition, (2) a truth condition, and (3) a reason or justification condition (so that accounts of this kind are often referred to as *justified true belief* accounts or definitions of knowledge). Other specific versions of this general account usually share Descartes's truth condition (2_C), but differ somewhat in their specification of the belief or acceptance condition parallel to (1_C) and to a wider and more serious extent in their specification of the reason or justification condition parallel to (3_C). As we will eventually see, there are also recent accounts that add a further condition (4), while still retaining conditions parallel to Descartes's three.

We will begin by examining the three general kinds of condition included in the traditional account, considering the rationale for including each of them as an essential part of the concept of knowledge, trying to understand the general nature of each condition, and discussing, briefly for condition (1) and more extensively for condition (3), some of the different ways in which the general condition in question has been further specified by different versions of the traditional account.

The Belief or Acceptance Condition

The basic rationale for this first general condition is quite straightforward: Someone who is in serious doubt as to whether a particular proposition is true or, perhaps even more obviously, who has never so much as considered or entertained that proposition can surely not be correctly said to have *knowledge* of it. If I am completely uncertain about whether it will rain tomorrow, then I do not know that it will (or that it won't). And if it has never so much as occurred to me that my roof might be leaking, then again I plainly do not know that it is—even if in fact it is leaking and even if I have what would be good evidence for this being so if I were to recognize it as such (there are damp spots on the rug and distinctive streaks on the walls).

The most obvious way to satisfy a condition of this general sort would be for the person in question to be in the conscious state of explicitly considering and assenting to the proposition in question. This might involve, as the formulation just given seems to suggest, a two-stage process: for example, my wife suggests to me that perhaps the roof is leaking, and after considering the evidence, I end up becoming convinced that this is what is going on. It is also possible, however, that the truth of the proposition strikes me as obvious as soon as it enters my mind, without any preliminary stage of consideration.

But while this is one way in which a condition of the indicated sort might be satisfied, it seems reasonably clear that it is not the only way, that people can and do know many things at a particular time that they do not have explicitly in mind at that time. I am about to give you an example of such a piece of knowledge, something that it seems plain that you in fact know even as you read these words though you do not at the moment have it explicitly in mind. (It was, of course, precisely to produce this situation that I didn't specify the proposition in question initially.) Consider, then, the claim that you are a human being, where what is intended is that each reader formulate the appropriate version of this general sort of claim, the one that applies to himself or herself. My suggestion is that the claim in question is something that you knew to be true while reading the earlier part of the present paragraph, even though you almost certainly did not have it explicitly in mind. If this is right, then a correct formulation of the belief or acceptance condition for knowledge should not require explicit, conscious acceptance of the relevant proposition at the time in question, even though this is clearly *one* way in which such a condition should be satisfiable.

Perhaps the most standard way of handling this point is to formulate the condition in question as the requirement that the person who has knowledge *believe* the proposition in question and then to distinguish two kinds of belief (or, as it is often put, two "senses" of the term "belief"): *occurrent* belief, which is what happens when the person has the proposition explicitly in mind and accepts or assents to it; and *dispositional* belief, where the person does not have the proposition explicitly in mind, but is *disposed* to accept or assent to it, that is, would accept or assent to it if the issue were raised. Thus in the case of the example just given, the suggestion would be that each of the readers of this book had a dispositional belief (or believed dispositionally) that he or she is a human being, though it is quite possible that none of them had an occurrent belief to this effect at the time just before the proposition was explicitly mentioned.

There is, however, a problem lurking here which needs to be dealt with. The following situation sometimes, perhaps even frequently occurs: there is a proposition that a person has *never* consciously or explicitly considered, still less consciously assented to, but which is in some way obvious enough that he or she would immediately accept or assent to it if it were proposed. In such a case, the requirements of the so-called dispositional sense of "belief," as just given, seem to be satisfied, but it still seems plainly wrong to say that the person believes the proposition in question—and even more plainly wrong to say that he or she knows it, even if all of the other conditions for knowledge should happen to be satisfied.[3] Consider as an example here the version of the leaking roof case discussed earlier in which I would accept at once the proposition that my roof is leaking if proposed by my wife or if it just happened to occur to me, but where I neither have it presently in mind nor have accepted or assented to it earlier, and suppose that Descartes's conditions are at least roughly on the right track. In such a situation, even if the evidence I have (the wet spots on the floor and distinctive streaks on the wall) would be enough to satisfy the correct version of the reason or justification condition, and even if the claim in question is in fact true (and even if whatever further conditions there might be in addition to or instead of these two are also satisfied), it still seems plainly wrong to say that I *know* that my roof is leaking—even though it does not seem wrong to say of the readers of this book that they knew that they were human beings even at the time prior to my explicitly suggesting this proposition to them.

For this reason, rather than defining dispositional belief in the way suggested earlier, it should be specified instead as the dispositional state in which (a) one has previously explicitly considered and consciously accepted or assented to the proposition in question, and (b) as a direct result of this prior acceptance or assent, would accept or assent to it again if the question were explicitly raised. It is also perhaps a bit clearer not to use the term "belief" for the alternative of conscious or explicit acceptance or assent. We can then say that condition (1) of the standard conception of knowledge should be understood to require that the person in question *either* explicitly and consciously accepts *or* else (dispositionally) believes the proposition in question at the time in question. (Having clarified the point, I will sometimes for the sake of brevity follow fairly standard philosophical practice by using the term "belief" to cover both dispositional belief under the corrected specification and conscious, explicit acceptance or assent.)

One further issue, the main one that distinguishes different versions of the belief or acceptance condition, is how *strongly* the person must accept or believe the proposition in question, that is, how strongly they must be convinced that it is true. The Cartesian view, as formulated earlier, requires that the person have no possible doubt that the proposition is true, a condition that is also sometimes formulated by saying that they must be *certain* of it. This is a very strong version of the belief or acceptance requirement. It is one that many or probably most of the things that we seem ordinarily to regard as instances of knowledge (see the list of examples in chapter 1) would not satisfy, though this fact is obscured somewhat by a tendency to exaggerate when saying that claims are certain or indubitable. Thus I might well say that I am certain that my dog is in the yard where I just left him or certain that Clinton was elected president in 1996 or certain that it is very hot in the center of the sun; but if pressed, I would have to admit that none of these claims is really beyond all possible doubt. (Try to think in each of these cases and in various others of ways in they might be false that are at least *possible*. Do so, if you can, without appealing to anything as outlandish as the Cartesian evil genius.)

A significantly weaker version of the belief or acceptance condition would say instead merely that the person must be fairly confident, reasonably sure in his or her belief or acceptance of the proposition in question. This is a requirement that seems to agree much better with our commonsense judgments as to the extent of our knowledge, as reflected in the earlier list. Is this a good reason for thinking that it is this second, weaker requirement that is in fact correct as one part of an account of the concept of knowledge?

A Digression on Method

There is an important and difficult issue of philosophical method pertaining to this last point, one that is indeed also relevant to the earlier examples, and this is as good a place as any to discuss it. There is, as we have already seen, a very long list of claims, roughly indicated in the earlier list, that from a "commonsense" or "intuitive" standpoint count as cases of knowledge (with obviously some significant variation from person to person). What this means is that most ordinary people and indeed most philosophers, if asked to consider whether one of these examples is a case of knowledge, would be inclined to say without much hesitation that it is. Thus we have (a) a proposed requirement for knowledge, the Cartesian requirement that a proposition that is known must be believed without any possible doubt or with certainty, together with (b) a large number of commonsense or intuitive cases of putative knowledge which do not satisfy the requirement in question and so, if it is correct, must not be genuine. Either the intuitive judgments in question or the proposed requirement must apparently be mistaken (assuming that the concept of knowledge is unambiguous), but how are we to decide between these two alternatives?

There are at least two reasonably clear things to be said about this issue, though they are, alas, not sufficient to resolve it. First, commonsense or intuitive judgments about particular cases are a central and essential part of our basis for understanding and delineating general concepts like the concept of knowledge. This is just to say that if all such judgments were dismissed as undependable, we would have little handle left on such concepts. (Imagine trying to figure out what knowledge is if you have no idea at all which particular examples in fact qualify as cases of knowledge. How would you begin? What would you rely on?)

But, second, while commonsense or intuitive judgments of the sort in question are in this way indispensable, there is no apparent reason to regard them as incapable of being mistaken. Indeed, this would be so even if it were not the case, as in fact it is, that the commonsense or intuitive judgments of different people or of the same person at different times often conflict. And if it is possible for such judgments to be mistaken, then it is hard to rule out completely the possibility that they might be largely or even entirely mistaken, so that some requirement that they all fail to satisfy might still be correct.

The upshot of these considerations is thus rather inconclusive. It seems right to say that the fact that the Cartesian version of the first condition conflicts with our commonsense or intuitive judgments about knowledge counts against it and in favor of the weaker version mentioned above. (Similarly, on an earlier issue, the fact that it seems intuitively wrong to say that I know that my roof is leaking when the proposition in question has never explicitly occurred to me counts in favor of a version of the first condition that would not be satisfied in that case.) But this resolution of the issue between the two versions of the first condition is not decisive, since there is no guarantee that the relevant "intuitions" are correct. At least some possibility remains that the Cartesian condition is correct after all—in which case, hopefully, we might be able to find further reasons of some sort that point in this direction. (In fact, it will turn out that there is an essential connection—see if you can figure out now what it might be—between the first and third conditions, whereby the discussion of the latter can shed at least some light on the former.)

The Truth Condition

The rationale for the truth condition is simply that one cannot know what is not the case, something that almost no philosopher has seriously disputed. If I know that my car is in the parking lot, then it must actually be there; if it is not, then I did not in fact *know* that it was there, no matter how sure I may have been and how strong my reasons or justification may have been.

One thing that sometimes makes people balk at accepting the truth condition is that someone can, of course, *think* that he or she knows something when in fact it is not true. Thus in the case just given, I may still think that I know that my car is in the parking lot. Similarly, many people living prior to the exploits of Columbus believed that the earth was flat and thought that this was something that they knew. And many scientists and others living prior the work of Einstein believed that Newtonian mechanics was an exactly correct description of the behavior of material bodies and again thought that this was a case of knowledge, indeed an exceptionally clear one. Moreover, in describing cases of this kind, it is sometimes tempting, and perhaps even valuable in some ways, to temporarily take the point of view of the people in question and thus describe the situation by saying that they knew the claim in question—that is, that from their perspective it clearly seemed that they knew. According to all versions of the traditional conception of knowledge, however, such ascriptions of knowledge where the proposition in question is false are always mistaken, however reasonable and obvious they may have seemed to the people in question.

Here we have a somewhat more subtle example of the appeal to intuitive or commonsense judgments. In general, it seems intuitively wrong to ascribe knowledge where the claim in question is not in fact true. This is why a person who claims to know something will normally withdraw that claim when it is demonstrated in some way that the claim in question is mistaken and will concede that he or she did not know after all. But there are also certain cases, such as that of beliefs about the shape of the earth prior to Columbus, where there seems to be *something* right about saying that the people in question knew something that wasn't so. This conflict is resolved by pointing out that the ascription of knowledge in such cases in effect reflects the point of view of the people in question, from which the proposition *seems* true; thus this ascription can still be said to be mistaken from a more objective standpoint in which the falsity of the claim is acknowledged.

A related problem that you may perhaps have with the truth condition arises from worrying about how you could ever tell that it is satisfied. As we will see further below, a person does in a way have to determine that the proposition is true, according to the traditional conception at least—something that is accomplished by appeal to the reasons or justification for it. But it is tempting to make the mistake of thinking of the truth condition as one whose satisfaction has to be somehow determined by the would-be knower independently of the satisfaction of the other two conditions, and the problem is then that there is no apparent way to do this. As the point is sometimes put, you cannot just "step outside" of your own subjective perspective and observe independently that the claim that you believe and for which you perhaps have reason or justification is also true—there is just no way to occupy such a "God's-eye" perspective. But a proponent of the traditional conception will reply that what this shows is not that the truth condition is mistaken, but rather that it is a mistake to think of it as a condition that a person must determine independently to be satisfied in order to have knowledge; instead it is just a condition that must in fact *be* satisfied (something that is in fact true of all of the conditions in question).

A useful way in which this point is sometimes put is to say that the concept of knowledge is a "success" concept, that is, that it describes the successful outcome of a certain kind of endeavor. The aim of the cognitive enterprise is truth: we want our beliefs to correctly describe the world. And, according to the traditional account of knowledge, we attempt to accomplish this by seeking beliefs for which we have good reasons or strong justification. When this endeavor is successful, that is, when the justified beliefs thus arrived at are in fact also true, then we have knowledge; when it fails, when the resulting strongly justified beliefs are not in fact true,[4] we have only what might be described as "attempted knowledge." But the distinction between genuine and merely attempted knowledge is not one that we have to, or indeed in the short run could, independently draw. (A crude but helpful comparison: When shooting an arrow at a target, the aim is to hit the target, and this is something that we attempt to achieve by aiming carefully. But whether or not we succeed depends entirely on whether the arrow does in fact hit the target, and this may be so, in which case we have succeeded, even if we have no independent way to establish that it is so.)

A deeper and more difficult question, one that is rather more metaphysical than epistemological in character, concerns the nature of truth itself: What does truth amount to? What does it mean to say that a particular proposition is true? Here there is one answer that is both the most widely accepted and also the one that is seemingly in accord with common sense. But it is an answer that philosophers of very different persuasions have often regarded as problematic or even as not fully intelligible. Thus we need to take a look at this controversy, even though a full discussion of it is beyond the scope of this book.

The widely accepted, commonsensical view is what has come to be known as "the correspondence theory of truth." It says that a proposition is true if it *corresponds to* or *agrees with* the relevant aspect or part of reality. Thus, for example, for the proposition that my car is in the parking lot to be true, according to the correspondence theory, is for the content of this proposition (that is, what I believe or accept when I believe or accept this proposition) to agree with or match the appropriate aspect or chunk of independent reality—in this case, that physical configuration that involves a certain complicated structure of metal, plastic, rubber, etc., (my car) being physically juxtaposed in the right way or not with a certain piece of asphalt (the parking lot). The physical configuration that would make the proposition true is something that one could point to or physically mark off (with police tape or by building a box around it) quite independently of the proposition or the various beliefs that involve it; the various ones that would make it false are in general less localized, but could also be pointed at in a way by indicating the two separate elements and their failure to realize the indicated relation.

Many different sorts of problems and objections have been raised in relation to the correspondence theory, but probably the most widespread of these involve doubts about how the relation of correspondence should itself be explicated or clarified—or indeed whether it can be intelligibly explicated at all. It has sometimes been suggested that correspondence must be construed as some sort of complicated structural isomorphism or relation of "picturing" between the components of the proposition, or perhaps of the linguistic expression of the proposition, and the relevant chunk or aspect of reality. And intelligibly defining or specifying a relation of this sort has been argued to be difficult or perhaps impossible. One reason offered for this claim is that the relation would have be realized by propositions about very widely different sorts of subject matter, such as concrete physical situations (as in the example just discussed), general physical laws, historical facts, facts about mental states, abstract logical and mathematical facts, and perhaps normative or valuational facts. But how, it is asked, could there be one relation of the sort in question that is realized in cases as different as these? How could the very same relation that obtains between the proposition that my car is in the parking lot and the physical configuration described earlier also obtain between the proposition that $2 + 3 = 5$ and the abstract mathematical fact to which it would presumably have to correspond? A second, perhaps even deeper reason often given for thinking that a specification of the correspondence relation is impossible is that to formulate such a specification, we would have to be able to talk about or indicate *both* sides of the relation: both the conceptually formulated, linguistically expressible propositional content and the mind-independent, nonconceptual aspect or chunk of reality. But, the argument goes, we have no way to get at the latter except via further conceptual, propositional descriptions, which thus, it is claimed, merely presuppose the correspondence relation (assuming for the sake of the argument that the correspondence theory is true) without really helping to explain it.

These reasons for doubting whether an intelligible specification of the correspondence relation is possible raise difficult issues and would take quite a bit of discussion, more than there is room for here, to get to the bottom of. Fortunately, however, there is a way of seeing that the problems they raise, though perhaps important in other ways, need not be solved in order to make sense of the correspondence theory of truth. The mistake that is made by these reasons and the objection that they support is thinking that the intelligibility of the correspondence theory requires a generally applicable specification of the relation of correspondence in the way that they suppose, at least if such a specification is supposed to be more than utterly straightforward and trivial. Any intelligible proposition, after all, says that reality (in the broadest sense of the term) is a certain way or has certain features that the content of the proposition specifies. And the best way to understand the correspondence theory, following Aristotle's original statement,[5] is to construe it as saying no more than that such a proposition is true if reality is *whatever* way or has *whatever* features the proposition describes it as having. In some cases, the content of a supposed proposition may be less than fully clear or intelligible, but that is a problem for that supposed proposition and not for the correspondence theory. A way of putting this point is to say that the only specification needed as to how reality would have to be to correspond to a particular proposition and so of what correspondence for that particular proposition involves is provided by the propositional content itself and need not be independently specified by the correspondence theory. (There is no room here for a consideration of the various other objections that have been raised against the correspondence theory, though none of these seems to me in the end to have any more force than the one just considered.)

The belief that the correspondence theory is untenable has also led philosophers to propose a variety of alternative theories or accounts of truth, some of which have also been motivated by doubts as to whether truth understood in the way indicated by the correspondence theory would be knowable or accessible. This is also much too large a topic for detailed discussion, but a brief enumeration of the most important alternatives and their main problems may help to give you some idea of what is involved:

(1) *The coherence theory of truth.* According to this view, the truth of a believed proposition simply consists in its fitting together coherently with other propositions that are believed, where coherence involves both logical consistency and (usually) other relations of mutual support or explanation. (It is important to understand that this is supposed to be what truth ulti-

mately *amounts to*, not merely—which would be substantially more plausible—a test or criterion for determining what is true.[6]) Since this view seems implicitly to deny the existence of any objects of knowledge beyond beliefs and their propositional contents (for admitting such objects would lead inevitably back to the correspondence theory), it seems to require an idealist metaphysics in which only mental states (and the minds that have them?[7]) genuinely exist.

In addition to the intuitive implausibility of this idealist view, there is the further objection that it seems possible for there to be many different and incompatible coherent systems of believed propositions, all of the members of which would be true according to the coherence theory—which appears (think about it) to be an absurd result. (This point is sometimes made by suggesting that the propositions reflected in a well-written novel would seemingly satisfy the requirement of coherence, so that the beliefs of someone who accepted all of them would thereby be true according to the coherence theory.)

(2) *The pragmatic theory of truth.* There are a number of different versions of this view, but we will limit ourselves here to the simplest, advanced by the American pragmatist William James,[8] which holds that the truth is what "works": that is, that for a believed proposition to be true is for the holding of that belief to lead in general to success in practice. Now there can be little doubt that believing true propositions often leads to success in this way and that believing false propositions often leads to failure: for example, if I have a true rather than a false belief about the location of my car, then my efforts to get to it and drive home are obviously much more likely to succeed.[9] But is such a belief true *because* it produces success, since producing success is just what truth is (as the pragmatic theory claims)? Or isn't it exactly the other way around: doesn't the belief lead to success because it is true (in the correspondence sense)?

(3) *The redundancy or "disappearance" theory of truth.* Some recent philosophers, seeking to avoid the problems that (as they see it) arise from the correspondence theory and these other theories of truth, have suggested that there is really no need for any philosophical theory of the nature of truth. They point out the necessary equivalence between assertions of the form "P is true," for some proposition P, and the simple assertion that P, for example between the assertion *that it is true that my car is in the parking lot* and the assertion simply *that my car is in the parking lot*: if one of these claims is true, then the other must be true also, and vice versa (think about it). But this equivalence means, they argue, that the assertion that a particular

proposition is true means or says no more than the simple assertion of that proposition, in which case the former can always be replaced by the latter, and any mention of truth thus disappears. Their conclusion is that talk of truth is simply *redundant*—nothing more than a needlessly elaborate way of asserting the propositions in question.

One problem with this view is that there are cases where the claim is made that something is true but where the proposition in question is left unstated ("what Tom said was true"), so that the proposed replacement doesn't work. A deeper problem is that the equivalence after all works both ways, and thus could at least as reasonably be taken to show that all propositional assertions are implicitly assertions that the proposition in question is true—which would make an understanding of truth essential for even understanding the idea of assertion or belief.

Having canvassed these alternatives, I propose to follow common sense and the main weight of philosophical opinion by assuming that it is the correspondence theory that gives the correct account of truth, and understanding the second condition for knowledge accordingly.[10]

The Reason or Justification Condition

The easiest way to understand the need for this third general condition as a part of concept of knowledge is to consider briefly the suggestion that no such condition (and no other condition beyond the two already discussed) is necessary, that knowledge can be correctly understood merely as true belief. In fact, there are a few kinds of situation where it does seem reasonably natural to say that a person knows something, even though only these two conditions are satisfied. Here the clearest examples are cases where (a) some secret is being hidden from someone, and (b) in which the purpose for the secrecy will be defeated if the person being kept in the dark comes to have a confident true belief about the matter in question, whether or not he or she has any reason or justification at all for this belief. Thus, for example, if I am hiding from Susan (whether seriously or in a game) and she confidently guesses my location and heads in that direction, I might say to myself or to someone hiding with me "Susan knows where I am hiding"—even if it is just a hunch for which she has no basis at all or even if it results somehow from some sort of mistake or confusion on her part.

But apart from such relatively rare cases in which the truth of the belief in question is in effect all that matters, it seems clear (a point that has been recognized at least since Plato[11]) that a mere lucky guess or hunch does not suffice for knowledge even though it undeniably may produce a true belief. Really clear illustrations of this point are not easy to find because it is unusual for a person to believe confidently that something is so even when he or she lacks any real basis for the belief. But what is clear is that in a case where the proposition believed happens to be true only by mere luck or accident, a person does not come to know merely by somehow managing to have a sufficiently confident belief. Thus, for example, if a person on a multiple-choice type quiz show has no idea at all about the answer to a particular question and simply hits the right answer by luck, it would be mistaken to ascribe knowledge to them (prior to their being told that the answer was correct) even if they did manage to believe confidently that the choice was correct. (Here again we have an appeal to intuition.) Similarly, a rabid sports fan who is utterly sure that his team will win a certain game even though there is no real evidence or other basis for this claim did not know beforehand that his team would win even if in fact it does. And even in the case discussed earlier, it would be easy to challenge the claim that Susan really *knows* where I am. The right account seems to be rather that in that specific case (and some others) a true belief is just as good as knowledge and can therefore, in what amounts to a kind of exaggeration, be described as such.

What more then is needed for knowledge than a true belief, perhaps a very highly confident one? The answer offered by the traditional conception of knowledge is that one further ingredient is needed: a sufficiently strong *reason* or *justification* for thinking that the claim in question is true. Here the last part of the specification is essential, for there are other sorts of reasons or justification that I might have for holding a belief that would not be of the right kind to yield knowledge. I might believe something out of loyalty to a friend or out of commitment to a religious tradition (also a sort of loyalty) or just because it makes me happier to do so, but such beliefs do not thereby constitute knowledge even if they should happen to be true. What is needed for knowledge, according to the traditional conception, is a reason or justification of the distinctive sort that is *truth conducive*: that increases or enhances (to the appropriate degree—see below) the likelihood that the belief is true. Such a reason or justification is standardly referred to as an *epistemic* reason or as *epistemic* justification.

The most familiar and obvious way to have an epistemic reason for something that I believe is to have *evidence* in favor of the truth of the proposition in question. In the clearest sort of case, evidence consists in further information of some appropriate sort in light of which it becomes *evident* that the proposition is true. Thus, for example, a police detective might have evidence in the form of fingerprints, eyewitness testimony, surveillance photographs, etc., pointing strongly to the conclusion that a particular person was guilty of the crime he or she is investigating. A scientist might have evidence in the form of instrumental readings and laboratory observations in favor of the truth of a particular scientific theory. And a historian might have evidence in the form of manuscripts and artifacts for the occurrence of a particular historical event.

It is less clear whether the concept of evidence can be extended to encompass all cases in which someone has an epistemic reason or epistemic justification. From an intuitive standpoint, it seems clear that my belief that 2 + 3 = 5 is epistemically justified, that I have a reason or basis of some sort for thinking that it is true. (I am not merely guessing, nor am I accepting the claim on the basis of authority; rather I see or grasp directly why the claim is true, indeed why it must be true.) But do I really have *evidence* that supports the proposition in question? If so, what exactly is it? Philosophers have spoken in cases of this kind of *self-evidence*, where this seems to mean that the very content of the proposition in question somehow provides or constitutes evidence for its own truth. We will investigate this idea of self-evidence more fully later on,[12] but it is clear at least that self-evidence does not involve evidence in the most ordinary sense—that is, it does not involve a separate body of information that supports the proposition in question, for otherwise it would not be *self*-evidence.

There are still other sorts of cases of apparent epistemic reasons or justification to which the concept of evidence does not comfortably apply. What about cases of ordinary sensory perception, for example, my present perception of a large green coniferous tree outside my window? Do I have *evidence* for the existence and character of the tree, and if so what might it be? Philosophers have sometimes spoken in such cases of "the evidence of the senses," but it is far from obvious how this idea should be understood or, here again, that it involves a separate body of supporting information. (Though it is worth noting that philosophers have also sometimes spoken of "sensory information"—can you see anything in such a case that this might refer to?) What about cases of memory? I believe and seem to know that I had Grape-Nuts for breakfast this morning, but do I have *evidence* for this claim when I simply remember it (as opposed to checking the traces left in the bowl)? And what about my apparent knowledge of my own states of mind, of my "immediate experience"? I believe and seem to know that I am currently thinking about the concept of knowledge, that there is a large patch of dark green in my visual field, that I have an itch in my left elbow, and that I am determined to finish this chapter today, but do I have *evidence* for any of these claims? In this last sort of case, philosophers have also sometimes appealed to the idea of self-evidence. This too will be considered later, but we can see immediately that this is again a rather strained use of the ordinary notion of evidence (and also not clearly parallel to the use of the idea of self-evidence in relation to the proposition that 2 + 3 = 5, since it does not seem to be simply the *contents* of propositions about my experience that gives me a reason for thinking that they are true—for those contents would be no different in cases where those propositions were obviously false and unjustified).

All of these matters will require further discussion later on in this book. For the moment, we can say that the concepts of an epistemic reason or of epistemic justification as they figure in the traditional concept of knowledge are, if not simply identical to the concept of evidence, at least fairly straightforward generalizations of that concept. First, they involve a *basis* of some sort for thinking that the proposition in question is true or likely to be true, even if not necessarily the sort of separate body of information that the idea of evidence most naturally suggests. Second, on their most standard and obvious interpretation, these concepts also seem to involve the idea that this truth-conducive basis is something that is within the cognitive possession of the person whose belief thereby comes to be justified, that is, that it is something that he or she is aware of in some way that would allow it to be cited as a reason or as giving justification for the belief in question.[13]

Yet a further issue pertaining to the reason or justification condition for knowledge is how *strong* the reason or justification must be, that is, how likely it must make it that the proposition in question is true, for knowledge to result. We have already seen Descartes's apparent view on this point: the reason must be *conclusive*, must *guarantee* the truth of the proposition in the sense that there is no possible way that the proposition could be false given that reason. Accounts of knowledge that, like the Cartesian account, involve this strong version of the reason or justification condition are sometimes referred to as versions of the "strong conception of knowledge" (or the strong sense of the term "knowledge").[14]

It is fairly easy to see the appeal of the strong version of the reason or justification condition and the strong conception of knowledge that results. If, as suggested earlier, the aim of our cognitive endeavors is truth and our reasons or justification are our means for achieving this goal, then only a reason or justification that satisfies the strong version of the condition allows us to be sure that the goal has in fact been achieved; with anything less than this, success would be to some extent uncertain. Moreover, this interpretation of the third condition for knowledge seems to agree with at least some of the ways in which we ordinarily use the term "know": given inconclusive evidence, it is natural for a person to say, at least if pushed, that he or she doesn't really *know* that the claim in question is true despite having a fairly good reason for believing it.

But the main problem with the strong conception of knowledge is that there seem to be many, many cases that we commonsensically or intuitively regard as cases of knowledge where the strong version of the reason or justification condition is clearly not satisfied. As we have learned from Descartes (even though he himself seems sometimes to lose sight of this lesson in the later stages of the *Meditations*), it is *very* hard to find beliefs for which there is not some *possible* way in which the proposition in question could be false in spite of the reasons or justification for thinking that it is true. Given possibilities like the evil genius, it is doubtful whether any beliefs about the material world outside of our minds or about the past will count as knowledge, according to the strong conception. Indeed, contrary to Descartes, it can even be questioned whether beliefs about our own states of minds will constitute knowledge according to this strong standard: is it really *impossible* (given my evidence or basis, whatever exactly it is) that I could be mistaken about whether I am experiencing a specific shade of color or about how severe a sensation of pain is? Thus if the strong conception is the right account of knowledge, it may well follow that we have virtually no knowledge at all, perhaps nothing beyond the minimal knowledge for each of us of his or her own existence. And this result seems to conflict both with commonsense intuition and with our ordinary usage of the terms "know" and "knowledge."

It is this sort of objection that has led an overwhelming majority of recent philosophers to adopt versions of what is sometimes referred to as the "weak conception of knowledge" (or the weak sense of "knowledge").[15] According to these views, the correct version of the reason or justification condition does not require *conclusive* reasons or justification for there to be knowledge. What is required is instead only *reasonably strong* reasons or justification, strong enough to make it quite *likely* that the proposition in question is true, but not necessarily strong enough to *guarantee* its truth. It is at least fairly plausible to suppose that most or all of the beliefs that we intuitively regard as cases of knowledge do in fact satisfy this less demanding condition.[16]

As noted earlier, there is a subtle connection between the first and the third conditions of any particular version of the traditional conception of knowledge, and we can now see what it is. It seems to be plainly irrational for a person to believe something more strongly than the strength of their reason or justification would warrant (and perhaps also, though less obviously so, to believe it less strongly). Thus if we assume, reasonably enough it would seem, that knowledge involves beliefs that are rationally held, then accepting the weak version of the reason or justification condition is a strong reason for also accepting the weaker version of the belief or acceptance condition that was mentioned at the end of the discussion of that condition; whereas one who accepts the strong version of the reason or justification condition has no reason not to accept (and perhaps good reason in favor of accepting) a comparably strong version of the belief or acceptance condition.

One very obvious question to ask about the weak conception is *how* likely the truth of the proposition must be to satisfy this weaker version of the reason or justification condition. If, as seems at least initially reasonable, the level of likelihood can correctly be thought of as a level of probability, then just *how* probable must it be in light of the reasons or justification available that the proposition is true in order for it to be adequately justified to count as knowledge? Presumably more than mere 51 percent probability is required, since it seems intuitively wrong to say that a person knows something that is only barely more likely to be true than false—and, of course, obviously wrong to say that something that is less likely to be true than false is known. But how much more is required? Is 80 percent probability adequate or is that still too low? Should it be 90 percent, or 95 percent, or 99 percent or 99.9 percent? There is no very obvious way of answering this question, and the even more striking fact is that almost none of the advocates of the weak conception of knowledge have ever seriously tried to do so.[17] Even more important, it is simply unclear what sort of basis or rationale there might be for fixing this level of justification in a non-arbitrary way. However problematic the strong conception of justification may be in other ways, its intuitive significance and importance is clear. But nothing like this seems to be true for the weak conception.

This problem by itself calls into serious question whether any clearly motivated version of the supposed weak conception of knowledge even exists as an alternative to the strong conception. But it will be convenient to defer further discussion of this issue until we have considered a quite different and somewhat surprising problem that has been recently (by philosophical standards) raised in relation to the traditional conception of knowledge.

The Gettier Problem

It is reasonable to say the some version or other of the traditional conception of knowledge was taken for granted, often without very much in the way of detailed specification, by virtually all philosophers seriously concerned with knowledge in the period from the time of Descartes until the middle of the twentieth century. In 1963, however, Edmund Gettier published a remarkably short (three-page) paper that seemed to many to show clearly that the traditional conception was at the very least seriously incomplete and quite possibly even more badly mistaken.[18]

Gettier's argument relies on examples (so-called Gettier cases) in which the conditions required by the traditional conception of knowledge are supposedly satisfied, but which are nonetheless intuitively not cases of knowledge. Here are two such examples:[19]

Case 1:
Eleanor works in an office in which one of the other workers, Tom, drives a Mercedes, talks about how much fun it is to own a Mercedes, wears Mercedes T-shirts, receives mail from the Mercedes owners club, etc. She infers and comes to strongly believe on this basis the proposition that one of her co-workers owns a Mercedes. In fact, however, Tom does not own a Mercedes: the car he has been seen driving is rented and all of the other evidence is part of an elaborate hoax aimed at convincing people that he owns a Mercedes. In fact, however, one of Eleanor's other co-workers, Samantha, does own a Mercedes, which she keeps garaged, hardly ever drives, and does not mention to anyone, though Eleanor has no evidence of this at all. (Note carefully: the belief at issue is the *general* belief that one or another of Eleanor's co-workers owns a Mercedes, *not* the specific belief that that co-worker Tom does, though Eleanor of course has the latter belief as well.)

Case 2:
Driving in the country, Alvin sees what looks like several sheep standing behind a fence beside the road and hence believes strongly that there are sheep in that field. In fact, there are sheep in the field in question, but they are out of sight behind a grove of trees, and the animals that Alvin sees are in fact large dogs bred and groomed so as to resemble sheep very closely. (Note carefully: the belief at issue is the general belief that there are sheep in the field in question, *not* the belief, which Alvin also has, that the particular animals he sees are sheep and are in the field.)

Gettier's first claim is that in cases of this sort, the three conditions of the traditional conception of knowledge are satisfied. Clearly this is so for the truth condition, but it is plausibly correct for the other conditions only if it is the weaker versions of those conditions and thus the weak conception of knowledge, as discussed above, that is in question—which is clearly what Gettier has in mind.[20] But, he claims further (think very carefully about this point), neither Eleanor nor Alvin has *knowledge* of the specific claim in question when this issue is judged from a commonsense or intuitive standpoint. Intuitively, though their beliefs are both justified (in the weak sense) and true, they are not true in the way that their reasons or justification suggest, but rather as a matter of something like a lucky accident. It is merely a lucky accident (without which her belief would have been justified but false) that one of Eleanor's other co-workers happens to own a Mercedes, even though the specific one to whom her evidence pertains does not. And the same sort of point is true in a different way of Alvin.

Think again of the archery analogy mentioned earlier. The analogy to a Gettier case would be one in which someone aims well but, because of the difficult conditions, would still have missed the target, and then hits it by accident, due, for example, to a random gust of wind at the last instant; such a person has indeed hit the target, but not as a result of their skill—their endeavor to hit the target by using their skill has in fact not succeeded. And analogously, in a Gettier case, the person in question has indeed achieved true belief, but not in the right way for knowledge: not as a result of his or her reasons or justification. (Here is a good place to stop and think: Do you see the problem with the traditional conception of knowledge clearly? If so, can you see any way around it? Does it show that the conception in question is mistaken, and if so, in what way?)

The conclusion reached by most of the philosophers who have discussed the Gettier problem is that the traditional conception of knowledge is incomplete, that a *fourth* condition has to be added to the standard three in order to rule out such cases as cases of knowledge. Many such conditions have been proposed, but we may focus here on one that has the virtue of being closely related to the intuitive account just given of what goes wrong in such cases. The proposed condition is that for a person to have knowledge, given the satisfaction of the other three conditions of the traditional conception in its weak version, it must also not be an *accident*, in relation to the person's justification, that their belief is true.[21]

Thus we would have the following modified version of the weak conception of knowledge. For person S to know proposition P at time t:

1_w. S must confidently *believe* or *accept* P at t.
2_w. P must be *true*.
3_w. S must have at t a *reason* or *justification* that makes it highly likely that P is true.
4_w. It must not be an *accident*, in relation to S's reason or justification, that P is true.

The Modified Weak Conception versus the Strong Conception

How are we to decide between the weak conception of knowledge (as modified to handle the Gettier problem) and the strong conception of knowledge, that is, the Cartesian conception formulated earlier? The main argument for the modified weak conception is that it seems to accord pretty well with our commonsense or intuitive judgments about whether or not we have knowledge in various particular cases, whereas the strong conception seems to lead to the skeptical conclusion that we have almost no knowledge, perhaps even that each person can only know of his or her own existence. Given that these intuitive judgments represent at the very least a large part of our basis for delineating the concept of knowledge, this is a very strong objection to the Cartesian conception and so a very strong argument in favor of the weak conception—one that may indeed seem at first to be totally decisive. But things are not quite this simple, as I will now attempt to show. For one thing, as we will see toward the end of our discussion, there is a way to mitigate at least somewhat the apparently decisive objection to the Cartesian conception just mentioned. And, moreover, it turns out that there are also the following pretty serious objections to the modified weak conception.

First. Though condition (4_W) was added to solve the Gettier problem, it is not clear that it entirely works. The problem is that in relation to the weak version (3_W) of the reason or justification condition, it could be argued that the truth of the belief is always *to some extent* an accident. There is always *some* chance that a belief that is only weakly justified will turn out to be false (since weak justification does not guarantee truth), and it thus seems to be always to *some* extent a matter of luck or accident whether this chance of falsity is realized in any specific case, as it will in fact inevitably be in some. And if this is so, then no case in which merely the weak justification condition (3_W) is satisfied will be able to fully satisfy condition (4_W) and qualify as knowledge.

Second. As we noticed earlier, there is a problem about the precise degree of justification that the weak conception requires, that is, about *how* likely the truth of the proposition must be in relation to the reason or justification that the person has. This is a very serious and quite possibly unsolvable problem. One thing that it calls into question is whether the concept of knowledge has the importance that is often attributed to it: how important can it be that the strength of one's reason or justification for a claim is above rather than below a line that cannot be clearly and nonarbitrarily defined?

Third. Another problem for the weak conception grows out of an elementary fact of probability theory, on the assumption again that levels of justification can be regarded as probabilities (or at least as behaving like probabilities). According to the weak conception, a person achieves knowledge (assuming that the other conditions are satisfied) when the level of their justification reaches a certain specific (though not yet clearly specified) level—that is, we are assuming, when the believed proposition is probable to that degree or greater in relation to their reason or justification. Suppose now that a person has knowledge, according to this account, of two propositions, P and Q. One of the strongest intuitions about knowledge is that he or she should then be able to infer the conjunctive proposition P-and-Q, together with any further consequences that follow from P-and-Q, and thereby have knowledge of these results. What, after all, is knowledge good for except to draw further conclusions that will usually involve other known premises? But it is a fact of probability theory that the probability of a conjunction is equal to the *product* of the probabilities of the conjuncts, which means that if the probabilities of P and Q separately just meet the required level of probability, whatever it is, the probability of the conjunction P-and-Q is guaranteed *not* to meet it. (For example, if the required level is 0.9, then the probability of the conjunction will be only 0.81, and similarly for any level of probability short of certainty.) Thus if the weak conception were the correct one, one would not in general have knowledge of the consequences of one's knowledge, making it again unclear whether and why the concept of knowledge has any real importance.

Fourth. A final problem for the weak conception grows out of what has become known as "the lottery paradox." Suppose that the weak conception is correct and, just to make the presentation of the argument simpler, that the "magic" level of probability required for adequate justification is 0.99. Suppose further now that a lottery is going to be held in which some prize (perhaps a turkey) will be awarded to the holder of the one ticket that is drawn out of the 100 tickets sold. It follows (assuming that the drawing is fair) that the probability that any particular ticket will win is 0.01 and the probability that it will lose is 0.99. Suppose then that I believe strongly of each ticket that it will lose (so that I thereby have 100 separate beliefs). Out of these, 99 are true, and for each of these true beliefs I have the "magic" level of justification. It is perhaps less clear, for the reason discussed in connection with the first of this series of objections, that condition (4_W) is satisfied; but if that condition is ever satisfied in a case of less than conclusive justification, it seems reasonable to suppose that it is here. Thus a proponent of the modified weak conception must apparently agree that I *know* that each of the losing tickets will lose (though I obviously do not know this about the winning ticket, since neither condition (2_W) nor condition (4_W) is satisfied there).

But from an intuitive standpoint this result seems plainly mistaken: in the case as described, I have no knowledge at all concerning which specific ticket will win (though I do know that each of them is quite unlikely to win).

These problems, of which the second is in my judgment the most important, seem to suggest strongly that all is not well with the modified weak conception of knowledge, thus raising the further question of whether any way can be found to make the strong, Cartesian conception more palatable from an intuitive standpoint.[22] The best suggestion that I know of in this connection is the following.[23] Think of the concept of knowledge as characterizing an *ideal* cognitive state: I am completely certain that a proposition is true, and I have reasons or justification adequate to guarantee that I am correct. Like many ideals, this ideal state is rarely achieved in practice; but, also as with many ideals, other states of the same general kind can be usefully viewed and assessed as *approximating*, in varying degrees, the conditions realized in the ideal state. And further, again in a way that seems to be true of other sorts of ideal states, common sense is characteristically inclined to underestimate the various reasons that make it difficult to achieve the ideal state and so to judge that it has been achieved in cases that actually fall short, perhaps even very significantly short.

Such a view of the concept of knowledge is supported to some extent at least by the fact that initially confident commonsense ascriptions of knowledge, to others or to oneself, often tend to be withdrawn in the face of serious challenge or especially when the issue at stake turns out to be very important. Thus, for example, I might be willing to say that I know that the liquid in a certain container is water or that the pills in a certain bottle are ibuprofen, but if challenged ("are you really sure?") or if the issue is whether the liquid can safely be poured on a fire or the pills safely consumed to relieve a headache by someone who is allergic to aspirin, I may well be willing to admit that I don't really *know*.

Nonetheless, in spite of this point, it still remains highly doubtful that commonsense assessments of knowledge, even in these relatively serious cases, ever come very close to employing the extremely high standard laid down by the Cartesian conception. It thus remains the case that the Cartesian conception is radically incompatible with our commonsense intuitions about cases of knowledge—which are, to repeat, our main and indispensable basis for deciding what the concept of knowledge really amounts to.

The apparent upshot of this discussion is that the traditional conception of knowledge is seriously problematic with regard to the strength of the reason or justification that should be required for knowledge (and, correlatively, with regard to the proper strength of the belief or acceptance condition). We seem forced to choose between (a) a view of knowledge that is so demanding that few if any of our ordinary beliefs even come close to satisfying it and (b) a view that leaves the required level of justification unspecified and probably unspecifiable, and that has other serious problems as well. In this way, the concept of knowledge turns out to be something of a mess.

This result might seem to seriously undermine epistemology itself, leaving it without any clearly defined subject matter. I believe, however, that the correct conclusion is substantially less dire. What reflection on this problem seems to me to suggest is instead that the concept of knowledge, though it provides a necessary starting point for epistemological reflection, is much less ultimately important in relation to the main epistemological issues than it has usually been thought to be. For whichever of the two main candidates for an account of the concept of knowledge should turn out to be correct, the main issues will be whether and how we have reasons or justification for our beliefs of various kinds and how just strong such reasons or justification in fact turn out to be. This will be so whether we think of our cognitive goal as approximating as closely as possible to the Olympian ideal of the strong, Cartesian conception or as seeking to achieve the ill-defined level prescribed by the modified weak conception.[24] And if we are unable to decide firmly between those two conceptions (or even come to suspect that there is no clearly correct choice to be made), the main questions just mentioned—(a) whether we have reasons or justification in light of which our various beliefs are likely to be true and (b) how strong or compelling such justification is— will be no less urgent or important.

For this reason, most of our concern in the succeeding chapters will be with issues pertaining to reasons and justification, with the concept of knowledge falling very much into the background. We begin in the next chapter by considering an issue that Descartes does not raise and that, surprisingly enough, neither he nor the philosophers that came before and even immediately after him seem to have even noticed clearly, even though it is quite important for other issues that they do discuss: the problem of induction.

Notes

1. We will understand a *proposition* as simply the *content* of a belief or acceptance (or other act of thought): thus someone who believes or accepts that grass is green has a belief or act of acceptance having the proposition that grass is green as its object. It is natural to take propositions to be abstract objects to which different believers, even those who speak different languages, can be related in this way. Thus if I believe that grass is

green, and my German friend Heinz believes what he would express in the German sentence "*der Rasen ist grün*," the most straightforward view would say that Heinz and I both stand in the relation of belief to the very same abstract proposition, a proposition that I express in one way in English and he expresses in a different way in German. Many recent philosophers have objected to this view of propositions and some have even gone so far as to claim that belief and other such modes of thought are instead relations to *sentences* (so that Heinz and I, assuming that neither of us speaks the other's language, could apparently not share any beliefs). Such a view seems rather preposterous. In this book, I will set views of this sort aside and speak throughout of propositions.

2. Note also that while a time specification has been included in conditions (1_C) and (3_C), no such specification has been included in (2_C). This reflects the generally accepted idea that the truth of a proposition does not vary over time, that propositions are either true or false once and for all. You should consider carefully whether this seems correct. (One case that is especially worth thinking about is that of propositions about the future.)

3. It is in fact not clear that all of the other requirements *could* be satisfied in such a case, not clear in particular that the reason or justification condition can be satisfied for a proposition that has never been considered. But if this were so, it would be just another reason for thinking that it is wrong or at least pointless to formulate the belief or acceptance condition in such a way that it would be satisfied in this sort of case.

4. Whether this is possible will depend, of course, on the specification of the reason or justification condition—see further below.

5. "To say that what is is not, or that what is not is, is false, while to say that what is, is, or that what is not is not, is true." Aristotle, *Metaphysics* 1011b26.

6. Tests of truth (that is, accounts of justification) that appeal to coherence will be considered in chapter 9.

7. If there are minds and we can have knowledge of them, then wouldn't the truth of propositions about those minds have to be understood as correspondence between such propositions and the mind or minds in question?

8. See James, *Pragmatism* (New York: Longmans, Green, & Co., 1907).

9. Must true beliefs *always* produce more success than false ones? See if you can think of counterexamples to such a claim. (What if I have a false belief about the lot my car is parked in but also a false belief about where the lot in question is in relation to my present location, and the two falsehoods "cancel each other out" so that I end up walking in the right direction to find my car?)

10. It should be noted, however, that adopting the correspondence theory has the effect of setting aside one historically important response to epistemological issues in general and skepticism in particular. As noted above, one motivation for alternative accounts of truth, especially the coherence theory of truth, is the conviction that truth in the correspondence sense is unknowable, so that insisting that truth must be understood as correspondence can lead only to skepticism. (Whether this is really so is something that we will be investigating throughout this book.) Thus the coherence theory is one example of a general sort of view that attempts to solve—or rather, I would prefer to say, evade—epistemological problems via the adoption of novel views of truth or of reality, thereby giving

what amounts to a *metaphysical* response to an epistemological issue. Perhaps the most important version of such a view is that of the eighteenth-century German philosopher Immanuel Kant, who claims that the truth of our ordinary beliefs about the world consists not in correspondence to independent (*"an sich"*) reality, but rather in correspondence to a peculiar sort of mind-dependent reality ("the world of appearances")—a view that is very hard to fully make sense of, but that may amount to a kind of coherence theory of truth. Since the issues raised by views of this kind are primarily metaphysical rather than epistemological in character, I have chosen not to discuss them further in the present book.

11. See his dialogue *Theaetetus*.

12. In chapter 5.

13. There are some recent epistemological views that reject this last requirement by holding that epistemic justification (though they do not usually extend this to epistemic *reasons*) need not involve anything that the believer is aware of or even necessarily could become aware of. On such *externalist* views, the factor in light of which the belief is likely to be true and is thereby epistemically justified may be wholly or partially *external* to the believer's own cognitive perspective. We will investigate such externalist accounts of epistemic justification later on (in chapter 10), but for the time being we will adopt the seemingly more natural *internalist* view that insists that an epistemic reason or epistemic justification must involve an *internal* awareness of whatever it is in virtue of which the belief is likely to be true.

14. The label derives originally from Norman Malcolm, in his paper "Knowledge and Belief," reprinted in Malcolm, *Knowledge and Certainty* (Ithaca, N.Y.: Cornell University Press, 1975).

15. This label was also first introduced by Malcolm, in the paper cited in note 14.

16. This is not to suggest that there are not still serious problems about whether and how various sorts of beliefs can satisfy even this condition, problems that will be considered in later chapters.

17. One exception here is Roderick Chisholm, who has offered a complicated series of attempts to precisely specify a weak version of the reason or justification condition in terms of other concepts like the relative reasonableness of believing, disbelieving, and "withholding" (that is, neither believing nor disbelieving an entertained proposition). (Chisholm uses the term "evident" to describe a belief having the level of justification that results in knowledge.) There is no space here for a detailed discussion of this attempt, but it is fair to say that almost no one would regard it as having clearly succeeded. See the three editions of Chisholm, *Theory of Knowledge* (Englewood Cliffs, N.J.: Prentice Hall, 1966, 1977, 1989).

18. Edmund L. Gettier, "Is Justified True Belief Knowledge?" *Analysis*, vol. 23 (1963), pp. 231–33; widely reprinted. It has been claimed, quite plausibly, that Gettier's paper has given rise to a larger body of philosophical literature, consisting of replies, criticisms of replies, etc., in proportion to its size than any other piece of philosophical writing.

19. Gettier's own examples are in fact somewhat less perspicuous than the ones that will be presented here.

20. You may doubt that the cases as described satisfy even the weak version of the reason or justification condition, though it would be hard to be sure about that without a clearer indication than we have been able to find of where exactly the line between inadequate and adequate reasons or justification falls. But it is very plausible at least that such cases could be further embellished so as to meet this requirement—think about ways in which this might be done.

21. A condition of this sort was first proposed by Peter Unger, in his paper "An Analysis of Factual Knowledge," *Journal of Philosophy*, vol. 65 (1968), pp. 157–70. His version, however, does not relate the idea that the belief's truth is accidental to the person's reason or justification in the way suggested here.

22. Notice carefully that the Cartesian conception requires no fourth, anti-Gettier condition. Gettier cases arise only under views according to which a justified belief can still turn out to be false, since only then could it also turn out to be true by accident.

23. Due to Panayot Butchvarov. See his *The Concept of Knowledge* (Evanston, Ill.: Northwestern University Press, 1970), pp. 54–58.

24. A further point worth noting is that even if we had somehow arrived at a specific version of the weak conception specifying a specific level of justification as adequate for knowledge, there would still be no reason not to seek still higher levels of justification for any claim whose truth was a matter of serious interest, nor would increases in justification become in any clear way less valuable once the "magic" level had been obtained. This again seems to call into question the very significance of the concept of knowledge as understood by the weak conception.

~

CHAPTER FOUR

The Problem of Induction

Having obtained, with Descartes's help, an initial overview of the epistemological landscape and having explored the general concept of knowledge, we now turn in this and the next several chapters to a consideration of some of the most fundamental epistemological problems or issues, all of which are focused on concerns having to do with justification. We will begin with a problem that has the merit of being relatively tightly focused in a way that makes the epistemological issue exceptionally clear. The problem of induction has to do with what reasons or justification there are for accepting *general* conclusions on the basis of observations of *particular* instances falling under them, for example, for accepting the general conclusion that a cube of sugar will always dissolve in a large glass of water at room temperature on the basis of many observations of such cubes dissolving under those conditions and none where they fail to dissolve. Clearly we often reason in this general way, but what may not be immediately apparent is how utterly central such reasoning is to most of our supposed knowledge of the world (a point that will be further discussed below).

What exactly is the *problem* about such reasoning? We commonly regard the observation of many particular instances as providing a good reason for the corresponding general conclusion, but are we in fact justified or rational in reasoning in this way? And if so, why? What specific form do the reasons or the justification take? How, that is, could you explain to someone who somehow failed to see the point just *why* a conclusion of this sort genuinely follows from the corresponding observational premises? Are there perhaps intermediate steps of some sort that could be filled in to make the reasoning clearer, or is there some other way to do this? Without some more specific account of this sort, the claim that reasoning of this sort is in fact good reasoning remains open to challenge—and it has in fact been very seriously challenged.

As mentioned earlier, the problem of induction is a relatively recent addition to the catalogue of fundamental epistemological problems, having almost entirely escaped the notice of Descartes, all of his predecessors, and his immediate successors. It was first explicitly formulated by David Hume,[1] who advocated the skeptical thesis that observations of particular instances provide *no good reason at all* for the corresponding general conclusions, that such inductive reasoning is reasoning in name only and is in fact quite unjustified. From the standpoint of common sense, this is quite a startling conclusion, and it should be even more surprising to you to learn that a very substantial majority of recent philosophers have agreed that Hume is essentially right—though many of them, as we shall see, have tried to find ways to put a cosmetically better face on this result. We will have to try to decide whether or not this intellectually pessimistic conclusion is correct.

Inductive Reasoning: Two Examples and a General Characterization

We will begin by trying to get a clearer and more detailed idea of the precise sort of (supposed) reasoning whose justification is in question. I begin with two relatively simple examples, one of them already briefly mentioned, on the basis of which we can arrive at a more general characterization of the essential features of inductive reasoning.

Example 1. I put a small cube of ordinary white sugar (sucrose) into a large (approximately 12-ounce) glass of tap water at room temperature (which I will specify broadly as the range from 60 to 80 degrees Fahrenheit), and in a fairly short time the cube dissolves completely. It occurs to me to wonder whether white sugar always behaves in this way, and so I proceed to do a series of tests. I purchase as many different brands and configurations of white sugar as I can find (beet sugar and cane sugar, sugar from different regions and countries, cubes and tablets, large bags and small packets) and put approximately the same quantity of each sample of sugar into the corresponding number of separate glasses of water, all of approximately the same volume and again at approximately room temperature. Though the time required varies somewhat, the sugar always dissolves. I do the same thing over and over, as I travel around the country and to different parts of the world. I also ask all of my friends and acquaintances in this country and abroad and perhaps even on the space shuttle to do likewise, and report the results to me. In this series of tests, the source and other specific details concerning the sugar vary widely, as do the source of the water, the shape of the container, the time of day, the day of the week, the season of the year, etc. Under all of these varied conditions, the sugar still *always* dissolves, as long as both it and the water are reasonably pure. Assume also that I have no relevant background information of any kind, that my information relevant to the behavior of sugar in this respect is entirely confined to these specific tests. Eventually I conclude on the basis of my information that small quantities of sugar (approximately one teaspoon in size) always dissolve when placed in 12 ounces of water at room temperature. Am I *epistemically justified* in accepting this conclusion? That is, do I have a good reason to think that the conclusion in question is highly likely to be *true*? And if so, what exactly is that reason? Does it depend only on the set of observations or is there perhaps some sort of further premise or principle involved? (Stop and think about this question for yourself before proceeding further. Do you think that this conclusion is justified, and if so, why?)

Example 2. I own a new air gun (essentially a fancier version of a BB gun), and I become curious about how consistently it shoots, that is, about how much variation there is in where the pellet hits that is due to the gun itself and not to the steadiness of aim of the person using it or to outside conditions that affect either the gun itself or the flight of the pellet. I therefore decide to perform the following experiment. I carefully and firmly fasten the gun to a fixed support (thereby avoiding the problem of steadiness of aim) so that it is aimed in a horizontal direction at a blank target. I proceed to fire an extended series of shots, using one specific kind of pellet and being careful to avoid gusts of wind and variations in the temperature of the gun itself (such as might be produced by sunlight). The result is that the shots cluster, with most of them in a very small area and the rest distributed fairly symmetrically around that area in different directions. Measuring and counting carefully, I determine that approximately 90 percent of the shots fall within a 2-inch-diameter circle centered on the area of greatest concentration. I repeat the experiment and have it repeated by others in many different locations, continuing to use the same pellets and new samples of the same brand and model of gun, having the target in a horizontal direction at the same approximate distance, keeping the temperature range fairly constant and avoiding windy conditions, but varying the other circumstances as much as possible. The results are always the same, within a close measure of approximation: the percentage of pellets within a 2-inch-diameter circle centered on the area of greatest concentration is always between 88 percent and 92 percent. Assume again that I have no relevant background information (though I have made the untested conjectures that wide temperature varia- tion might affect the behavior of the gun and that wind might affect the flight of the pellets). I eventually conclude that under the specified condi- tions, approximately 90 percent of the shots from a new gun of that brand and model using those pellets will fall within such a 2-inch circle. Do the ex- periments described give me a good reason for thinking that this conclusion is highly likely to be true? (Though these are quite simple examples, notice how carefully I have to describe them in trying to make sure that nothing relevant has been left out—something that in fact took repeated additions and corrections when I was writing this section. Have I succeeded in this, or can you think of further things that should have been mentioned?)

How might we give a more general characterization of the structure of these and similar examples and of the reasoning involved? First, we have two observationally determinable features or conditions (which may be as com- plicated as we choose): first, the feature or condition that fixes the general sort of case being investigated (call this A); and, second, a further indepen- dently observable feature or condition that may or may not result from or be associated with a particular instance of condition A (call this B). Thus in ex- ample 1, condition A would be the specified quantity of sugar being placed in the specified quantity of water with the temperature falling in the indi- cated range; and condition B would be the subsequent dissolving of the sugar. And in example 2, condition A would be an air gun of a certain specific type being fixed in place and fired with a certain specific kind of pellet at a target a certain horizontal distance away under the further conditions specified; and condition B would be the clustering of the shots within the specified area to the degree indicated. Second, we have many observed cases of A, with the observers and other circumstances (those not specified in the description of A) being varied as widely as possible, out of which some fraction that we may formulate as m/n are also observed to be cases of B. (In the first case, this frac- tion is just all or 100 percent, while in the second case it is 90 percent.) A full description of all of these observations is what I will call a *standard in- ductive premise*. Third, on the basis of this premise and with no other relevant information, the conclusion is drawn that *approximately* m/n of *all* cases of A will also be cases of B (a *standard inductive conclusion*). This is intended to be understood as claiming not only that this will be true of past, present, and fu- ture cases, but also that it would have been true of *possible* cases that never became actual: sugar that was never put in water or even sugar that might have been produced but never was; guns that could have been so tested but weren't and even guns that might have been manufactured but weren't. *Inductive reasoning* or an *inductive inference* is just reasoning from a standard inductive premise to the corresponding standard inductive conclusion, that is, concluding on the basis of this kind of premise (and no other information) that this kind of conclusion is highly likely to be true.

The problem of induction then is just whether or not, and of course why, reasoning of this sort is rationally cogent: whether such a premise does indeed provide a good epistemic reason or strong epistemic justification for the resulting conclusion; that is, whether and why the truth of a standard inductive premise makes it highly likely—or even, for that matter, likely to any degree at all—that the corresponding standard inductive conclusion is true.[2]

Sometimes the issue is formulated in terms of an envisaged further premise that could be added to the argument so as to make the reasoning more obviously cogent. Such a premise, often labeled the Principle of Induction, is sometimes formulated as the claim that the future will resemble the past, but this is not really adequate to justify the full scope of the standard inductive conclusion. A somewhat better version would say that unobserved and merely possible cases are likely to resemble observed cases. But if such a premise were added, this would merely shift the issue to that of how this new premise is itself justified. Thus adding such a further premise really does nothing to advance the issue.

We will first look at Hume's argument for a skeptical response to this problem, an argument that is interesting on its own and has also had an enormous impact on subsequent discussions of the issue.

Hume's Dilemma

Hume begins by raising a challenge to those who think that inductive inference is rationally cogent. A standard inductive premise and the corresponding standard inductive conclusion are, he points out, two quite distinct propositions. The transition from the one to the other thus requires some inferential "process of thought" that needs to be spelled out and explained:

> If you insist that the inference is made by a chain of reasoning, I desire you to produce that reasoning. The connection between these propositions is not intuitive [that is, not just self-evident]. There is required a medium which may enable the mind to draw such an inference, if indeed it may be drawn by reasoning and argument.[3]

Hume's point here, briefly noticed earlier, is that the supposed inferential connection between a standard inductive premise and a standard inductive conclusion is certainly not so straightforward and obvious as not to require any sort of explanation.

One way to see this point more clearly is to notice that the conclusion of such an inference goes *very far* beyond the information contained in the premise, making claims about indefinitely many unobserved cases and even about merely possible ones. Why then should the relatively narrow information in the premise be regarded as a reason for thinking that this much wider and more sweeping conclusion is true? This is not something that can be just taken for granted or assumed without question. If the conclusion is to be reasonable at all, Hume is suggesting, then some further account must be possible of the inferential process of thought or the steps of reasoning whereby it is reached. Hume confesses that he is unable to arrive at any satisfactory account of this reasoning, and suggests that others will do no better. (As already suggested, this is an exceptionally clear example of the general form that epistemological problems typically take: we have some sort of evidence or basis E upon the strength of which some sort of further claim or conclusion C is accepted, and the question is whether and why the transition from E to C is rationally cogent.)

While the force of a challenge of the sort that Hume is raising obviously increases as philosophers over the years try and apparently fail to meet it, this failure alone obviously cannot establish conclusively that, as Hume claims, there is no such account to be given because the so-called inference is in fact not rationally cogent at all. As he himself suggests [48–49], perhaps the reasoning in question is very subtle or very difficult, and this accounts for the repeated failure to give a clear account of it. Hume's response to this suggestion is that the reasoning cannot be as difficult as that, indeed cannot be very difficult at all, since it is apparently familiar to young children and even animals, who seem to generalize from experience in more or less the same way. This, however, is inconclusive: it is certainly possible that a cogent line of reasoning of the sort in question genuinely exists, even though animals, children, and even unsophisticated adults arrive at their conclusions in some other way—perhaps by a process of arational conditioned habit (Hume's eventual suggestion for a general account of how such conclusions are arrived at—but *not* justified).

In any case, Hume also offers a much more powerful line of argument, one that purports to show quite conclusively that no cogent reasoning of the sort in question is even possible. The argument in question is what logicians call a *dilemma*: that is, it argues (a) that there are only two relevant possibilities (in this case two possibilities for the sort of reasoning that might justify induction), and (b) that each of these possibilities leads to the same conclusion, which must therefore be correct (in this case the conclusion that no reasoning that would genuinely justify an inductive inference is possible). More specifically, Hume claims that there are two and only two general kinds of reasoning: what he calls "demonstrative reasoning," which proceeds *a priori* (by thought or reason alone, without reliance on experience), and what he calls "moral reasoning" (or, later and much more clearly for a modern reader, "experimental reasoning" [51]), which relies on experience [49]. His claim is that neither of these two fundamental sorts of reasoning can do the job of showing that a standard inductive conclusion genuinely follows from the corresponding standard inductive premise.

Consider first demonstrative or *a priori* reasoning. Hume here advances, without very much in the way of argument, the claim that all demonstrative or *a priori* reasoning (i) pertains only to "relations of ideas," that is, to relations among our concepts, and (ii) relies essentially on the avoidance of contradiction.[4] It is part (ii) of this claim that is most immediately relevant to the present discussion. Here it is important to see clearly that what we are concerned with is the justification of the *inference* or *transition* from the premise to the conclusion of an inductive argument; the standard inductive premise itself is, of course justified by experience, specifically the experiences involved in making the various observations, but that fact has no direct bearing on how the inference *from* that premise *to* the inductive conclusion is justified. Hume is claiming that the only way to be justified on a purely demonstrative, *a priori* basis in inferring from a premise to a conclusion, that is, without relying in any way on experience to justify this transition, is if accepting that premise and rejecting that conclusion leads to a contradiction. Thus, to take a very simple example, the reason that *it is raining* follows demonstratively from the claim that *today is Monday, and it is raining* is that it would be contradictory to deny the former claim (by saying that it is *not* raining) while accepting the latter (that today is Monday, and it is raining): this would amount to saying that it is both false and true that it is raining, which is an explicit contradiction.[5]

But this does not work for the inference we are interested in, for:

> it implies no contradiction [to say] that the course of nature may change and that an object, seemingly like those which we have experienced, may be attended with different or contrary effects. [49]

Applied to our examples, the point is that there is no *contradiction* involved in saying that all of the observed quantities of sugar have dissolved under the conditions indicated earlier, but that others have not or will not or would not; and similarly that there is no *contradiction* involved in saying that in the observed cases 90 percent of the pellets fired from air guns under the conditions indicated have hit in the indicated area, but that this is not true for other actual or possible cases where no such tally has been made. Therefore, Hume concludes, these alleged inferences cannot be justified by demonstrative or *a priori* reasoning.

Hume's discussion of the second alternative, namely reasoning that relies on experience, is a bit less straightforward and introduces some irrelevant complications having to do with causality. But the essential point can be seen by asking how an appeal to experience could possibly justify an inference from a particular standard inductive premise to the corresponding standard inductive conclusion. Clearly the correctness of such a conclusion is not itself a matter of direct observation, since it makes a claim about unobserved instances (and if it were, the inductive inference would of course not be necessary). Thus the only apparent way that experience could play a justificatory role would be by (i) appealing to particular observed cases in the past where standard inductive premises were observed to be true and where the corresponding standard inductive conclusion turned out to be true also (and the absence or rarity of contrary cases), (ii) concluding on that basis to the general thesis that when a standard inductive premise is true, the corresponding standard inductive conclusion is highly likely to be true also, and then (iii) using this general thesis to justify the particular inductive inference in question.

There are, however, two difficulties with an attempted justification of this sort (only the second of which is mentioned explicitly by Hume). The first difficulty is that the truth of even past inductive conclusions in fact never becomes something that can be simply observed: because such conclusions apply to indefinitely many future, possible, and almost surely unobserved past cases, the most that can be known by observation is that they have never (or probably rather only very rarely) been subsequently refuted. And this does not seem to be a strong enough result to do the justificatory work that is needed: that past arguments of this sort have usually led to true conclusions *as far as we can tell* does not show that the conclusion of the argument we are interested in will be true without this qualification. (This is a tricky point that you should think about carefully.)

The second, much more fundamental and obvious difficulty, is that the inference from the observations in step (i) of the proposed justification to the general thesis in step (ii) is *itself* just another instance of inductive reasoning (think carefully about just how this is so), whose rational cogency is just as much in question as that of any other instance. Thus, Hume argues, to attempt to justify inductive inferences in general by appeal to this particular instance of such an inference "must be evidently going in a circle and taking that for granted which is the very point in question" [50]. As long as it is inductive reasoning in general whose justification is in question, the cogency of the foregoing argument is just as much in doubt as that of any other case of such reasoning and so cannot help to remove that doubt.[6]

Thus, according to Hume, inductive inferences cannot be justified by either of the two possible kinds of reasoning, and so *cannot be justified at all!* In thinking about the significance of this claim, it is important to be clear about an aspect of the point that has in fact been mentioned above, but not emphasized: Hume's claim is not merely that such inferences are not *conclusive*, that we cannot be *completely certain* that the conclusions are true, a claim that would be at most mildly unsettling. It is rather that inductive inferences yield *no justification at all* for their conclusions, that is, that they fail to increase or enhance *to even the smallest degree* the likelihood that their conclusions are true. If he is right, then what we call "inductive reasoning" does not really deserve that label, for it is in fact of no value at all for supporting its supposed conclusions.

The Implications of Hume's Conclusion

Before turning to a consideration of the ways in which subsequent philosophers have responded to Hume's argument, we should pause to become a bit clearer about the consequences that would follow if he were correct—consequences that seem[7] from an epistemological standpoint to amount to almost total catastrophe. It is hard to develop this point fully at this stage in our discussion, but we can get some idea of it by considering briefly how some major kinds of belief and putative knowledge seem to depend, directly or indirectly, on inductive reasoning for their justification.

First, consider beliefs about the properties of various kinds of material objects and material substances. What justification do I have for the belief that the wooden floor I am walking on will support my weight, that various kinds of food will nourish rather than poison me, that the detergent I use to wash dishes will clean them rather than exploding in my face, and so on? The issues here are complicated by the presence of background knowledge and many levels of reasoning, but it is nonetheless impossible to see how beliefs of this kind could be justified without relying on inductive generalizations about the behavior of the objects and substances in question. (In fact, the first of our examples was a simple case of this kind of reasoning.) One particularly important category of belief included under this general heading is beliefs about the persistence of various kinds of objects and substances through time—what reason do I have for thinking that an object, such as a tree or a building, that I observe at one time continues to exist at later times (unless disturbed or destroyed in some definite way)? How do I know that such objects don't just vanish or pop into and out of existence for no reason? (Think carefully about this last point.)

Second, consider scientific beliefs about causal laws and also about various kinds of unobservable entities and processes (electrons, radioactivity, and the like). Contrary to what Hume suggests,[8] there is almost certainly more to causality than just the regular succession of the events in question, but it is still impossible to see how we could have any justification for beliefs that one specific kind of event causes another without relying on inductive generalizations about the sequences in which events of those kinds or perhaps similar kinds occur. Moreover, though theories about unobservable entities and processes clearly cannot be directly justified by inductive inferences based on observation, the main arguments for the truth of such theories is that they provide the best *explanations* for patterns or regularities pertaining to things that are observable in various sorts of experimental situations, with these patterns or regularities being themselves established by induction. Thus if inductive inference is unjustified, so also apparently are all such scientific beliefs.

Third, consider my beliefs about the past that are not based on memory of my own direct observations. Any justification that I have for such beliefs must clearly rely on *evidence* falling into various general categories: written evidence of various kinds, reported memories of other people, photographs, artifacts of various kinds, and so forth. But how could I be justified in thinking that any of these sorts of alleged evidence are genuinely reliable indications of the sorts of events that they are alleged to be evidence for without relying in some way on inductively established generalizations pertaining to the relation between such events and the production of the corresponding evidence, for example, between the occurrence of major political or social events and the production of written accounts of them that are at least roughly accurate? (None of these last three points is particularly obvious, and a full explanation of them would take us too far afield. For the time being you should take them as challenges to think about how beliefs of the various kinds might be justified and see whether you can think of any sort of justification that does not rely at some point on inductive conclusions.)

Later on, we will see how the justification of beliefs about the material world in general and also of beliefs about the mental states of other people arguably rests in large part on generalizations that are in turn established by inductive reasoning. In fact, it has been argued pretty convincingly (see if you can see how the argument would go) that without inductive reasoning, I would be justified only in beliefs about my own existence and subjective experience at the present moment. For now, we need not decide in any firm way whether this extreme conclusion is really correct; but we can at least agree that the skeptical consequences of accepting Hume's conclusion that there is no justification for inductive inferences are very severe indeed.

How, then, have other philosophers responded to Hume's arguments, especially the dilemma argument? Although there have been a number of attempts through the years to show that Hume is mistaken, none of these has ever been very widely accepted. On the contrary, as noted earlier, the prevailing response, especially in the twentieth century, has been that Hume is basically correct, that his argument succeeds in showing that inductive inferences cannot be justified *if* that means showing that such inferences establish that their conclusions are *to any degree* likely to be true on the basis of the truth of their premises. Indeed, the main recent responses to Hume have been to concede completely this central point and then try to soften or mitigate its significance by arguing that inductive reasoning can still be said to be justified or rationally acceptable in other ways that do not conflict with Hume's conclusion. We will consider next the two main versions of this sort of attempt: first, the pragmatic "vindication" of induction; and, second, the "ordinary language" justification of induction.

The Pragmatic "Vindication" of Induction[9]

The main idea of the pragmatic approach to induction is that while *inductive reasoning* cannot, as the pragmatist agrees that Hume showed, be justified by showing that it is likely to lead to true conclusions, the *inductive method* of arriving at general statements about the world can nonetheless be "vindicated" by showing that in the long run it is *guaranteed* to find the truth, *if* there is a truth of the relevant sort to be found. As thus summarily formulated, the pragmatic thesis should seem extremely puzzling (how, you should be asking, can there be such a guarantee if Hume is right?), and it will take some careful work to arrive at a clear understanding of it.

We must first try to understand what the pragmatist has in mind by the *inductive method*. Consider again the air gun example given earlier, but think now of the investigation as an extended process in time during which I gradually acquire more and more evidence, from my own experiments and those of others, concerning the behavior in the relevant respect of air guns of the kind in question. Suppose that I am at a relatively early stage in this process: I have done a few trials and perhaps received a relatively small amount of similar information from others. Then what the inductive method instructs me to do is to (i) *tentatively* accept the claim that the proportion of pellets falling in the indicated sort of 2-inch circle so far is the true or correct proportion in general, and then (ii) revise this claim when and if the overall observed proportion changes as new trials are performed. (Of course, if the proportion remains approximately constant, then no actual revision may be necessary. And this would be the case if in particular, as in the other example, the observed proportion was and remained simply all or 100 percent.)

The pragmatist uses a special term to refer to these tentative claims about the proportion of A's that are B's that we are instructed by the inductive method to adopt in such a case: he calls them *posits*. A posit is a statement or claim that is not *asserted* or *believed* to be true or even probable, but is rather temporarily adopted and *treated*, for some further purpose, *as though it were true*—in the case of induction so that it can gradually be modified, hopefully in the direction of something closer to the real truth. (But whether there is any real basis for such a hope is, of course, a large part of the issue.) Such a posit is regarded by the pragmatist as a kind of intellectual *wager*: it is analogous, according to him, to a *bet* made in a gambling situation, for example, to betting that the ball in the roulette wheel will land on red. But whereas in at least many gambling situations, such a bet is an "appraised posit," in that the gambler knows the odds that it will be correct (slightly less than 50 percent in the example just given), an inductive posit, according to the pragmatist, is a "blind posit," for which it is impossible to know the chances of success—or even that there is any chance at all![10]

To see why this is so, we need to consider more explicitly what "success" in the inductive case, according to the pragmatist, would amount to. What we are seeking is a statement of the *true* proportion of A's that are B's, as opposed to the proportion that has been observed so far. But what exactly would such truth amount to? In fact, there is a problem here that is easy to miss. We understand what a true proportion would be where the cases of A are a fixed, definitely delimited set. Thus if A's are just the people in a certain classroom at a certain time and B's are the females, then the true proportion of A's that are B's is just the ratio of the number of females in the room to the total number of people in the room. But this simple account does not apply straightforwardly to the issue we are mainly concerned with, which concerns not only *indefinitely* many actual cases of A, but also merely *possible* cases of A. In this sort of issue, it is much less clear what the "true" proportion even amounts to.

The pragmatist approaches this issue by drawing an analogy with mathematics (though it must be clearly borne in mind that this is *only* an analogy).

Mathematicians speak of what they call *limits*: thus the limit of the value of the mathematical expression $1/x$ as the value of x increases infinitely, that is, gets larger and larger without ever stopping, is zero. Of course for any specific value of x, however large, $1/x$ does not equal zero, but rather is equal to some small positive value. But as the values of x get larger and larger, the value of $1/x$ gets closer and closer to zero, *converges* on zero, so that the *difference* between that value and zero can be made smaller than any fixed value just by making the value of x large enough; and this is precisely what it means to say that the limit is zero. Analogously, according to the pragmatist, the true proportion of A's that are B's is what he calls "the limit of the frequency": the value, *if any*, on which the observed proportion of A's that are B's converges, in approximately the same sense,[11] as the number of observed cases increases indefinitely. Thus if there is such a limit in, for example, the air gun case, then the difference between the observed proportion of pellets hitting inside the specified circle and the limit value can be made smaller than any small fixed value—and made to remain smaller for all larger numbers of observed pellets—simply by making the number of observed pellets sufficiently large.[12]

It should be obvious that there is no guarantee or even likelihood that the method of induction will arrive at such a limit value in any relatively short number of trials. In the short run, chance variation could always yield values that are quite different from the limit value, in principle different to *any* specified degree. For the pragmatist, this point is really just an application of Hume's original argument: there is no contradiction between (1) the claim that the limit of the frequency has one value and (2) the claim that the observed proportion in any finite number of cases has some different value; and any appeal to experience would again be circular.

Moreover, much more seriously, there is no guarantee or even likelihood, according to the pragmatist, that the inductive method will find such a limit even if pursued in the long run, *even the infinitely long run*, for the very simple reason that there is no guarantee or even likelihood in general that such a limit even *exists*. Again apply Hume's argument, which the pragmatist endorses: there is no contradiction in saying that such-and-such proportions are observed at various times, but that the series of observed proportions *never* converges on a definite limit value; and again there is no noncircular way to argue for the existence of such a limit by appeal to experience.

This is perhaps a surprising result, but it is in fact fairly easy to think of examples where it is not at all implausible to doubt the existence of such a limit. Consider the proportion of people who are left-handed: perhaps left-handedness results from cultural and/or environmental factors that vary enough over time to prevent the proportion from ever converging on a limit.

Or for an even clearer example, consider the proportion of people who wear pink shirts on Tuesdays: here it is very plausible that this proportion varies according to fads and fashions, the discovery and availability of dyes, religious or cultural values, changes in the work week, etc., so as to vary widely over time and never converge on a limit.

The pragmatist's point is then that any case we happen to be interested in *might* turn out to be like these, with no limit value to be found. Thus if inductive success means finding such a limit value, there is no guarantee or even likelihood that induction will succeed in any given case. This is in fact the fundamental reason, according to the pragmatist, why inductive reasoning cannot be justified in the sense of showing that it is likely to lead to the truth.

What we *can* be sure of, according to the pragmatist, is that following the inductive method will succeed in finding the truth *if* such success is possible, that is, *if* there is a truth of the kind in question, a "limit of the frequency," to be found—or rather, strictly speaking, that the inductive method will yield a value for the proportion of A's that are B's that *approximates* the true or limiting proportion to any degree of closeness that we desire. And this is so simply because of the way that the limit in question was defined. *If* there is such a limit, then a large enough number of observations *must*, by definition, bring the observed value within any specified distance of the limit value. It would be a contradiction to deny that this is so, to say that there is a limit but that the observed proportion never approaches it, no matter how large the number of observed cases. (Read the previous paragraph again if this point doesn't seem clear.)

Thus this guarantee of success *if* success is possible is a demonstrative or *a priori* result that even Hume can and should accept. Moreover, the pragmatist claims, nothing better can be established for *any* other method of arriving at general conclusions on the basis of observation. Thus while the pragmatist's argument does not, for the reasons already discussed, constitute a *justification* of inductive reasoning, it does, according to him, constitute a *vindication* of the inductive method by showing that it is rational or reasonable to adopt it: what could be more reasonable than to adopt a method that is guaranteed to succeed if success is possible when there is nothing better than this to be had?

Is the pragmatic vindication of induction an adequate response to the problem of induction? In particular, is it plausible that this is really the best we can do? Though the account of why adopting the inductive method is reasonable sounds initially pretty good, there are in fact two large problems with it. These do not show that the pragmatist's claims are mistaken in themselves, but they do suggest strongly that their significance is much more limited, and the resulting skepticism much more dire, than it might at first appear.[13]

First, given the claim that induction will succeed in the long run *if* success is possible, we need to ask *how long* the long run in question must be. The answer, already implicit in our earlier discussion, is that no run of *any* finite length is guaranteed *or even likely* to be long enough. The pragmatist argument guarantees success eventually (if such success is possible), but not success by *any* particular point in the sequence of observations. (If you don't see *clearly* why this is so, you should reread the three paragraphs before the previous one.) This means that for any actual application of induction we are interested in, such as the two earlier examples, there is no number of trials, however large, for which we can have *any* degree of justified confidence that the observed proportion is a reasonable approximation of the limit even if such a limit does exist. At any given point, we *might* in fact have succeeded in approximating the limit, but we can *never* have any justification at all for thinking that this is so—or, accordingly, for being confident that we can safely act on our results in ways that depend for success on their being true. This seems to mean that induction is practically next to useless if the pragmatic vindication is the best we can do. Indeed, while induction is guaranteed to succeed in the long run if success is possible, its likelihood of success in any short run is on the pragmatic view apparently no better than that of a random guess—and guessing is of course a much less labor-intensive "method" than careful experimentation.

Second, if this is really the best we can do in justifying induction, the result is of course skepticism—and, as we saw briefly above, very probably a quite deep and severe version of skepticism that would leave little of our supposed knowledge standing. Here is a rather picturesque description of our resulting epistemic situation, given in fact by the leading advocate of the pragmatic approach:

> A blind man who has lost his way in the mountains feels a trail with his stick. He does not know where the path will lead him, or whether it may take him so close to the edge of a precipice that he will be plunged into the abyss. Yet he follows the path, groping his way step by step; for if there is any possibility of getting out of the wilderness, it is by feeling his way along the path. As blind men we face the future, but we feel a path. And we know: if we can find a way through the future it is by feeling our way along this path.[14]

And even this seems too optimistic: probably he should have said that it is only an apparent path that may in fact lead directly into the abyss. And in any case, we will also never be able to be justifiably confident to any degree that we have in fact emerged from the wilderness.

It is surely overwhelmingly implausible, as we look around at our orderly world and at the various scientific and technological marvels that it contains, that our epistemic situation is as dismal as this. While this does not show conclusively that the pragmatist is wrong that no better justification for induction is to be found, it surely gives us very strong reasons both to seek one and to anticipate with some confidence that it is there to be found.

The "Ordinary Language" Justification of Induction[15]

A second, quite different attempt to defend the rationality of induction while still conceding the correctness of Hume's basic argument has been advanced by adherents of the approach to philosophy known as "ordinary language philosophy." The basic claim of this once popular philosophical approach is that the traditional problems of philosophy, including the problem of induction and the other main problems of epistemology, are "pseudo-problems" that arise from misuse of language or inadequate attention to ordinary linguistic usage. Such supposed problems, it is claimed, need to be "dissolved" rather than solved: they evaporate under careful scrutiny.

In fact, as we will see, the appeal to linguistic usage is rather inessential, particularly in the case of induction, and the specific view in question could just as well be described as the commonsense justification of induction. The main claim is that inductive reasoning is reasonable or justified simply because reasoning in this way is what we commonsensically call "reasonable" in the kinds of cases in question. Consider again the examples described earlier in this chapter. Clearly, from a commonsense standpoint, a person who, on the basis of the evidence indicated in the first example, accepted the conclusion that small quantities of sugar always dissolve in the way indicated would be described as having drawn the reasonable conclusion; and someone who concluded instead that such quantities will sometimes fail to thus dissolve would be said to be unreasonable. Similarly, in the second example, drawing the indicated conclusion would be described as reasonable, and drawing any significantly different conclusion as unreasonable. Thus, the ordinary language philosopher claims, there is no meaningful issue to be raised about the reasonableness or justification of reasoning inductively—or at least none that cannot be easily and trivially dealt with.

Therefore, according to the ordinary language philosopher, the very idea that there exists a significant "problem of induction" is a mistake, a kind of intellectual illusion. One account[16] of how this illusion arises is the following. The basic mistake is to demand implicitly that *inductive* reasoning meet the standards of *deductive* reasoning if it is to be reasonable or justified. In a deductive argument, such as the ones that occur in areas like logic and mathematics, the conclusions follow *conclusively* from the premises, so that it is impossible to consistently accept the latter and deny the former. It is noticing that this is not so for inductive arguments, that (as Hume pointed out) it is possible to consistently accept the premise of such an argument and deny the conclusion, that allegedly leads philosophers to think that there is a problem about whether and why induction is reasonable—one that might perhaps be solved by adding something like the Principle of Induction mentioned earlier, if only that principle could itself be somehow justified. But this whole approach, according to the ordinary language philosopher, is just a confusion. Deduction is one kind of reasoning, and induction is simply a distinct, fundamentally different kind of reasoning. Each of the two possesses its own autonomous standards of correctness or reasonableness, and there is no reason at all to expect one kind of reasoning to meet the standards of the other or for demanding that it do so. And if this mistake is not made, then it is obvious at once that induction is reasonable or justified by *inductive* standards, those reflected in ordinary usage and common sense, which are the only standards that are genuinely relevant in this sort of case. Thus the supposed problem allegedly disappears.

But there is in fact very much less force to this supposed dissolution of the problem than there at first seems. For the main concern underlying the problem of induction is *not* whether inductive reasoning is "reasonable" or "justified" when judged by the standards that are implicit in ordinary usage and common sense, something about which there is no serious doubt, and which Hume, for example, does not question. It is rather whether those standards are themselves correct or reasonable or justified in a deeper sense: whether reasoning in accordance with those standards is in fact likely (as common sense of course would say) to lead to conclusions that are *true*. And this is not a question that is in any way answered by pointing out that the standards in question are the ones that we commonsensically accept. Nor, in fact, does the proponent of the ordinary language solution in fact claim that it is. On the contrary, proponents of this approach commonly concede, as indeed they must, that the fact that inductive reasoning is "justified" or "reasonable" in the way that they have explained does *not* mean or in any way suggest that conclusions reached in this way are likely to be true.[17] Thus the real problem of induction has been neither shown to be senseless nor in any real way dissolved.

An analogy may help to bring out the point more clearly. Suppose that there is a religious community that accepts the practice of settling various kinds of issues, including many issues that we would regard as factual or scientific in character, by appeal to a body of sacred texts. Imagine that a skeptic about this practice emerges in the community in question, someone who asks whether there is any good reason or justification for thinking that the answers yielded by the texts are in fact likely to be true. And imagine an ordinary language philosopher, who attempts to meet this challenge by pointing out that accepting the answers that are indicated by the texts is just what being reasonable means in the kinds of cases in question (according to the community in question). Clearly this does not genuinely answer the skeptic's challenge, which is really a challenge to the practice of appealing to the texts itself and so cannot be satisfactorily answered by simply invoking that practice. And the situation is no different with the analogous case of induction. As one critic has nicely put the point, the ordinary language defense of induction seems to amount to no more than this: "If you use inductive procedures you can call yourself 'reasonable' [by commonsense standards]—*and isn't that nice!*"[18]

Can Inductive Reasoning Be Justified A *Priori*?

Thus the most prominent recent attempts to show that it is possible to accept Hume's conclusion while still defending inductive reasoning as in some way reasonable or justified seem to come to very little. In particular, the skeptical implications of Hume's argument remain as deep and troubling as ever. Since there is no other attempt in this direction that seems to do any better, it seems pretty clear that the only way to avoid these deeply skeptical results is to find some more direct answer to Hume's dilemma that allows us to avoid his conclusion. This means either finding some third alternative as to how inductive reasoning can be justified (thus "going between the horns" of Hume's dilemma), or else showing that one of the two alternatives that Hume considers (the two "horns" of the dilemma) does not in fact lead to Hume's conclusion.

There appears to be no hope of refuting Hume's argument that induction cannot be justified by appeal to experience. Though a few recent philosophers have made attempts in this direction, the circular or question-begging character of such a justification seems too clear to be denied. Thus any defense of induction will apparently have to be independent of experience—that is, a priori. It also seems undeniable that Hume is again right that there is no *contradiction* involved in accepting a standard inductive premise and rejecting the corresponding standard inductive conclusion, so that an *a priori* argument defending induction cannot be of the simple, straightforward type that is based on avoiding contradiction. What is much less clear, as will be suggested here for this specific issue and defended in a more general way and at much greater length in the next chapter, is that Hume is correct that all *a priori* reasoning must be based in this way on the avoidance of contradiction—where, to repeat, a contradiction is being understood here as the simultaneous assertion and denial of the very same proposition. (The possibility to be discussed could in fact be regarded either as a third alternative to Hume's two, a different kind of *a priori* reasoning, or as a challenge to Hume's construal of the demonstrative, *a priori* alternative, but it makes no ultimate difference in which of these ways it is put.)

Reflect again on the two examples of inductive reasoning offered above and on other examples of the same kind. It certainly *seems* intellectually compelling to reason in this way in such cases, and there seems to be no particular plausibility to holding that this seeming reasonableness is somehow based on experience or observation (beyond that required to establish the standard inductive premises), nor that it is (as in the religious community case) merely a reflection of communal standards that we just happen, for no good reason, to accept. On the contrary, that the likelihood that the conclusions in question are true is substantially increased or enhanced by the corresponding premises *seems* very obvious, indeed just as intellectually obvious as the conclusion in many cases of logical or mathematical reasoning (even though the *degree* of support is less than conclusive). All this could still, for all we have seen so far, be an illusion of some sort, but if so, it is an extremely powerful and persistent illusion, and it is time to see whether we can find some better way of making sense of it.

What sort of an *a priori* reason might there be, then, for thinking that a standard inductive conclusion is likely to be true if the corresponding standard inductive premise is true? Here there is an important lesson to be learned from our earlier discussion of the pragmatic approach. The pragmatist claimed that there is in fact no guarantee or independent likelihood of any sort that in a series of observations of the sort that is summarized in a standard inductive premise, the proportion of A's that are B's will in fact converge on a definite value, rather than varying irregularly among very different values, and I think he is right about this. Consider, then, a series of nonconverging observations, one in which the observed value over time does not approach closer and closer to any particular value, but simply wanders through the range of possible values in a way that exhibits no discernible pattern (perhaps the series of observed values of the proportion of people who wear pink shirts on Tuesdays). At any particular point in such a series, there will of course be some definite value so far of the observed proportion of A's that are B's, one that merely summarizes the observations to that point, and this fact could of course be formulated in a standard inductive premise. But does such a premise constitute any reason at all in this kind of case for thinking that the corresponding standard inductive conclusion is true? My suggestion is that the answer to this question is plainly "no." Without any appearance of convergence, such a conclusion may represent only one temporary stage in an irregular series of values, and there is no reason at all to ascribe to it any more significance than that.

Consider in contrast the sort of case in which there is apparent convergence, that is, in which the observed values seem on the whole to be approaching closer and closer to one particular value, albeit perhaps with small fluctuations along the way (and let us modify the idea of a standard inductive premise for the rest of this discussion so as to include the stipulation that such apparent convergence has taken place). Now we do seem intuitively to have a good reason to accept the corresponding standard inductive conclusion, which in effect states that the convergence value is (approximately) the true value of the proportion of A's that are B's. But why? Why think that observations that apparently converge in this way can provide a kind of justification for a corresponding conclusion that nonconverging observations cannot? My suggestion is that we now have a fact, the fact of apparent convergence, that seems to demand some sort of *explanation*. To be sure, it is always logically possible that such apparent convergence results merely from chance, but this becomes more and more unlikely the longer it persists. (Think very carefully about this point: If only chance is at work, then convergence of the sort in question represents a striking coincidence, one that is unlikely to occur just because there are so many other possibilities that are equally likely, so many other patterns in which A's that are and are not B's could occur—all of which would destroy the apparent convergence.)

How then might such a convergent series of observations be explained? The most obvious and straightforward explanation would be (i) that there is an objective regularity in the world, due in some way to the natures of A and B and the way in which they relate to each other, according to which just that (approximate) proportion of A's tend to be B's, and (ii) that a series of observations of the sort in question naturally tends to reflect that regularity, once enough cases have been observed to cancel out the effects of chance variation with regard to just which A's happen to be observed. Thus in the case of the air gun example, the idea would be that there is something about the construction and materials and operation of the guns in question that is regularly correlated, and in this case no doubt causes, the pattern of pellet distribution that is observed. And *if* this sort of explanation is the right explanation in such a case, then the proportion reflected in the convergent observations is (approximately) the true proportion, and the standard inductive conclusion is true. (Notice that we have here an account of what it is for a given proportion to be the true proportion in such a case that is significantly different from the pragmatist's and rather more natural: it is for it to reflect such an objective regularity in nature.)

Is there any reasonably plausible competing explanation for such a convergent series of observations that might upset this conclusion? Once chance has been ruled out as extremely unlikely, the only other possibility seems to be (i) that there is indeed an objective regularity involving A's and B's, but that the true proportion involved in this regularity is substantially different from that reflected in the convergence, and (ii) that in some way or other the A's that are observed represent a *skewed* or *unrepresentative* sample from the total set of A's. But *why* would the skewing reflected in (ii) occur, that is, *why* would the sample of A's be unrepresentative in spite of the variation of conditions, observers, etc., that is part of what is claimed by a standard inductive premise? A skewing due merely to chance would be extremely unlikely to produce regular enough results to account for the observed convergence. Thus the skewing in question would itself have to be *systematic*, that is, would itself have to result from some regular process or mechanism, which in this case could apparently only be due to the fact of observation itself: it would have to be that observation affects or somehow selects A's whose likelihood of being B's differs from that of the overall population of A's.

It is in fact very hard to be sure in a particular case that a possibility of this sort does not obtain. In the case of the air gun example, perhaps merely the proximity of an observer somehow affects the gun so as to alter the results. This might be due to heat from handling the gun to the degree necessary to fire it repeatedly or to quantum mechanical effects of some sort[19] or to some still further, perhaps unknown mechanism. The crucial point to appreciate is that this possibility, if carefully considered, has (somewhat surprisingly) *no bearing at all* on the justification of inductive reasoning. It is just too obvious that in at least some cases observational results are influenced by the fact that observation has taken place, and the claim that inductive reasoning is justified should not be construed as denying this obvious fact. Observational results involving such influence *obviously* have no genuine value as evidence of what would take place if observation were not occurring, and generalizing from them would clearly be a mistake.

The problem of induction is not concerned with this possibility, but is rather the problem of whether and why observational results of the sort summarized in a standard inductive premise (including the claim of convergence) provide good evidence for a standard inductive conclusion—that is, as we now see, for the existence of an objective regularity—*on the assumption that this sort of observational influence does not occur*. Thus the only apparent competitor to the explanation which makes the standard inductive conclusion true turns out not to be a genuine competitor at all, but rather reflects a possible circumstance that would make inductive reasoning simply inapplicable to the case. And, therefore, in the cases where the assumption just indicated holds, where the fact of observation does not itself affect the results, we have good reason to think that the standard inductive conclusion, representing as it does the only nonchance explanation available of the fact of apparent convergence, is true.

There is one further potential objection to be considered. As quoted in our earlier discussion, one of the things that Hume says is that inductive conclusions cannot be shown to be likely to be true because "the course of nature may change." Doesn't this possibility still defeat our attempted justification? Even if the convergent observations were due to an objective regularity of the sort indicated, couldn't that regularity simply change in the next instant, so that even if the standard inductive conclusion still correctly describes at least part of the past, it no longer correctly describes future or possible cases? This objection raises metaphysical issues that we cannot go very far into here. But the simple answer, which I believe to be correct, is that the regularity in question is not supposed to be just an ungrounded, coincidental pattern, but rather something that results in some way from the natures of A and B themselves. Thus as long as those natures persist, that is, as long as there are A's and B's at all, the regularity in question is also at least very likely to persist, which is enough to safeguard our conclusion.

The foregoing defense of induction at least appears to be purely *a priori* in character. At no time did any sort of observational or experiential evidence (beyond the standard inductive premise itself) seem to be brought in and appealed to in order to show either (i) that the truth of a standard inductive premise (understood as including the appearance of convergence) requires some explanation or (ii) that the existence of an objective regularity that would make the corresponding standard inductive conclusion true is the best explanation for such a fact. Instead, both of these points were defended on what appear to be entirely *a priori* grounds. Nonetheless, there are many philosophers who doubt strongly whether an *a priori* argument of this sort of can genuinely be cogent. Their reservations have mainly to do, not with the specific issues surrounding induction, but rather with general views of the possibility and nature of *a priori* reasoning generally, a topic we will turn to in the next chapter.

Notes

1. In his book *A Treatise of Human Nature* (1739), Book One, Part III; and, somewhat more explicitly, in his later book *An Inquiry concerning Human Understanding* (1748), section 4.

2. This problem is sometimes referred to as "the traditional problem of induction" or perhaps "the Humean problem of induction," in order to distinguish it from other problems pertaining to induction that have been raised more recently, especially Nelson Goodman's so-called New Riddle of Induction. See his *Fact, Fiction and Forecast* (New York: Bobbs-Merrill, 1965). A consideration of these further problems is, however, beyond the scope of the present book.

3. David Hume, *An Inquiry concerning Human Understanding*, ed. C. W. Hendel (Indianapolis, Ind.: Bobbs-Merrill, 1955), p. 48. (Subsequent references in the text are to the pages of this book.)

4. As we will see more fully in the next chapter, this two-part claim is in fact one version of the central thesis of one main variety of *empiricism*, the general view that all knowledge or at least all significant or substantive knowledge derives from experience.

5. This assumes that a contradiction is to be understood as the simultaneous assertion and denial of the very same proposition. As we will see in the next chapter, philosophers have not always been careful to confine themselves to this clear idea of a contradiction.

6. Hume's main formulation of this point is in relation to his version of the Principle of Induction: the claim "that the future will resemble the past and that similar powers [for example, solubility] will be conjoined with similar sensible qualities" [51]. The point is then that if this principle is essential to the justification of inductive reasoning, then to argue for its justification by appeal to its apparent truth in observed cases in the past would be in effect to appeal to the principle for its own justification, thus arguing in a circle or begging the question.

7. I say "seem" only because of the yet unexplored possibility of *externalist* views of justification or knowledge. See chapter 10.

8. In both *A Treatise of Human Nature*, Book I, Part III, section 14; and *An Inquiry concerning Human Understanding*, section 7.

9. The main proponent of the pragmatic solution to the problem of induction is the German-American philosopher of science Hans Reichenbach, and we will largely follow his presentation of this view. See his *Experience and Prediction* (Chicago: University of Chicago Press, 1938), pp. 339–63; and his *Theory of Probability* (Berkeley: University of California Press, 1949), pp. 469–82.

10. See Reichenbach, *Experience and Prediction*, pp. 352–53.

11. The convergence in this sort of case will normally not be as smooth and regular as that in typical mathematical cases.

12. Is the pragmatist right that the true proportion is just "the limit of the frequency," as thus understood? The answer is not immediately obvious. One problem is the possibility, which is a serious concern in certain sorts of cases, that the fact of observation might itself influence whether an A is a B. But if that concern is set aside for now (see further

below), we can at least agree that it is plausible that this limit should closely correspond to the true proportion (if there is one).

13. A third, more technical problem is that there are other "methods" for which the same sort of vindication can be given, but which can be formulated so as to yield any specific answer at all in a particular case. See the works of Reichenbach cited in note 9 and also my *In Defense of Pure Reason* (Cambridge: Cambridge University Press, 1998), p. 194.

14. Reichenbach, *Theory of Probability*, p. 482.

15. Different versions of this general approach to induction have been put forward by a number of different philosophers. Here I largely follow the version offered by P. F. Strawson, *Introduction to Logical Theory* (London: Methuen, 1952), chapter 9.

16. See Strawson, pp. 441–42.

17. See Strawson, pp. 449–50.

18. Wesley Salmon, "Should We Attempt to Justify Induction?" *Philosophical Studies*, vol. 8 (1957), p. 42.

19. Analogous to those involved in the famous case of Schrödinger's Cat, who is allegedly neither alive nor dead until someone observes its condition.

~

CHAPTER FIVE

A *Priori* Justification and Knowledge

As we saw in chapter 2, one of Descartes's fundamental epistemological assumptions is that certain propositions can be justified and known purely via
"the natural light of reason," that is, purely in virtue of their self-evidence,
without any essential reliance on experience: in the traditional terminology,
a priori. Propositions justified in this way are for Descartes one part of the ultimate basis or "foundation" upon which all the rest of our knowledge rests,
with the other part being constituted by immediate experience of one's own
existence and specific states of mind.[1] As discussed earlier, it is self-evidence
or *a priori* insight to which Descartes appeals for the justification of the general principles that he attempts to use to go beyond his knowledge of his own
mind to knowledge of the material world. We have also seen in the previous
chapter that a somewhat similar appeal to *a priori* justification appears to be
essential for a nonskeptical justification of inductive reasoning, at least for
one that yields the result that inductive conclusions are likely to be true.

How plausible is this idea of *a priori* justification (and resulting *a priori*
knowledge)? It is easy to be suspicious here. The way in which sensory or introspective experience can justify claims about the world is—or at least initially seems—straightforward and obvious. But the idea of a reason for thinking something to be true that does not depend, directly or even indirectly, on
such experience may seem puzzling or even paradoxical. Where is the justification for an allegedly *a priori* or self-evident claim supposed to come from?
What does such justification really amount to? What is the difference, you
may want to ask, between a claim of self-evidence and a purely dogmatic assertion with no real justification at all?

We will begin by exploring the idea of *a priori* justification, trying first to get clearer about what it really amounts to and then considering two fundamental reasons for believing that such justification genuinely exists. Only then will we be in a position to investigate the main philosophical views about the ultimate nature and significance of this alleged species of justification.

What Is A *Priori* Justification?

The initial conception of *a priori* justification is that it is justification that does not *depend* at all on *experience*. But in order to understand clearly what that means, both the relevant conception of experience and the relevant sort of dependence need to be explicated further.

What then is *experience*? Clearly my *sensory experiences* of various specific sensory qualities count as kinds of experience: for example, my awareness of patches of a distinctive slightly yellowish green color (which leads me to believe and seemingly be—somehow—justified in believing that there are new leaves on the tree outside my window) or my consciousness of a faint whooshing sound (which leads me to believe, again seemingly with justification, that the furnace has come on). Also included in the general category of experience are my ongoing *introspective* experiences of my own specific conscious mental states and processes (which again may lead to apparently justified beliefs): my conscious awareness of a very light background headache, of the nagging background thought that I really ought to reply to my e-mail, or of the foreground thought that I need to find good, clear examples of experience. Another kind of experience worth mentioning is *memory experience*, the experience of recalling various events that I experienced at some earlier time, from eating toast for breakfast this morning to breaking my collarbone in a touch football game many years ago. A *priori* justification, then, is supposed to be justification that is independent (in the relevant sense, not yet clarified) of experiences of all these various sorts.[2]

Contrast the justification derived from experiences of these various sorts with the following two fairly typical examples of (allegedly) *a priori* justification. Seeking a really clear example of *a priori* justification, I focus on the claim that $2 + 3 = 5$ and consider very carefully whether and (if so) why I am justified in accepting it (something that I would, of course, be very unlikely to do under ordinary circumstances). Presumably this simple arithmetical fact is something that I learned long ago in grade school, and perhaps the resulting memory is somehow a basis for justification (though I certainly have no specific memory of the occasion in question). But it at least *seems* quite clear that I need not rely on such a memory, that even if my teachers somehow inadvertently failed to mention this specific proposition or if I have in the mean-time entirely forgotten it, I can still come to be justified in the belief in ques-tion just by thinking carefully about the proposition in question and its in-gredients. One way to do this, though it is probably not essential, would be to run through my mind several specific imagined scenarios in which I have two objects of a certain kind and three more of the same kind (and none beyond those) and thus inevitably five altogether. Or perhaps I just think very care-fully about the claim in the abstract. Either way, it appears that just by think-ing about this proposition, I can come to see clearly that it is true and indeed that it *must* be true, that it could not be false. As this is sometimes put, I seem to grasp that the proposition in question is *necessary*: that it must be true in any possible world or situation.[3] And this in turn *seems* to be a perfectly ade-quate basis for justification: that the claim apparently cannot fail to be true seems to be a good, indeed an excellent reason for thinking that it is true. (If this still strikes you as inadequate because, after all, it only *seems* that the proposition in question must be true, you should ask yourself carefully whether *any* basis for justification, even the (seemingly!) clearest sense perception, ul-timately offers any more basis for justification than this.)

Consider a second example, this time one involving an inference. Won-dering whether the weather will be conducive to taking my dogs for a walk this afternoon, I consult the morning paper, which predicts rain later in the day. I proceed to reason as follows: (1) Whenever the paper predicts rain that doesn't start until later, the afternoon turns out in fact to be sunny and pleas-ant. (2) The paper today predicts rain arriving later. Hence, the afternoon will be sunny and pleasant. (And I anticipate a nice walk.) You might well question whether the track record of the paper is really so dismal as to make me justified in accepting premise (1) of this little argument. And, as we will see later,[4] there are problems of a much less obvious sort pertaining to the jus-tification of premise (2). Our immediate concern, however, is with the in-ference from premises (1) and (2) to the conclusion (or, equivalently—think about this—with the hypothetical proposition that *if* (1) and (2) are true, then the conclusion is true). Here again it seems that if I think about the case carefully, I can simply see (where this is *intellectual*, not sensory seeing) that the conclusion follows from the premises, that it *must* be true if they are. And again this *seems* to be a perfectly adequate basis for justification.

But is the justification in these two cases, supposing for the moment that it is genuine, really independent of experience in the way required for it to count as *a priori*? One issue here concerns the *understanding* of the allegedly self-evident propositions or inferences, which is clearly an essential precondi-tion for grasping their (apparent) necessity. To understand these propositions requires understanding the *concepts* that they contain. But it is plausible to suppose that the understanding of at least some of the relevant concepts depends on sensory experience: that understanding the concepts of 2 and 3 and 5 depends on sensory experiences of the appropriate-sized collections; and, even more plausibly, that understanding the concepts of a sunny day and of rain and of the newspaper depends on sensory experiences of the corresponding sorts of situations and objects. If this is right, then the alleged justification in each case does depend, albeit indirectly, on sensory experience, and so is apparently not *a priori* after all.[5]

As the concept of *a priori* justification is standardly understood, however, this objection, though initially plausible, is in fact mistaken. The key point is that while not only the allegedly *a priori* justification in these cases, but indeed *any* sort of justification *of course* presupposes an understanding of the proposition (or propositions) in question, that understanding does not thereby constitute a part of the justification itself, that is, a part of the reason for thinking that the proposition in question is true. And the issue on the basis of which the distinction between *a priori* and empirical ("*a posteriori*") justification is drawn is precisely whether the justification itself involves as an essential part an appeal to experience of the relevant sort—that is, whether, *assuming* that the claim in question has been understood (whatever that may require), a further appeal to experience is still needed to provide a reason to think that it is true. Thus while justification of the sort that seems to be present in the two examples plausibly depends *in a way* on sensory experience, that dependence is not of the right sort to prevent the justification from being *a priori*. (Note carefully, however, that the justification in question would *not* count as *a priori* if the experience needed to acquire the concepts needed for understanding the claim had to be appealed to *again* as evidence in order to have a reason for thinking that the claim is true.)[6]

Thus we may sum up the discussion so far by saying that *a priori* justification is justification that does not depend (a) on sensory or introspective or memory experience[7] in a way that (b) makes that experience constitute an essential part of the very justification or reason in question. But it may depend on experience as an essential precondition for understanding the concepts in question, as long as that experience does not *also* function as part of the justification or reason.

The Epistemological Indispensability of A *Priori* Justification

But why should we believe that *a priori* justification as thus understood genuinely exists? We have examined two examples for which such a claim is at least reasonably plausible, and it would in fact be easy to offer many more broadly similar ones. But while a careful consideration of such examples may be fairly persuasive, it is probably not sufficient by itself to settle the issue to the satisfaction of anyone who is initially inclined to be skeptical. While the justification that seems to exist in such cases does not depend on experience of the relevant sort in any easily discernible way, perhaps there is a dependence of some more subtle sort. Or perhaps (a much more skeptical thought) the claims in question are not really justified after all.

We have also seen how the notion of *a priori* justification plays an indispensable role in Cartesian epistemology and how it is apparently the only available hope for a justification of inductive reasoning. These two considerations, especially the second, are more powerful, but still inconclusive, at least until it can be shown more clearly that there is no alternative to *a priori* justification for the justification of induction and, more generally, of claims that go beyond direct experience. But reflection on them leads in fact to two more general arguments, the second in effect a generalization of the first, that give very strong reasons for thinking that *a priori* justification exists—or at least that it must exist if extremely pervasive and intuitively implausible versions of skepticism are to be avoided.

To understand the first argument, we need to focus on the general issue of how claims that go beyond what can be justified by *direct* observation or experience alone are justified. In the Cartesian view, as we have understood it, direct observation by itself justifies only claims about the existence and specific mental states of the person in question, leaving all other knowledge (assuming of course that there is any) to be justified via some sort of inference from this directly experiential knowledge. We will consider in the following two chapters whether the Cartesian view is right about this and what alternative construals of the scope of what is justified by direct observation or experience alone there might be. All that matters for the moment, however, is that on any view of the scope of direct observation or experience that has ever been seriously advanced, it is completely obvious that a large proportion of the things that we commonsensically think that we know (see again the list in chapter 1) are not and could not be simply justified by direct observation alone—whether we think (as would Descartes) in terms of the direct observations of a single person or instead somehow manage to pool together the direct observations of all persons.

These things that are not justified by direct experience would include claims about the past, especially about matters that were not directly observed by anyone (but even things justified by memories of past direct observations still are not, at a later time, justified by direct observation alone[8]);

claims about present but unobserved objects and situations; claims about the future; claims about unobservable entities, as in theoretical science; and general claims about such things as laws of nature. How then are claims of these various sorts justified? A possible answer, of course, is that they are not in fact justified at all, but this is very implausible from the standpoint of common-sense intuition and would result in a very deep version of skepticism (how deep obviously depending on what the right account of the scope of direct observation turns out to be).

A helpful way to think about this issue in relation to a particular claim that is not justified by direct observation alone is to imagine forming a *conditional* proposition (that is a proposition of the "if . . . then . . ." form) in the following way: The *antecedent* (the "if" part) is to include *everything* that is justified by direct observation or experience alone (at the time in question), that is, everything that is justified directly by the relevant kinds of experience without the need for any further inference. Much of this will presumably be irrelevant to any particular proposition whose content goes beyond direct observation (a *trans-observational proposition*), but it is simpler to include it anyway. The *consequent* (the "then" part) of the conditional is to be just the particular trans-observational proposition we are interested in. The conditional proposition as a whole thus says that *if* the various things justified by direct observation or experience alone are true, *then* this further trans-observational claim is true also. (Pretty obviously we can't actually formulate this proposition, since the list of things that would go into the antecedent is impossibly long. But we can still think about it clearly enough for the following argument—can't we?)

Ask yourself now whether this conditional proposition is itself justified in some way. If you consider this question carefully, it becomes clear that the conditional proposition is at least *not* justified by direct observation or experience alone: direct observation alone cannot tell us that if the results of direct observation are true, then something further that is not a result of direct observation is true.[9] But if this conditional proposition is not justified at all, then it is apparently impossible for the trans-observational proposition in the consequent to be genuinely justified by inference from the things known by direct observation: for how could I be justified in inferring from the antecedent claim to the consequent claim if I have no justification, no reason, for thinking that the latter claim will be true if the former claim is true? It apparently follows that there are only two possible ways in which the trans-observational claim in the consequent could be justified: either (i) it is justified on its own, independent of any inference from the antecedent claim, in a way that does not depend on direct observation or experience—that is, is justified *a priori*; or (ii) the whole conditional proposition is justified *a priori*, and the consequent, trans-observational claim is justified by inference from this conditional claim and the observationally justified antecedent claim.[10]

It apparently follows that if there is no *a priori* justification, then it is impossible for *any* trans-observational claim to be justified, so that justified belief and knowledge is limited to what can be justified by direct observation alone. This would amount to a quite severe and intuitively implausible version of skepticism (though just how severe and implausible will again depend on the scope of direct observation). Thus if commonsense intuition is even approximately correct about the scope of our knowledge (and assuming, as we are for now,[11] that internally accessible justification is indeed a requirement for knowledge), it follows that *a priori* justification must exist.[12]

A closely related but even more powerful argument for the existence of *a priori* justification, one that does not depend in any specific way on claims about the scope of our knowledge or the falsity of skepticism, can be arrived at by reflecting on the very notion of reasoning. To *reason* is to make a transition in thought from one (perhaps complex) proposition to a second proposition in a way that involves at least *conditional* justification: justification for the claim that *if* the first proposition is true, *then* the second one will be true also. Reasoning is thus quite different from mere free association, in which no conditional justification of the sort indicated need be involved. It is also obviously quite different from being justified in adopting the second claim by appeal to direct observation or experience. My suggestion is that the very idea of reasoning really only makes sense if the conditional justification in question (as opposed to the justification of the first of the two propositions) is *a priori* in character. Observation or experience can of course play a role by justifying part or all of the initial proposition. But once observation or experience has done its job, once all the claims that are directly justified by observation or experience have been accepted, either there is no justification for any further transition, and accordingly no genuine reasoning can take place, or else there is *a priori* justification of at least a conditional sort for the reasoned transitions. (Reasoning can also, of course, involve drawing the conclusions that would follow from propositions that are merely possible, even from those that are known in fact to be false. But this would still have to involve conditional justification of the sort indicated.)

Think about this very carefully. Perhaps we can just barely imagine a being who is entirely unable to reason, whose justified claims are limited to the results of direct observation or experience alone. Such a being would also, of course, be unable to engage in *practical* reasoning to decide what to do or how to act on the basis of its directly observational knowledge, and so would have to simply have its actions or behavior spontaneously triggered somehow by its observational states. It would also be unable to reason hypothetically, that is, unable to consider the hypothetical results of various possible actions or occurrences. It would be unable to plan for the future or wonder about alternative possibilities in the past. The content of its justified beliefs would be limited to whatever it is that can be justified by direct observation or experience alone, and would have no further significance or implications of any sort—at least none that such a being could appreciate. Whether beings of this sort are really imaginable is perhaps uncertain, but what does not seem at all uncertain is that we ourselves are *not* at all like that. And it is also clear that there could be no reason or argument for the conclusion that we *are* after all like that which was not intrinsically self-defeating—since it would itself have to be an instance of the very reasoning that it seemingly rules out as impossible for us. (Think about this point very carefully: is there any further possibility that is being overlooked?)

Together these two arguments seem more than sufficient reasons for accepting the idea of *a priori* justification and proceeding to investigate the two main philosophical views of how it works and what it amounts to, which is what we will now proceed to do. We will first investigate a relatively modern view, *moderate empiricism*, which holds that *a priori* justification, while perfectly genuine, is limited to the consequences of definitions or meanings—and so is, in a sense to be further explained below, essentially trivial or verbal in character.[13] This view is very probably the most widely held position on the nature of *a priori* justification, and we will accordingly devote the most space to it here. Later we will turn more briefly to a more traditional and in some ways much more ambitious view, *rationalism*, according to which *a priori* justification depends on genuine insight into the necessary character of reality.

Moderate Empiricism

Someone who is skeptical of the very idea of *a priori* justification but who has become convinced by the foregoing examples and arguments that its existence is undeniable—or at least can only be denied by accepting skeptical results that are even more implausible—is very likely to hit upon and be strongly tempted by the idea that such justification is merely a matter of *meaning* or *definition* or *conceptual content*. In fact we have already encountered the first relatively clear historical version of this idea in Hume's view that demonstrative or *a priori* knowledge derives from "relations of ideas" and depends entirely on the avoidance of contradiction. In Hume's view, such knowledge, although perfectly genuine in its own way, really tells us nothing substantive about the world (which is why it cannot, according to him, be used to justify the substantive claims made in inductive reasoning), but instead merely spells out the content of our ideas and the way they are related to each other. Such a view would make *a priori* justification much less puzzling and problematic than it might otherwise seem, and it accordingly deserves careful consideration. As will emerge, however, it is also a slippery view, difficult to come to grips with clearly and cleanly, and we will have to proceed very carefully.

The best way to explain the moderate empiricist view more fully is to begin with an example for which its main claim is initially quite plausible. Consider the proposition that *all bachelors are unmarried*. It seems plain that this proposition is one for which *a priori* justification is available. To be sure, it is perhaps barely imaginable that someone might not realize this, and might accordingly seek empirical justification for such a claim, say by knocking on lots of doors, collecting statistics as to the proportion of those who identify themselves as bachelors who also say that they are unmarried, and then reasoning inductively. But it is clear that this is unnecessary, that merely thinking about the content of the proposition in question, without any reliance on experience, will enable one to see readily that it is and indeed *must* be true. (A reminder: whenever I say that anything is thus clear or obvious, part of your job as a budding philosopher is to satisfy yourself that it really is clear, that there are no problems or doubts that you can find.)

But how does such *a priori* justification work in this case? Where does it come from? The moderate empiricist answer is that it derives from the definition or meaning of the term "bachelor" or, perhaps equivalently, from the content of the concept *bachelor*. A bachelor is, *by definition*, an unmarried adult male, and so any person who is in fact a bachelor must also be unmarried.[14] Perhaps the most famous formulation of this point is due to the German philosopher Immanuel Kant[15]: the proposition in question is justified on an *a priori* basis because its predicate concept (the concept of being unmarried) is *included* or *contained* in its subject concept (the concept of a bachelor, that is, of an unmarried adult male); thus to deny that the predicate is true of the subject would be to implicitly contradict the very content of the subject concept. Kant calls propositions having this feature "analytic"; his view is that the *a priori* justification of analytic propositions is in this way straightforward and obvious, not in any way puzzling or problematic from an epistemological standpoint. And the moderate empiricist claim, which Kant—on the surface at least[16]—does not accept, is that *something* like this is true of *all* genuine cases of *a priori* justification, thus allegedly establishing that *a priori* justifiable claims are mere matters of definition, trivial or *tautological* (look up this word in a dictionary) in character, and thus say nothing substantive about the world.

Something like this, perhaps, but not exactly this in all cases. One problem with the Kantian conception of analyticity is that there are other propositions that have seemed to many to have essentially the same tautological status, but that are not of subject-predicate form at all and so obviously cannot satisfy Kant's definition. Consider, for example, the proposition that *either the tallest tree in the quad is a redwood or the tallest tree in the quad is not a redwood.* Assuming that the criteria for being a redwood are clear and sharp, and that is it is also clear which quad is intended and what its boundaries are, it seems obvious that this proposition is also one that is justified *a priori* and also plausible that it has something like the same trivial, nonsubstantive quality as does the bachelor example.[17] But this proposition has no subject and predicate as a whole (though its two component propositions do), and it is thus not analytic under Kant's conception of analyticity.

Moderate empiricists have reacted to this problem, and to more serious ones yet to come, by adopting expanded or modified concepts of analyticity (or definitions of "analytic"), concepts that allegedly amount to much the same thing and have the same epistemological significance as the Kantian conception, but that nonetheless apply to a wider range of cases. The result of this strategy is that the term "analytic" has in fact no univocal meaning, but has rather been used to express a fairly large number of allegedly similar, but nonetheless distinct concepts. And this in turn has, not surprisingly, been a source of both confusion and occasional obfuscation.

The crucial point to bear in mind here is that whether moderate empiricism really succeeds in accounting for all *a priori* justification in the way that it claims to do depends not on the mere applicability of the technical term "analytic" to all *a priori* justifiable propositions, but rather on the underlying claim that the applicability of this term is supposed to support: the claim that all *a priori* justifiable propositions are, like the original bachelor example, nonsubstantive, trivial or tautological consequences of something like meaning or definition or conceptual content. The truth of this claim in a particular case seems to follow fairly straightforwardly from the applicability to the proposition in question of Kant's conception of analyticity (though, as we will see, there is at least a small problem even here), but it cannot be just assumed to follow from the applicability of these other, different conceptions of analyticity simply because the same word is used to express them. What matters is not the use of the term "analytic," but rather the particular conception that this word is used by a given version of moderate empiricism to express. (As an example that will turn out to be less far-fetched than it might at first seem, suppose that some philosopher were to define "analytic" as meaning simply the same thing as "justified *a priori*." Obviously on this conception of analyticity, all *a priori* justified propositions would be analytic, but equally obviously this would do nothing at all to explain how *a priori* justification is possible.)

The Fregean Conception of Analyticity

The modified concept of analyticity that deals most straightforwardly with the redwood example and others like it is one due originally to the nineteenth-century German logician and philosopher of language Gottlob Frege. Frege defined an analytic proposition as one that (i) is a substitution instance of a truth of logic or (ii) can be transformed into such a substitution instance by replacing one or more of its component concepts with synonymous or definitionally equivalent concepts.[18] Here a truth of logic is to be understood as a general, abstract proposition that is true on logical grounds alone and so would be provable as a theorem in an adequate system of logic. Thus the relevant truth of logic for the redwood example is the abstract proposition that *for any proposition P, either it is the case that P or it is not the case that P*—something that you should be able to see intuitively to be true solely on logical grounds, simply because of the meaning or significance of the logical idea of disjunction expressed by the word "or" and the logical idea of negation expressed by the word "not." This proposition says in effect that the either-or part will be true no matter what proposition is substituted for the variable P. The original redwood proposition is then clearly such a substitution instance, with the proposition that *the tallest tree in the quad is a redwood* substituted in this case for P. Thus the original redwood proposition qualifies as analytic under the Fregean definition, specifically under clause (i).

What about clause (ii) of Frege's definition? The significance of this clause can in fact be illustrated by returning to the bachelor example. The proposition that *all bachelors are unmarried* is not a substitution instance of a truth of logic as it stands. Its explicit logical form would be *all F's are non-G*, and this is clearly not a truth of logic since there are many instances of it that are not even true (for example, *all snakes are nonreptiles*). But if we replace the concept *bachelor* with the equivalent or in some sense identical concept *unmarried adult male*,[19] we get the proposition that *all unmarried adult males are unmarried*, which is a substitution instance of the logical truth that *for any properties or classes F, G, H, all FGH's are F*—which again you should be able to intuitively recognize as having that status. Thus the bachelor proposition too is analytic under the Fregean conception, which we thus see includes or subsumes the Kantian conception as a special case.[20]

One specific version of the general moderate empiricist thesis would then be that all *a priori* justifiable propositions (a) are analytic according to Frege's conception of analyticity, and therefore (b) are merely trivial or verbal in character and hence nonsubstantive. Here part (b) is supposed to imply that there is no epistemological problem or puzzle about how such propositions could be justified *a priori*, that their *a priori* justification is, as I will say, *epistemologically unproblematic*, not in need of any further explanation from an epistemological standpoint. But, as we will see next, there are in fact serious problems with both parts of this thesis.

The problem with part (a) is that there are many examples of propositions that are seemingly justifiable *a priori* but that do not seem to be analytic according to Frege's conception. Here is a short list of examples, including one of our original ones, that could easily be expanded with further examples of these same general kinds and others:

> Nothing can be red and green all over at the same time.
> For any solid objects A, B, and C, if A is larger in volume than B, and B is larger in volume than C, then A is larger in volume than C.
> All triangles have three sides.[21]
> 2 + 3 = 5.
> No object can be spherical and cubical at the same time.

None of these propositions is a substitution instance of a truth of logic as it stands.[22] Nor is there any clear way to transform any of them into such a substitution instance by substituting synonyms. (This issue will be discussed below in relation to some of these examples, but you should think about it yourself for the others.) Thus, an opponent will claim, the version of moderate empiricism just offered is mistaken, because there are clear examples of *a priori* justifiable claims that are not analytic (in Frege's sense), but instead are *synthetic* (*nonanalytic*). (And that there is justified belief and knowledge that is in this way synthetic *a priori* is one formulation, albeit not the most perspicuous, of the opposed view known as *rationalism*.[23])

To more fully appreciate the force of this objection, we will consider two of these examples more fully, starting with the first, the proposition that nothing can be red and green all over at the same time. I will assume that you are in agreement that this proposition is justifiable *a priori* and also that it is not as it stands a substitution instance of a truth of logic. But might there not be, contrary to what was just claimed, a way to transform this proposition into such a substitution instance? Let's think about how this might be done. Pretty clearly the key terms or concepts in the proposition are *red* and *green*, so that it would be a definition or equivalent concept for one or both of these that would be required. Moreover, these conceptual equivalents would seemingly have to connect somehow with each other, for if they were entirely unrelated, the resulting form could still not be a substitution instance of a truth of logic: it could not be a truth of logic that two unrelated concepts could not both apply to the same thing. (Think about this until you see clearly why it is so.)

Do you see any way to define one of these concepts so as to yield this result? Indeed, are they definable at all? (Think a bit about these questions before proceeding.) Well, one initial thought at this point is that since red things cannot also be green, maybe *red* could simply defined as *not green*. Then the original proposition would say that nothing can be not green and green all over at the same time, which does seem like a substitution instance of a truth of logic. But is this a correct definition of red? (Think again before you read on.) The answer seems to be plainly "no," for if we also defined *blue* in a parallel fashion as *not green*, we would get the obviously absurd result that *red* and *blue* are equivalent, indeed identical, concepts.

But suppose we consider defining *red* instead as *not green and not blue and not yellow . . .* and so on, for all of the other possible colors. One problem with this is that it is less than clear exactly which and how many colors would have to go into the list of negations or exclusions, but this might be manageable. (Is it?) Is such a definition of *red* plausibly correct otherwise? (Think about this question for yourself before reading further.)

In fact, it is pretty clear that both of these suggested definitions of *red* are simply wrong, in two related ways, as an account of the actual meaning or content of the concept *red* (don't forget that this is what such a definition is supposed to give!). The basic point here is that *red* is a *positive* concept, the concept of the *presence* of a certain property, and not merely a *negative* concept having to do with the *absence* of certain other properties. This can be seen clearly by imagining two unlikely, but still possible cases. Imagine first someone who has never experienced or even hallucinated anything red, but is familiar with all of the other colors whose negations or exclusions are listed in the proposed definition. Such a person would have no problem understanding that definition, but would seemingly still not understand the concept of *red*, that is, would have no conception of the specific positive property in question.[24] Now imagine what is in a way the opposite case: someone who lives in a world where *everything* is red, and who has never experienced or even hallucinated any other color. Such a person could presumably understand the concept *red*, but would seemingly be utterly unable to understand the proposed definition or allegedly equivalent concept. Either of these cases seems to show that the concept *red* and the proposed definitionally equivalent concept are not in fact the same concept.

Is there any way to do any better than this with the red-green example? It is far from obvious that there is or what it might be, and in fact philosophers disposed toward moderate empiricism have struggled mightily without much success.[25] This is a good (though not quite conclusive) reason for thinking that there is no equivalent concept that can replace the concept *red* in the example in question in such a way as to turn that proposition into a substitution instance of a logical truth (and, of course, an exactly parallel argument would apply to *green*). If this is right, then the red-green proposition, though justified *a priori*, is not analytic in the Fregean sense, in which case the version of moderate empiricism that uses that conception of analyticity is mistaken.

There is no space here for a thorough discussion of each of the other examples given, so I will consider only one more of them, namely the proposition that 2 + 3 = 5, which is in fact the one out of this list that was historically regarded as the most hopeful for the moderate empiricist and also the one most explicitly considered by Frege himself. (A warning: the discussion of this example is unavoidably a bit technical—be prepared.)

Here the obvious candidates for definition are the numerical concepts 2, 3, and 5, and this time there are much more plausible definitions available. If we take 1 as the undefined starting point, then 2 can be defined as *the successor of 1*, that is, as *the number that is greater than 1 by 1*, that is, as 1 + 1. And analogously, 3 can be defined as *the successor of 2*, that is, as (1 + 1) + 1. Here the parentheses are crucial: 3 is *arithmetically equal* to 1 + 1 + 1, but that is not its *definition* (any more than 3 is to be *defined* as, say, 7 − 4). Finally, 5 can be analogously defined as *the successor of the successor of 3*, that is, as {[(1 + 1) + 1] + 1} + 1 (with all of the parentheses again essential, for the same reason). Given these definitions, which I am willing to accept as correct, the original proposition can be transformed into:

$$(1 + 1) + [(1 + 1) + 1] = \{[(1 + 1) + 1] + 1\} + 1$$

Here, though this is inessential to the main point to be made, extra fences have been added on the left-hand side of the equation to make it clear that it is conceptually equivalent to 2 + 3, rather than to 1 + 1 + 2 + 1, which is quite a different concept, even though the two numbers are again arithmetically equal.

The problem now is that while there is no doubt that this equation is correct, its correctness does not seem to be merely a matter of logic, as it would have to be if it were just a substitution instance of a truth of logic. Intuitively, what is needed to make the two sides identical is the addition or subtraction or movement of some parentheses. The needed adjustments do not affect the correctness of the equation, but this is again not a matter of sheer logic, but rather depends on the specific subject matter in question (numbers and the addition relation); for example, if the plus signs were replaced by minus signs, the equation would no longer be correct, even though the logical form would be exactly the same. (Check this for yourself.) Thus the equation resulting from the substitutions could itself just as well have been on the list of those which are not analytic on the Fregean conception.

We have been talking about the main problem that arises for part (a) of the version of the moderate empiricist thesis that employs the Fregean conception of analyticity, but now it is time to turn to part (b), the claim that propositions that are analytic on Frege's conception are, as I put it earlier, epistemologically unproblematic, because their being justifiable *a priori* is due merely to their trivial, definitional and hence nonsubstantive character. Consider again the proposition, discussed earlier, that *either the tallest tree in the quad is a redwood or the tallest tree in the quad is not a redwood*. This proposition is, as we saw, justified *a priori*: one need not look in the quad nor know anything about redwoods to be able to see that it is true. But we now need to think harder than we have so far about what exactly the version of moderate empiricism that we are now considering has to say about how this proposition is justified.

Pretty obviously *part* of the account is that the proposition in question is justified by virtue of being recognized as a substitution instance of the general truth of logic that was also cited earlier, namely that *for any proposition P, either it is the case that P or it is not the case that P*. No definitional or conceptual replacement is involved in this case, making it a bit artificial to describe the justification in question as a matter of definition or conceptual equivalence, but perhaps this can be thought of as the limiting case in which the propositions occurring in the propositions can serve as their own definitions for the purpose in question. The real problem, however, is that in order for this specific proposition to be justified *a priori* in virtue of being a substitution instance of the indicated general logical truth, the logical proposition in question must *itself* be justified and indeed justified *a priori*. Though masked somewhat by referring to this more general proposition as a "logical *truth*" and by pointing out that it is intuitively obvious that it has that status, this point is still essential. If one were not justified *a priori* in accepting the logical truth itself, then merely recognizing that the specific proposition was an instance of the general form in question would yield no reason to think that the specific proposition was true and so such recognition would yield no justification. And the same issue also arises about our other example, the proposition that *all bachelors are unmarried*, and indeed about *any* application of the Fregean conception of analyticity.

Does the version of moderate empiricism that we are considering have any account to offer of how such truths of logic are themselves justified *a priori*? It seems clear on reflection that in fact, perhaps surprisingly, it does not. The whole idea of this version and of the conception of analyticity that it appeals to is, after all, that *a priori* justification can be accounted for by showing that the proposition in question is transformable into, reducible to, an instance of a truth of logic, but this idea is obviously incapable of accounting fully for the justification of logic itself. Perhaps some truths of logic are themselves transformable into instances of still more general truths of logic, but this process must come to an end at some point, leaving the justification of the remaining, most general truths of logic unaccounted for. But if this is so, then the justification of the other propositions that were reduced to these most general logical truths was not really *fully* accounted for either.

This is a subtle point, and we need to reflect on it carefully, "chew" on it a little, to make sure that its full significance has been grasped. Moderate empiricism offers the hopeful promise that *a priori* justification can be accounted for in a way that removes the aura of mystery that allegedly surrounds it. This is supposedly to be done by showing that such justification is really just a matter of meaning or definition or conceptual content, so that the *a priori* justified claims in question do not really say anything substantive about the world, but, as it is sometimes put, are "merely a matter of semantics." But the version of moderate empiricism that we are presently dealing with has failed to fulfill this promise. It turns out to explain the *a priori* justifiable propositions that it does apply to only by showing that they are instances of, reducible to, more general truths, whose justification it does not account for. But then even the justification of the truths that are in this way explained has not been shown to be *merely* a matter of definition, *merely* semantical. What has been shown is only that the more specific, less general truths are applications of the more general truths of logic. But if the latter are themselves substantive, genuinely about the world, not merely matters of definition—and no reason at all has been offered so far for denying or questioning this—then so also, it would seem, are their specific applications, with meaning or definition or conceptual content being relevant only to revealing that these applications do indeed have that status. (And we are now in a position to see that even the Kantian conception of analyticity faces the same objection: it too relies on truths of logic, albeit very simple and seemingly obvious ones, whose *a priori* justification it does not *and cannot in principle* account for.)

In addition, remember that there is also the other, previously discussed objection that there are many seemingly clear examples of *a priori* justification to which this version of moderate empiricism does not seem to apply at all. (Like the other objection, this one too also applies to a conception of moderate empiricism built around the Kantian conception of analyticity, for many of the examples in question are of subject-predicate form.) Thus the version of moderate empiricism we have been considering clearly does not succeed. (But, something that applies to every such claim in this book, this does *not* mean that you should agree until and unless you have thought carefully on your own about whether this is right, whether there is any good reply on behalf of the view in question that has been overlooked.) The question to which we must now turn, necessarily more briefly, is whether any other version of moderate empiricism, based on some different concept of analyticity, can do any better.

Another Conception of Analyticity

There are in fact, as already suggested, *many* other conceptions of analyticity and corresponding versions of moderate empiricism, far too many for them all to be considered in this book. Here I will focus on only one of these, chosen because it is probably one of the two versions of moderate empiricism that are mostly widely held (the other being the version already discussed).[26] This version offers a much simpler conception of analyticity, defining an analytic proposition as simply one that is true solely by virtue of its content or meaning. The advantage offered by this conception of analyticity is that it may seem on the surface to handle the cases that caused problems for the Fregean conception, such as the examples listed above and the truths of logic, while dealing just as well with the examples to which the Fregean and Kantian conceptions apply.

But does it really? Indeed, does this conception of analyticity really offer a satisfactory explanation of *any* case of *a priori* justification? To try to get a handle on this issue, let us consider again one of the examples discussed earlier, the proposition that *nothing can be red all over and green all over at the same time*. Is this proposition true *solely* by virtue of its content or meaning in a way that explains how it is justified *a priori*?

Here we need to think very carefully and make sure that we keep the issue clearly in focus. Clearly, as we have already seen, the content is at least *relevant* to the issue of justification: One who did not understand that content could not be justified in accepting the proposition. (This, however, seems true for *any* sort of justification, shedding no special light on *a priori* justification in particular.) Moreover, anyone who understands that content can apparently also see at once that the proposition must be true—but this is just to say that this proposition is justified *a priori* and rather obviously so, while saying nothing yet about how or why this *a priori* justification obtains.

Thus the real issue here is not whether the content or meaning of the proposition is relevant in these ways, as it obviously is, but whether it is somehow by itself *sufficient* for justification. And if this issue is carefully considered, the answer seems to be "no." To understand this content is to understand both which two specific properties are in question and the idea of there being an incompatibility between them. But to have a reason to think that the proposition is true, one must *also* see further that the two specific properties in question really *do* stand in this relationship of incompatibility, that redness and greenness *are* in fact so related that they cannot occupy the same region—and that is something over and above merely understanding the claim at issue, something which thus seems to require a further, independent act of intellectual insight. It may be hard to imagine someone who grasps the content of this proposition without also at once having this further insight, but that does not in any way show that these are just the same thing. Thus, it seems, this version of moderate empiricism fails to really explain the *a priori* justification of this proposition.

My suggestion is that what is true in this case is true in general: that this version of moderate empiricism fails in fact to offer *any* genuine explanation of the *a priori* justification of *any* proposition—or at least none over and above the partial insight offered by the version previously discussed. In every case, seeing that the proposition in question must be true will be an insight that goes beyond a mere understanding of its content, however invariably this further insight may in fact occur (which will in fact vary substantially from case to case). In effect, this version of moderate empiricism relies in an illegitimate way on the intuitive obviousness of many (though decidedly not all) *a priori* justified propositions. Because the truth of the propositions in question is so obvious once their content is understood, it is easy to think that an understanding of this content is all that is required for justification. But this, I am suggesting, is an illusion. Given a grasp of the content, there is *always* the further question of whether the claim in question is true, and this will be so no matter how obvious the answer to this further question might be. Indeed, it is just this obviousness, which is of course just self-evidence under another name, that needs to be accounted for, not just taken for granted. (That this further question always exists is again a claim that you should carefully reconsider on your own, thinking about the various examples that have been given here and about others that you think up for yourself.)

I would also suggest more generally that all other versions of moderate empiricism (and correlative conceptions of analyticity) have in fact one or the other of the same kinds of failings that we have found in the ones we have considered explicitly: either they merely *reduce* some cases of *a priori* justification to others, while leaving these remaining ones unaccounted for; or else, when carefully considered, they turn out to fail to really explain or account for *a priori* justification at all, relying tacitly on the very intuitive obviousness (or seeming necessity) that is most in need of explanation. (Some few versions manage to combine both of these mistakes.) But this is not something that can be demonstrated or even further discussed here.[27] Instead I will conclude this chapter with a briefer examination of the other main position regarding the nature of *a priori* justification: the traditional rationalist view held by Descartes, Plato, and many other historical philosophers.

Rationalism

The central idea of the rationalist view concerning the nature of *a priori* justification is at least initially extremely simple and straightforward: *a priori* justification involves a direct insight (or apparent insight[28]) into the nature and structure of reality—where successful, one whose content is *necessary*, reflecting features and relations that could not fail to obtain. Consider again the proposition that *nothing can be red and green all over at the same time*. According to the rationalist, once I understand this proposition, I am apparently able to see or apprehend directly that the two properties do stand necessarily in the indicated relation of incompatibility, that each of them necessarily excludes the presence of the other, and so also that the proposition in question must be true. Similarly when I consider and understand the proposition that 2 + 3 = 5, I am apparently able to see or grasp directly that the sum indicated on the left-hand side of the equation is necessarily equal to the number indicated on the right-hand side, that is, that in any situation in which there are 2 things of some relevant kind and 3 more things of that kind and no more, there will necessarily always be exactly 5 things of the kind in question.

These *a priori* insights (as I will refer to them) obviously depend on an understanding of the content or meaning of each proposition, but they are not somehow merely reducible to that understanding. According to the rationalist, this is what is involved in *every* case of *a priori* justification, even those that conform to the Kantian or Fregean conceptions of analyticity. All that is special in those cases is that the insights in question conform to certain structural patterns that are shared by other parallel insights, where one can also see or grasp in a more general way that any proposition having that same structure must be true. But there is no apparent reason to think either that such common structures can be identified for all cases of *a priori* justification, nor, more importantly, that the presence of such a general structure somehow removes the need for the sort of insight upon which the rationalist insists.

What should we think about this view? At one level, it accurately reflects what seems intuitively to go on in a case of *a priori* justification—seems, that is, before doubts and criticism have set in. Many philosophers would argue, however, that the simplicity and initial intuitive plausibility of the view are purchased at the severe price of making it utterly mysterious at a deeper, more reflective level what *a priori* justification really amounts to or how it is supposed to work. Indeed, rationalism, though accepted more or less without question by almost all philosophers from Plato and Aristotle down to Descartes and his immediate successors (especially Locke), has been more or less constantly under attack since the time of Hume and Kant, and especially so for most of the twentieth century. We must attempt to understand why this is so, what is supposed to be so objectionable or problematic about the rationalist view. I will approach this issue by considering some of the main questions and objections that have been raised in relation to the rationalist view.[29]

First, one important issue is how strong a claim the rationalist view can or should make about the *a priori* insights to which it appeals. Historically, most rationalists have claimed, or at least have seemed to claim, that *a priori* insight is *infallible*, that is, that claims justified in this way can never be mistaken—and indeed that this is itself a necessary fact that can be known *a priori*.[30] But is such a claim at all plausible? And is there any good reason why the rationalist needs to make it?

The answer to both of these questions appears to be "no." With regard to the first, it is hard to see how *any* human cognitive process could be entirely free from the possibility of error. What possible reason could there be for thinking that *a priori* insight is not affected by such things as lack of full attention, failure to notice subtle detail, confusion, distraction, etc., factors that seem to afflict every other sort of human cognitive operation? Moreover, this general reason to suspect fallibility is strongly reinforced by what seem to be clear examples of actual mistakes, including routine errors of calculation and reasoning, apparently clear but paradox-inducing insights in logic and mathematics, and at least many of the errors that the history of philosophy is littered with (a point that does not depend on being able to decide *which* philosophical views are mistaken or correct, but just on noticing the pervasive disagreement that makes it impossible for all or even very many of the historical views to be correct).

Is there any room for serious disagreement about this point? A proponent of infallibility might perhaps insist that the apparent *a priori* insights from which the erroneous judgments resulted were not genuine, that genuine *a priori* insight is and must be infallible. But apart from any clear rationale for this claim, it is inherently futile if *a priori* insight is to be regarded as a basis for *internalist* justification in the way that the Cartesian view and most historical rationalists insist.[31] If mock *a priori* insights (as we might call them) at least sometimes cannot be distinguished from genuine ones by the person who has them, as the cases of error seem to plainly show, then the consequence of saying that justification results only from genuine insights will be that a person will be unable to tell whether or not a belief is justified on this basis—until its truth or falsity is established in some other way, making the justification supposedly provided by the insight no longer essential.[32] Thus the rationalist must apparently say that the basis for *a priori* justification is the *appearance* of *a priori* insight: the person's *seeming*, given adequate understanding and reasonably careful reflection, to find a proposition to be necessary.[33] The belief that results from such an insight *might* still be mistaken (though there is no reason to think that the chance of error is very large—is there?). And such an error might be corrected in at least two ways: (i) by comparing that *a priori* belief with other, related ones, or (ii) by thinking about the claim in question even more carefully and fully and thereby coming to see the mistake.

Second, a closely related issue is whether beliefs justified *a priori* must be, as the historical rationalist tradition again on the whole seems to claim, immune to any possibility of *refutation* by *experience*. It is again unclear why a rationalist needs to make such a claim. His main thesis is that *a priori* insight provides a source of justification distinct from experience, a thesis that is seemingly unaffected by the further issue of whether and to what extent the resulting justification is capable of being defeated or overridden by other sources of justification, whether by other *a priori* insights or by experience or by anything else.

But a further question is whether experience, and here we may limit ourselves for simplicity to sensory experience, does ever in fact conflict *directly* with *a priori* insight. Think about this in relation to the various examples discussed in this chapter: What sort of sensory or perceptual experience would conflict with the insight that *nothing can be red and green all over at the same time?* Or with the insight that $2 + 3 = 5$? In a way it is easy to specify such conflicting experiences: they would be experiences of something that is red and green all over at the same time or of a situation in which there are 2 things and 3 more and no others, but still somehow not 5 altogether. But what is extremely doubtful is whether we can make sense of such specifications in any genuinely intelligible way, that is, whether we have any real idea of what such experiences could possibly be like. (Consider this question on your own: Do you think that you can clearly imagine such experiences?)

What this suggests (but obviously does not fully establish) is that in fact the issue of *direct* conflict between experience and *a priori* insight simply does not arise in any significant way. This would not mean that experience is simply irrelevant to claims supposedly justified *a priori*. What it would mean instead is that conflicts between experience and *a priori* justification are always *indirect*, depending on inferential connections of some sort whose justification can in the end only be *a priori*.[34] And this would mean in turn that experience could undercut or refute one *a priori* claim only in a way that relies at the same time on other *a priori* justified claims, and thus could not pose a challenge to *a priori* justification in general.

Third, a fairly pervasive, but rarely fully articulated concern among philosophers about the idea of *a priori* insight focuses on its nondiscursive character: on the fact that appeals to direct *a priori* insight involve in general nothing like steps of reasoning or the appeal to independent criteria or standards (for how would *those* be justified?—think about it), nothing but the bare and seemingly brute fact of the insight itself.[35] Is it not fundamentally irrational to rely on something as unargued, as inarticulate as this? This description is at least a bit misleading in that the insights in question can often be elaborated to some degree or intellectually displayed and discussed, but it is fundamentally correct that for rationalism the *a priori* insight is an autonomous and irreplaceable basis for justification that cannot be somehow translated into or reduced to something more discursive.

The question is whether there is any real objection to be found in the vicinity of this point. The rationalist will happily agree on the fundamentally unargued, direct or immediate character of *a priori* insight, but will insist that any nonskeptical view must accept *something* having this sort of status. For what is the alternative? Criteria or standards must themselves be justified. Steps of reasoning require premises, not all of which can be derived from further steps, on pain of an infinite regress; and the correctness of the steps still has to be directly, nondiscursively recognized. Thus some nondiscursive basis is apparently required if there is to be any justification at all, and (as argued above) a nonexperiential one if there are to be any justified claims that transcend experience—so that its having that character is in itself no objection to *a priori* insight.

Fourth, a closely related concern focuses on the possibility that the *a priori* insights of different people, or even of the same person at different times, might conflict with each other. This, it might be argued, is what is wrong with the appeal to brute, nondiscursive insight: it leaves no recourse in cases of disagreement. Of course, if the point just made that discursive procedures must ultimately rely on such nondiscursive insights is correct, then such procedures could not, even if available, provide a general solution to this problem. (Think carefully why this is so.) But even if this is right, the issue of how to resolve conflicts of *a priori* insight still remains.

Probably there is no general solution to this problem. There are many things that can be tried: Those involved can investigate separately or, even better, together whether there is some ambiguity or unclarity in their understandings of the claim or claims in question that accounts for the disagreement. They can look for independent premises, some justified *a priori* and some perhaps empirically, which they both accept, that can be used in various ways to resolve the conflict. They can each try to articulate their insights in different, perhaps somewhat more detailed ways, in the hope that some change or refinement in one or both insights will occur in a way that resolves the dispute. They can enlist the aid of others, who may be able to find ways to help one or both to see how their seeming insights were mistaken. They can each ponder and reflect on their own to try to find some mistake or confusion. In other words, they can do all of the various things that people have always done in such situations. But there is also no guarantee that any of these approaches will work in a particular case, and thus the possibility at least exists that some such conflicts will persist even though all such means of resolution have been thoroughly tried. (Though it is doubtful that this situation occurs very frequently.) What each person should do or think in a case where the conflict remains unresolved is a difficult and subtle issue, one that depends on the details of the case and on the apparent clarity and sureness of their individual insight. But does the possibility of such cases pose any general objection to the reliance on *a priori* insight—even in the many cases where no such conflict occurs? It is hard to see why it should. (Is this an adequate response, or can you see some way to push the objection further?)

Fifth, many philosophers have worried about what *metaphysical* picture lies behind the appeal to *a priori* insight. Here the most obvious and standard answer was well articulated by the British philosopher Bertrand Russell, in a relatively early work,[36] and I will briefly summarize his view. For Russell, *a priori* knowledge ultimately has to do with relations of *universals*. These are *abstract* entities: such things as properties (redness or being a tree), relations (being larger than, being a necessary consequence of), numbers (2, π), etc. Such entities are, according to Russell, part of reality, but are neither physical nor mental in character. They do not exist in time or space. (Russell puts this by saying that they do not *exist* at all, though they do *subsist* or have *being*.) Not only *a priori* justifiable truths but in fact all truths of any kind have at least partially to do with such universals. Thus in order to know any truths, we must directly apprehend (or, as Russell puts it, must be *acquainted with*) universals. One way to do this, according to him, is to *abstract* from the experience of particular instances of the universals in question: for example, one who experiences several different red items can thereby become acquainted with the general property that they all possess.

According to Russell, we have *a priori* knowledge by directly apprehending necessary relations between the universals with which we are acquainted.

This is, in his view, what is happening in examples like the ones involving the proposition that *nothing can be red and green all over at the same time* or that $2 + 3 = 5$, as discussed earlier in this section. Such propositions are self-evident. That is, they are evident by virtue of the very content of the propositions itself: the particular universals they involve and the specific way in which they are put together or configured in each case. (Look back at our earlier discussion of these examples to see how well it fits this picture.) Many other philosophers, both rationalists and nonrationalists, have believed that the rationalist account of *a priori* insight and its role in justification implicitly involves a metaphysical picture of at least approximately this sort. And many recent philosophers especially have thought that such a "Platonistic" metaphysics is fundamentally untenable, so that this would constitute a further objection to rationalism, perhaps the most serious of all. In fact, however, neither of these claims is obviously correct. While there is undeniably some plausibility to the idea that rationalism is ultimately committed to the sort of picture that Russell presents, this has surely not been established or even investigated in anything like a thorough way. And, more importantly, the supposed objections to such a view are, in my judgment, much less compelling than they are usually taken to be. But further discussion of these matters is impossible in this book, so I will have to leave them to your further consideration, in light of whatever background in metaphysics you either presently have or eventually acquire.

I have suggested that there are serious problems with moderate empiricism and have tried to suggest that rationalism presents at least a more attractive option than it is usually regarded as doing. But, like all the discussions in the present book, our discussion of *a priori* justification has been very much less than conclusive, with plenty of loose ends and further issues left for you to pursue.

There is, however, one important further point to be made about the choice between these two views, before we turn to issues having to do with empirical justification. We saw in chapter 4 that an appeal to *a priori* justification seems to offer the only hope for a nonskeptical response to the problem of induction,[37] and we will see in chapter 7 that something similar seems to be true for the problem of justifying beliefs about the material world on the basis of our sense experience. In fact, however, it is very doubtful that either of these appeals to *a priori* justification, or indeed the *a priori* justification of any inference whose conclusion goes beyond direct experience, could succeed if the moderate empiricist view of *a priori* justification were correct. Here I will focus on the issue of induction, leaving the application of essentially the same point to the issue of the external world to be made after you have learned about that issue. The basic question is whether, given a moderate empiricist view, it could possibly be justifiable *a priori* that a standard inductive conclusion is likely to be true if the corresponding standard inductive premise is true. And the answer seems to be that it could not, that the latter claim obviously goes beyond the meaning or content of the former in a way that would rule out its being merely a tautological consequence of that meaning or content.[38] (Seeing this point clearly will require getting really clear, probably clearer than you are so far, about just what the moderate empiricist is saying.) This does not, of course, resolve the issue between the two views of *a priori* justification, but it does perhaps bring out a little more clearly just how much is at stake.

Notes

1. The second part of the foundation is discussed further in chapter 6.

2. A few recent philosophers have restricted the relevant sort of experience to sensory experience, thus counting even the introspective justification of claims about my own mental states as a kind of *a priori* justification. But while there can be no objection to a purely stipulative definition of this sort, it clearly draws the line in the wrong place with respect to the historical discussion of the *a priori* and also lumps together very disparate things as instances of *a priori* justification.

A further issue, which I will mention but not pursue, is whether there are still other sorts of experience of which genuinely *a priori* justification must be independent: the experiences involved in cases of clairvoyance (if such cases actually exist) or, less controversially, the experiences involved in cases of *blindsight*, in which blind people are able to fairly accurately report the presence of various sorts of large objects in their vicinity, without any physical contact with them. Such examples seem to involve something strongly analogous to sense perception: a presumably causal process of some sort in which something like *information* is transmitted from the event in question to the mind of the cognitive subject. My suggestion would be that the results of any such process should also count as a kind of experience, so that the justification involved (assuming that there is any) would not count as *a priori*.

3. There is one possible source of confusion that must be avoided. Objects can of course multiply (insects or animals of various sorts, given a bit of time; soap bubbles, given the right sort of winds) or diminish (soap bubbles again, fish in a tank where piranhas are included, particles of matter and antimatter in close proximity). But the claim that 2 + 3 = 5 says nothing for or against such changes over time. It says only that at any moment or in any fixed situation in which there are 2 things and 3 more (and none beyond those), there will be 5.

4. In chapter 7.

5. In fact, the idea that concepts of these sorts and others are derived from experience turns out to be much harder to make clear sense of than one might suspect. But

the general idea that experience is somehow required for the acquisition of such concepts still seems extremely plausible.

6. This point may seem like hairsplitting, but in fact it is not. The role of experience in providing reasons or justification is quite different from its role in concept acquisition. Each of the two roles raises quite different issues, and only confusion can result from running them together. In particular, the basic reasons, discussed next below, for regarding *a priori* justification as epistemologically indispensable are perfectly compatible with a dependence on experience for the understanding of concepts.

7. Or on other experiences that are strongly analogous to these. See note 2, above.

8. How we should think about the role of memory in justification is a very tricky issue. It will be considered, though only fairly briefly, in chapter 8.

9. If this doesn't seem obvious, think of it this way: the only way that direct observation could justify such a conditional would be if we could directly observe that when the other things known by direct observation (listed in the antecedent) are true, then the further thing we are interested in (given in the consequent) is true also; but this could be so only if we were able to directly observe that the claim in the consequent is true, in which case it would not be trans-observational after all.

10. It is worth noting that these two possibilities overlap to some extent. If the consequent is justified *a priori*, then so also is the conditional as a whole (on the standard truth-functional—so-called material—interpretation of conditionals): to establish that some claim P is true is also automatically to justify that if anything else you like is true, then P is true. But this makes no real difference to the result.

11. See chapter 10.

12. For some further elaboration of this argument, see chapter 11.

13. In chapter 11, we will consider a more radical version of empiricism that at least purports to reject *a priori* justification entirely, while still allegedly avoiding skepticism.

14. I believe that this definition is correct, but some philosophers have raised doubts about it, which you should at least consider. Is the Pope a bachelor? What about a man who is legally married but is separated from his wife and has lived alone for many years? What about a man who is not (legally) married, but has lived with a female partner in a stable, relatively permanent arrangement for many years?

15. In the introduction to his *Critique of Pure Reason* (1st edition,1781; 2nd edition, 1787).

16. Because of his apparent rejection of the moderate empiricist claim, Kant is often classified as a rationalist. My own view is that this classification, while superficially correct, can be seen to be seriously mistaken when one asks what Kant's view, at a deeper level, really amounts to. There is no space here to sort out the details of Kant's view, but those who are curious may consult my book *In Defense of Pure Reason* (Cambridge: Cambridge University Press, 1998), § 1.5. (This book will be hereafter referred to as *IDPR*.)

17. Imagine a weather forecaster who predicts that either it will rain tomorrow or it will not rain tomorrow. This is a less good example because of the possibility of borderline cases where it is neither clearly raining nor clearly not raining, but it still does not seem

to make a substantive claim about the weather. Such a forecaster would probably not keep his job very long.

18. It might be questioned whether the notion of synonymy really applies to *concepts*, as opposed to words or expressions, but I will assume here that it either does or can be extended in the obvious way to do so. There is an alternative, more standard formulation of Frege's conception that speaks instead of sentences and component words, but this seems to me to be at least somewhat misleading, since it is not the justification and knowledge of *sentences* (strings of linguistic symbols) that is the ultimate issue. Here I will generally speak of concepts, even though this will complicate the formulations in some places. (It is also worth adding that Frege himself was not a moderate empiricist: while he believed that many examples of a *priori* justifiable propositions are analytic in the sense he defined, he also believed that there are also important ones that are not.)

19. There is a problem lurking here called "the paradox of analysis," which you might want to pursue further: are the supposed concepts in question really just the same concept? And, if so, how are we to think about the "replacement" referred to in the text? A good place to start is C. H. Langford, "The Notion of Analysis in Moore's Philosophy," in *The Philosophy of G. E. Moore*, ed. P. A. Schilpp (Evanston, Ill.: Northwestern University Press, 1958), pp. 319–43, together with Moore's reply in the same volume.

20. A proposition will be analytic under the Kantian conception if and only if (a) it is also analytic under the Fregean conception, and (b) the relevant truth of logic is of approximately the form given, with perhaps more or fewer elements in the subject and predicate, but where each element in the predicate is also present in the subject.

21. Here I follow the etymology of the word in assuming that *triangle* is defined as *a 3-angled plane rectilinear figure*, not as *a 3-sided plane rectilinear figure* (which should really be called a *trilateral*). But if you prefer the alternative conception of a triangle, substitute the proposition that all triangles have three angles.

22. Think carefully about this claim. It amounts to saying that the general, abstract *form* in each case is not one that has only true substitution instances. Thus the form of the first proposition would be *nothing can be F and G all over at the same time*, something that is plainly not true for all substitutions for F and G (for example, substitute *red* for F and *smooth* for G, and think of a smooth, uniformly red billiard ball).

23. As noted, "synthetic" just means nonanalytic, so that any proposition is either analytic or synthetic and no proposition is both. But philosophers have occasionally become confused on this point. Thus the British philosopher A. J. Ayer, in a widely reprinted discussion of the issue of a *priori* justification, offers the following definitions: "a proposition is analytic when its validity [i.e., justification] depends solely on the definitions of the symbols its contains and synthetic when its validity is determined by the facts of experience." Ayer, *Language, Truth and Logic* (New York: Dover, 1946), p. 78. Under *these* definitions, there can of course be no synthetic propositions that are justified a *priori* (think carefully about why), but there might still be *nonanalytic* propositions that are justified a *priori*—which would be enough to refute moderate empiricism.

24. Part of the idea here is that redness is a property that must somehow be experienced in order to be grasped or understood. Do you think that this assumption is correct?

25. See, for example, the exchange between Hilary Putnam and Arthur Pap, originally in the *Philosophical Review*, vol. 65 and 66 (1956 and 1957), reprinted in *Necessary Truth*, ed. L. W. Sumner and John Wood (New York Random House, 1969), pp. 71–93.

26. Actually this isn't quite right. What is very widely held, more widely probably than either version separately, is rather a kind of uneasy amalgam of the two, one that shifts in an unprincipled way between the two correlative conceptions of analyticity, employing at a given moment whichever one works better for the purpose at hand. This, of course, is a kind of cheat, since it hides the fact that neither conception can do the whole job.

27. For a much more extensive canvassing of the main conceptions of analyticity and correlative versions of moderate empiricism, see *IDPR*, chapter 2.

28. The need for and significance of this qualification is discussed below. Ignore it for now.

29. Most of the points in this section are considered more fully in *IDPR*.

30. This is presumably Descartes's view, though he oddly undercuts it by seeming to say that the claims in question cannot be fully trusted until the existence of God has been proved and that of the evil genius thus ruled out—which is, of course, what leads to the Cartesian circle. (See chapter 2.)

31. To repeat (see endnote 13 of chapter 3 and the associated text), an internalist view is one according to which the reason for thinking that the belief is true must be something that the person in question is or at least can be aware of. See chapter 10 for much more discussion of internalism and of the opposed externalist view.

32. There also seems to be room here for something analogous to a Gettier case (see chapter 3). If there can be mock *a priori* insights yielding beliefs that are mistaken, there can also presumably be cases of such mock insight where the claim in question happens, by accident, to be true. Thus even determining truth or falsity independently would not be enough to determine whether an apparent insight is genuine or mock.

33. In *IDPR*, I refer to this position as *moderate* rationalism, as distinct from the extreme rationalism apparently exemplified in most of the historical tradition.

34. See again the discussion above of why experience cannot justify reasoning.

35. The perceived need to replace brute insight of this sort with something more discursively articulated is one prime motivation for moderate empiricism—though it should be noted that the second of the two main versions of moderate empiricism discussed above does not really do this.

36. *The Problems of Philosophy* (London: Oxford University Press, 1912), chapters 9 and 10.

37. It would be a very good idea to reread and reconsider that earlier discussion in light of the fuller understanding of the idea of *a priori* justification that you have now acquired.

38. In fact, as you may be able to see if you think about it a bit, both of the modern views considered in chapter 4, the pragmatic view and the ordinary language view, take a moderate empiricist view of *a priori* justification for granted, which is a large part of the reason why the proponents of those views are so sure that Hume is right and that no better justification of induction is to be had.

CHAPTER SIX

~

Immediate Experience

We have now examined the first main part of what many, beginning with Descartes, have regarded as the initial basis or *foundation* for justification and knowledge, namely *a priori* insight and the beliefs that it allegedly justifies. In this chapter, we turn to what has been regarded as the second main foundational component: immediate experience and the justification that allegedly results from it. Though we will have to discuss the general idea of immediate experience, our main focus is on the particular variety of immediate experience allegedly involved in sense perception—for it is here, according to most philosophers in the general Cartesian tradition, that the main basis for knowledge of the material world "external" to mind is to be found.

The Concept of Immediacy

What then is *immediate* experience? What exactly is the significance of describing it as "immediate" (or, alternatively, as "direct")? The contrast, as the term itself suggests, is with things that although still experienced in some sense, are experienced via the *mediation* of something else, something that is itself experienced more directly or immediately. But just what sort of mediation is at issue here?

Perhaps the clearest examples of less than fully immediate experience are those involving explicit *inference*. Thus, for example, suppose that upon hearing a certain distinctive thumping or vibrating noise, I am puzzled (and perhaps slightly alarmed) for just a moment, and then realize (because this is the overwhelmingly best explanation for the sound) that my dog Willie is scratching himself, as he often does, and bumping against the dining room table as he does it. Here it would be quite natural to say that I *hear*, and thus *experience*, my dog scratching and the table being bumped. But it also seems reasonable to say that my experience of the scratching and bumping is *mediated* by my more direct experience or awareness of the sound this activity produces.

Why exactly are we tempted to say this? In the first place, my awareness of the dog's activity is obviously *caused* by my awareness of the sound, which is thus in a sense prior. And, second, the *reason* or *justification* both (i) for the belief that I come to have in this case that the dog is indeed scratching and bumping, and (ii) for the belief (whether held by me or by an external observer) that I do hear the dog behaving in this way (think carefully about the difference between these two beliefs) clearly depends on my having an awareness of the sound.[1] We need not worry for the moment about whether my inference is really justified and, if so, how. All that matters for the moment is that it takes place and that my experience of the dog's activity consequently depends on my prior experience of the noise in both of these ways.[2]

Consider now a series of modified examples. As I become more familiar with this particular doggy activity, my momentary hesitation becomes briefer and briefer and the inference in question becomes less and less considered and explicit. Eventually we reach a case where it is no longer clear that any inference is taking place at all: one in which I just think at once, with no hesitation or uncertainty at all, that the dog is again scratching and bumping the table. In this last case, I may no longer focus on the noise in any very explicit way, and it might even be questioned whether I am explicitly aware of it at all. Intuitively, what I am primarily aware of experiencing is just the scratching and bumping of the dog. But even in this case, it seems clear that my experience or awareness of the dog's activity is still causally dependent on an awareness of some sort of the sound. After all, if my ears were plugged or otherwise disabled, I would obviously no longer be aware in any sense of the dog's activity (assuming, of course, that I do not perceive it in some other way). Moreover, if someone (perhaps someone who does not know what is causing the sound) were to ask whether I was aware of that funny thumping and vibrating noise, the answer would plainly be "yes"; and (a trickier and less obvious point—think carefully about it) it would also be true that my awareness of the sound did not just begin at the point when the question was asked, but rather was present earlier as an element in my total conscious experience, even though I was not focusing on it explicitly. In addition, the most crucial point, both the belief that the dog's activity is taking place and

the belief that I am hearing this activity still seem to depend for their justification (assuming for the moment that they are justified at all) on my awareness of the sound, even though there is no longer an explicit inference involved—at least, this is something that many, many philosophers have taken
to be obviously true.³ The main reasons for such a view are, first, the continuity of this case with the earlier ones in which the justificational dependence is clearer and also, second, the alleged absence of any good alternative
account of where the justification might come from.⁴

We now have a reasonably clear set of examples in which one thing (the
noise produced by the dog's activity) is experienced *more* immediately than
something else (that activity itself). But for most if not all philosophers who
have ever invoked the notion of immediate experience, it would nonetheless
not be the case that the sound is immediately experienced either. The sound
is, after all, still a physical occurrence external to the mind, a vibration in the
air. As Descartes would have been quick to point out, it is thus something
about which the evil genius might deceive me. Hence, he might argue, what
is experienced *most* immediately in this situation is not the external, physical sound, but rather something subjective and mental, about which, in his
view, I could not be deceived: the aural *sensations* or apparent aural qualities
that would still occur even if the evil genius were deceiving me about the
physical sound or, alternatively, even if I were merely hallucinating it or experiencing it in a dream.⁵ And here too the claim would be, first, that my experience of the physical sound, assuming that I really am experiencing one,
clearly depends on or results from my experience or awareness of these subjective sensations, even though it may not be clear that this is a causal dependence; and, second, that my reason or justification (if any) for thinking
both that such a sound has actually occurred and that I have experienced it
also depends on my experience of these sensations, making that experience
also prior from a justificatory standpoint.

In fact, according to the general view held by Descartes and many others,
the same thing is true of *all* cases in which we experience or seem to experience external material objects or processes: in each such case, it is subjective
sensations or subjectively experienced qualities that are experienced most
immediately; and it is upon the experience of these subjective entities or
processes or whatever exactly they are (more on this shortly) that the justification, if any, for the resulting claims about both the material world and my
(less immediate) experiencing of it depends. This is obviously a major and
not at all initially obvious philosophical thesis, for which some substantial argument is accordingly required. One argument here is Descartes's own, invoking the specter of the evil genius. (This argument was briefly suggested

but not developed in the previous paragraph—you should think more about just how much force, if any, it has.) We will look at some further, more widely advocated arguments shortly.

Before doing that, however, we need to probe a bit more deeply into the idea of immediacy itself. If something is experienced *less* immediately when the experience of it is dependent in these ways on an experience of something else, so that the latter experience is prior in both the causal and justificatory order, then a thing that is experienced *fully* immediately would be one the experience of which is not in these ways dependent on the experience of *anything* else. The intuitive picture that proponents of immediacy seem to have in mind, often without articulating it very explicitly, is that the object of immediate experience is directly before "the eye of the mind," directly present to its mental gaze. This is why the awareness of this object is not dependent in any way on the awareness of anything else. The fundamental Cartesian assumption in this area is that it is with such immediate awareness that *all* justification that is not purely *a priori* begins.

Another quasi-metaphorical term that has sometimes been used to express this idea of immediate experience is *acquaintance*, sometimes also with the added adjectives "immediate" or "direct."[6] Again the suggestion is that there is no gap of any sort between the mind and the object with which it is immediately or directly acquainted—as seems commonsensically to be the case when a person is directly introduced to someone else, thus no need for anything like inference, and accordingly also no room for doubt of any sort. (It is important to recognize that both such talk of acquaintance and the invocation of the "eye of the mind" are highly metaphorical in character; a large part of the issue here is just how appropriate these metaphors really are and how much weight they can bear.)

What things are we supposed to be immediately aware of or "acquainted" with in this sense? As we saw earlier, Descartes's view is apparently that we are immediately aware of the existence and contents of all of our conscious states of mind, a view that has been adopted by many others. These would include, first, sensory experiences of the sort that we have just been discussing, about which we will shortly have a good deal more to say. Included also would be, second, bodily sensations, such as itches, pains, tingles, etc. These are naturally regarded as experiences of various events and processes in the physical body, but Descartes's point again would be that there is in each of these cases something directly or immediately present to consciousness, something that cannot be doubted, even though the more remote bodily cause certainly can be.[7] The third main category of states of whose existence and content we are (allegedly) immediately aware are conscious instances of what are sometimes referred to as "propositional attitudes": conscious beliefs or acceptances of propositions, together with conscious wonderings, fearings, doubtings, desirings, intendings, and so forth, also having propositional content. In these cases, the view would be that I am immediately aware both of the propositional content (what it is that is believed, doubted, or whatever) and of the distinctive attitude toward that content that such a state involves (believing or accepting it, wondering whether it is true, fearing that it might be true, etc.). On the other hand, I am of course *not* immediately aware of the contents of those merely dispositional states that are also often classified as mental: dispositional beliefs and desires, emotions like fear or hatred or anger (as opposed to the conscious manifestations of those emotions), traits of character, etc. (Think carefully about the difference between these two general kinds of things that are standardly included in the category of "mental states.")

For epistemological purposes, the most important—and commonsensically implausible—part of this general set of doctrines is the view that in ordinary sensory perception, I *never* immediately or directly experience the ordinary objects and events in the material world that I seem to be perceiving, but instead only objects or processes or states (the right category is not quite clear at this point) of the sort that have so far been indicated with the perhaps not altogether appropriate term "sensation." If this view is correct, as was believed without much question by Descartes and his immediate successors (again, especially Locke), then, as we will see in the next chapter, it has very momentous consequences for the further issue of how beliefs about the material world are justified and indeed of whether they can be justified at all. We will look next at the two main arguments, over and above Descartes's appeal to the evil genius, that have been offered for this view.

The Argument from Illusion: First Stage

The standard label for the first argument is in fact something of a misnomer: it would be better described, as we will see, as "the argument from illusion, hallucination, and perceptual relativity," with these two added kinds of examples probably playing in the end a more important role than examples of illusion proper. The argument was first stated explicitly by Berkeley,[8] but it is hard to avoid thinking that Descartes and Locke also had something like it in mind. The argument falls fairly naturally into two main stages.

We will honor the traditional label by starting with an example of *illusion*. Consider the case of the straight stick, say an ordinary broomstick, that looks bent when half of it is immersed in reasonably clear water. (If you have never actually encountered such a case, it might be a good idea to perform this or a similar experiment yourself: a pencil in a clear glass of water will do fine.) The argument would then be as follows. What I am *immediately* aware of, the thing that is directly before my mind, that object or entity or whatever it is that is just *there* in my "visual field" in such a case, is undeniably bent: I observe directly that it has two straight sections that are clearly at an angle to one another. But the only relevant material object, the broomstick itself, is not bent in this way (as determined by viewing it out of water, feeling along it, inserting it successfully into a straight piece of pipe, etc.). Therefore, by the logical law that things having different, incompatible properties cannot be identical (one version of what is often referred to as "Leibniz's Law"), the *immediate* object of my experience, the thing that according to the proponents of this argument really is bent, cannot be the physical broomstick, but must instead be something else that is apparently not to be found in the material world at all, but rather exists only in or in relation to my experience. The British philosophers John Locke and George Berkeley spoke here of "ideas" or "ideas of sense," while more recent philosophers have used the term "sense-data" (singular: "sense-datum"—see further below).[9] But this latter term, especially, introduces a substantial amount of theoretical baggage that will be considered later on, but should not be presupposed yet. (You should try to think of other examples that are referred to as examples of perceptual "illusions," and see if a parallel argument seems to apply to them; in some cases it will, but in others the application is at least not so straightforward.)

Consider now a second example, this time an example of *hallucination*. Having had quite a bit too much to drink, I seem to see very lifelike pink rats scurrying around me, darting between my legs and under the furniture. In this case, so the argument goes, the things that I am *immediately* experiencing are undeniably pink and variously rat-shaped: again such objects (or instances of whatever metaphysical category they ultimately fall into—see below) are just *there* in my visual field, not arrived at by inference or anything analogous to inference, but just basic, undeniable elements of my experience. But, although I may not fully realize this at the moment in question, there is in fact nothing at all in the immediately adjacent material world that has these two properties of being pink and rat-shaped, nor indeed, we may easily suppose, either one of them. I might come to know this by asking other people or perhaps by closing and locking the door and looking carefully after I have sobered up, but all that really matters is that it is true. Thus here too, it is argued, the pink and rat-shaped elements undeniably present in my immediate experience cannot be identified with anything physical,[10] but must again apparently be entities that somehow exist only in or in relation to that experience. (Again, you should try to think of parallel examples and assess this general line of argument in relation to them.)

Consider, finally, an example of *perceptual relativity*. Looking from some distance at what I know independently to be a table with a rectangular top, I am immediately aware of a roughly trapezoidal shape, with what I think of as the closer edge of the table presenting an appearance that is quite discernibly longer than that presented by the farther edge. But there is once again no external material surface in the vicinity having such a trapezoidal shape, something that could again be determined in a variety of ways. Thus, it is argued once again, the trapezoidal element present in my immediate experience, since it has a shape that nothing material in the relevant vicinity has, cannot be identified with anything in the external material world and so must once more be some distinct experiential or experience-related entity that actually has the trapezoidal shape that I experience.[11] (Here too, you should try to think of parallel examples, which are in this case much more numerous and easy to find.)

The conclusion so far is that in all three of these examples and in others that are similar, the *immediate* object of my experience is not something in the external material world,[12] but rather some other sort of entity or entities with quite a different sort of nature and status (to be discussed further below). Obviously the first two examples, especially the second, are relatively unusual in character. But examples like the third one are much more common, reflecting an aspect that seems to be present in one way or another in much or all of our perceptual experience. It is very, very common when perceiving a material object or situation to be immediately aware, at least in part, of properties, including relational properties, that the object or objects in question do not, according to our best judgments about them, actually possess: colors that are affected or distorted by such things as reflections, varied lighting, and colored glasses or windows; shapes that are in part a reflection of perspective and distance; perceived relative sizes that are do not correspond to the actual sizes of the relevant objects; felt temperatures that are affected by whatever was handled just before; etc.

The Argument from Illusion: Second Stage

If this conclusion is right (something that we will eventually have to consider further), then there are at least *many* cases of sensory experience (or, in the examples of hallucination, apparent sensory experience) in which what we immediately experience is something other than material objects and situations:

relatively rare cases of illusion and hallucination and much more common cases of perceptual relativity. But nothing said so far comes even close to justifying the stronger thesis mentioned earlier: the thesis that what we are immediately aware of in *all* cases of sensory experience, whether actual or apparent, is *never* an ordinary, external material object. To support this much more sweeping conclusion, a second, supplementary stage of argument is needed, comprising three distinct, but mutually supporting subarguments.

First, it is possible to extend the result of the discussion of perceptual relativity in the following way. There are obviously lots of examples where a material object is experienced in which some of the immediately experienced qualities are *not* different from and incompatible with (at least not clearly so) the relevant qualities that commonsense judgment ascribes to that object. Thus, for example, although I can immediately experience a trapezoidal shape in connection with the table, I can also, by putting myself in an optimum position (think about how I might have to do this!), immediately experience a rectangular shape, one whose proportions correspond more or less exactly to the "real" shape of the table (as specified by common sense). And similarly for color, temperature, and many other kinds of perceivable qualities.[13] So far, then, the foregoing line of argument would provide no reason for thinking that when I experience these "true" qualities, I am immediately experiencing anything other than a material object itself.

But there is an important feature of at least many such cases that we need to take note of. Think again of the table example. Suppose that I have obtained a perspective from which I experience the "true" rectangular shape of the table. But suppose that I am, from that perspective, still not experiencing the "true" *color* of the table: in reality, it is a light blond color, but due to my colored glasses or the dim lighting I am experiencing a much darker, more reddish shade of brown. Think now of what my actual experience would be like in such a case. What would happen, at least roughly, is that there would be a rectangular patch of reddish brown color in my visual field. The issue we are presently considering is whether although my immediate experience of the color is not an immediate experience of the material table (since that isn't its "true" color), my immediate experience of the "true" rectangular shape might still be an immediate experience of the table. But does this view really make good sense? After all, what both outlines and fills the rectangular shape that I experience is precisely the very reddish brown color that I experience, so that apart from the awareness of the color, I would have no awareness of the shape. Given this intimate connection between them, it is hard to see how *that very shape* and *that very color* could be immediately experienced features of two quite different kinds of objects or entities, one an external, independently existing material object and the other an object, entity, or whatever it is that, as we have been putting it so far, exists only in or in relation to my experience. On the contrary, the immediately experienced object or entity or whatever it is that has the immediately experienced "true" shape seems necessarily to be the very same one that has the immediately experienced non-"true" color, so that if the latter is not the material table, then neither is the former.[14]

And there seem to be many other examples of the same general sort: examples (i) where though some of the immediately experienced qualities are those that commonsensically are the "true" qualities of the material object, others are not; and (ii) where the "true" qualities are related in experience to the "false" ones in such a way as it make it difficult or impossible to make sense of the idea that the entities to which the two kinds of qualities belong are distinct. To give one more example, if what I immediately experience in relation to a sound has a pitch that is different from the sound's true pitch, but a timbre that is the same as its true timbre, then neither my immediate experience of the pitch nor my immediate experience of the inextricably connected timbre can be an immediate experience of the sound. If this is right, then even many cases in which we immediately experience some of the "true" qualities of material objects will turn out not to involve immediate experiences of those material objects themselves. Exactly how far this argument can be pushed is not altogether clear, however, and it is at least not entirely clear that it has the result that ordinary, external material objects are *never* immediately experienced. (Think about this issue by considering a variety of examples for yourself. The main question is whether there are any clear examples of perception in which *all* of the set of immediately experienced qualities, or at least all those that are inextricably bound up with each other in the way indicated, can be plausibly regarded as the "true" qualities of the relevant material objects.)

Second, philosophers attempting to extend the conclusion of the first stage of the argument from illusion have pointed also to the fact that the intrinsic character of an immediate experience in which (assuming that we accept the first stage) we are immediately experiencing something other than a material object is often *indiscernible* from the intrinsic character of an immediate experience in which we might still, for all that has been shown so far (not counting, for the moment, the first of the second-stage arguments just given), be immediately experiencing a material object itself. Thus if my experience of the pink rats is sufficiently lifelike, which is apparently often true in such cases, I may well be unable to tell whether it is an experience of real pink rats or not by simply scrutinizing the specific experience itself. Instead, I will have to appeal to collateral information involving such things as my failure to find any trace of rats when I wake up in the morning or the fact that rats of that color do not occur naturally or perhaps my general awareness of my state of inebriation. Similarly, and even more obviously, if I want to distinguish cases where I am experiencing the "true" color of an object from cases in which I am not, it will do no good to carefully scrutinize the color experiences themselves. Instead, I have to rely on further information about lighting conditions, the presence of glasses, previous knowledge of the specific objects or kinds of objects in question, knowledge of the way in which light reflecting of a surface can produce a glare that distorts the "true" color, etc.

The case of shape is more complicated and at least somewhat debatable. Clearly I can normally tell when I am looking at an ordinary object from the sort of perspective that makes something other than its "true" shape appear as the immediately perceived quality in my visual field. (Thus, while I am often fooled about the colors of things, I am much more rarely fooled about their shape.) But even here it is doubtful that my experience of the trapezoidal shape could be distinguished from my experience (from a different perspective) of the "true" rectangular shape of the tabletop simply by examining the intrinsic character of those experiences themselves. Instead, I am able to tell when I am experiencing the "true" shape by relying on cues having to do with my perceptions of the legs and other distinct parts of the table, my perceptions of other objects in the vicinity of or lying on the table, my knowledge of how light looks when reflected off such a surface at an angle, my background knowledge of this table and of tables in general, etc. What I am suggesting is that in a case where all of these background elements were systematically eliminated, the immediate experience of the "true" shape would be indiscernible in its intrinsic character from the perspectively distorted experiences that did not reflect the true shape. (Imagine a set of table tops of various regular and irregular shapes, thin enough for the edges not to be very distinctly perceivable, hung at different angles to the observer by thin, invisible wires, and so lighted and of such surface reflectance as to give no clue to the angle on the basis of anything like the presence or absence of glare. Then the point is that the immediate experiences of the various shapes would not be distinguishable as experiences of the "true" shapes or not simply by appeal to the character of the experiences themselves.)

Suppose we accept, at least for the moment, this claim that immediate experiences of "true" qualities are not distinguishable by appeal to their intrinsic character from immediate experiences of "false" qualities. The further argument is then that if in some cases the immediate object of experience is really an ordinary, external material object (such as the table), while in others it is something other than any such object, something that exists only in or in relation to the experience itself, then it would surely be reasonable to expect there to be *some* discernible difference between the intrinsic characters of these two sorts of experiences. The idea here is that if what is "directly before the mind" in these two sorts of cases is as different in nature as an external material object is from these subjective, mind-dependent or mind-related entities (whose nature we have admittedly not yet said anything very specific about), then this difference should surely make *some* difference to the character of the experience itself. Thus if the two experiences are really indistinguishable in their intrinsic character, and if the immediate experiences involving "false" qualities cannot, as already argued, be immediate experiences of external material objects, it would follow that the immediate experiences involving "true" qualities are not *immediate* experiences of the external material objects either. Instead, it is suggested, what is *immediately* experienced in both sorts of cases are objects or entities or whatever exactly they are of the same basic kind, ones that exists only in or in relation to the experience. At least in the cases involving the "true" qualities, we can also be properly said to experience the material object that really has those qualities—but not *immediately*.

Third, in addition to the indiscernibility in intrinsic character of the immediate experiences involving "true" qualities and those involving "false" ones, there is also in many cases a striking *continuity* between immediate experiences of these two kinds. Consider the table case again, and suppose that I am able to move continuously from the immediate experience of the trapezoidal shape to an immediate experience of the "true" rectangular shape. (Perhaps I am lying at the end of the sort of mechanically controlled movable platform used in making motion pictures.) Think of the series of immediate experiences that I would have in such a situation: first, of the clearly trapezoidal shape; then, as I move closer to being directly over the table, a series of less and less trapezoidal shapes (that is, shapes in which the angles of the sides in relation to the farther edge become smaller and those in relation to the nearer edge larger, so that all of these angles gradually get closer to right angles); then finally an immediate experience of an exactly rectangular shape; and then, if I look back and continue to move, a series of shapes that are at first again slightly trapezoidal and then become more and more so.

According to the hypothesis being argued against, the one that accepts the first stage of the argument from illusion but still holds that at least some immediate experiences involving "true" qualities are immediate experiences of the external material object itself, all of the immediate experiences in this sequence except the one involving the exactly rectangular shape are immediate experiences of entities or whatever existing only in or in relation to experience, but that single immediate experience is an immediate experience of the table top itself. But, the argument now goes, this is very difficult to believe in light of the continuity just described. How can it be, given a series of immediate experiences that shade into each other so gradually and continuously, that at some point there is a radical shift of this sort in the object or entity or whatever it is that is being immediate experienced? Surely this sort of "jump" from the entities existing only in or in relation to experience (whatever exactly their nature may be) to an external material object would have to involve some sort of break or discontinuity in the experiential sequence? Thus if, as seems to be the case, no such break or discontinuity can be found, the conclusion indicated is that no such "jump" occurs, that the object or entity or whatever it is that is being *immediately* experienced at the instant when the shape is perfectly rectangular is of the same general sort as those being immediate experienced in the other cases, and thus not an external material object.

The same sort of argument can be made for many of the other examples in which there are immediate experiences of both "false" and "true" qualities: lighting can be gradually varied, the darkness and tint of glasses gradually increased or decreased (think here of the sunglasses that darken gradually when exposed to sunlight and then lighten gradually when such light is absent), the broomstick can be very slowly and gradually immersed in the water, the motion that distorts the pitch of sounds can be varied gradually, etc. To be sure, it does not seem to work for at least the most striking cases of hallucinations, such as the pink rats, to which only the second of the three subarguments is really applicable.

The Argument from Illusion: Evaluation

What evaluation should we make of the argument from illusion? Does it really establish the conclusion that it purports to establish, namely, that in sensory experiences (and apparent sensory experiences, as in the hallucination case), we never *immediately* experience external material objects in the way that that we commonsensically think that we do? This is a very complicated question that I will largely leave to you to consider and discuss, offering only a few further suggestions as to some of the issues involved. Pretty clearly in thinking about this question, you should think separately about the two main stages of the argument.

First, is there any defensible way to reject the conclusion of the first stage? This is very hard to do in the hallucination case, in which it is the clearest that there is *something* (though not necessarily, as we will see, a genuine *ob-*

ject or *entity*) being immediately experienced that cannot be an external material object. Could the conclusion be rationally rejected in the other sorts of cases? Could we say, for example, in the stick in water case that what is being immediately experienced is just the two parts of the material stick, with the circumstances merely creating the illusion that they are at an angle to each other? (But isn't it the *result* of that illusion that is immediately experienced, and what exactly is *that*?) Could we say in the table case that even where the immediately experienced shape is trapezoidal, we are still experiencing the material table, which merely *looks* trapezoidal from that perspective? (But what is it for it to *look* trapezoidal?) Could we perhaps even deny that there is anything genuinely trapezoidal involved? (But then what about that apparent shape in my visual field? What exactly is it?)[15]

Second, even if we suppose that the first stage of the argument cannot be rejected, is there perhaps some defensible way to reject the conclusion of the second stage? Here the three subarguments need to be separately assessed. In fact, it is pretty clear that none of these subarguments is conclusive by itself, and hence also that they are not conclusive together.[16] Thus, for the first subargument, isn't it still possible that the immediate experience of the "true" shape could be an immediate experience of the material object, even though the conjoined immediate experience of the "false" color is not? And, in addition, it would be very difficult to show conclusively that *all* cases in which a "true" quality is immediately experienced are also cases in which at least one "false" quality is also immediate experienced in the closely connected way discussed earlier. (Again, can you think of clear cases to the contrary?) As for the second subargument, it is surely not impossible that immediate experiences of very different sorts of objects or entities might be indiscernible in their intrinsic character. (But isn't it nonetheless seriously unlikely, especially when the difference is this large?) And as for the third subargument, it is surely also not impossible that a shift in what is being immediately experienced could occur in an experientially continuous series of such experiences. (But isn't it again quite unlikely?) The issue that you should think about is thus how strongly these subarguments separately and together support the conclusion in question.

The Causal or Scientific Argument

The second main argument for the thesis that the immediate object of sensory (or apparently sensory) experience is never the external material object that we seem commonsensically to be perceiving (assuming that such an object is actually present) appeals to broadly scientific facts about the perceptual processes that are causally responsible, in at least normal, nonhallucinatory cases, for such experiences. Consider a perceptual experience in which I seem to see a light yellow ball about the size of a basketball sitting on the ground some distance away on the other side of my yard. What I immediately experience is something that occupies a round region in my visual field and is light yellow (with the sorts of perceived variations in color that seem to reflect the curvature of the ball's surface and the effects due to lighting and shadow). As so far described (and setting aside the argument from illusion for present purposes), this immediately experienced entity could just *be* a material ball. But is this really plausible, given our commonsense and scientific knowledge of the process of perception?[17]

If there really is a material ball of at least approximately the sort in question, then it may very well be *part* of the cause of my having that immediate experience. But it is surely not *all* of the cause. Think what else is involved and how these other elements could and perhaps do affect the experience that results. In the first place, my seeing of the ball depends on there being light of the right sort present in the situation and reflected off the ball toward my eyes. If the color or intensity of the light were different, the qualities that I immediately experience would also be different, even though the ball itself might be exactly the same. Second, the reflected light must be transmitted through the space separating me from the ball, and there are a variety of ways in which what occurs there could affect the experienced result, even though the ball itself is again unchanged. For example, if there were a colored haze in the air, this would affect the color that I experience. Or if there were panes of glass or pieces of transparent plastic, either large ones off in the distance or small ones that I wear like glasses, then they could affect either the color or the shape that I experience. Third, what I immediately experience depends on the functioning of the eye and the optic nerve, and there are a variety of ways in which defects or abnormalities here can affect what is ultimately experienced, even though the ball itself is again unchanged. Finally, the signal from the eye needs to be received and processed in the brain, and again there are a variety of ways in which changes or abnormalities at this level can affect what I immediately experience, even though the material ball, assuming that there is one, once again remains unchanged. (There are lots of possibilities at each of these stages, and you should again use your imagination to explore and assess some of them.)

It is possible that in an actual case of the sort described, the character of my immediate experience is being affected in one or more of these ways. Perhaps, for example, I am suffering from jaundice, and this accounts for the yellow color; and my glasses are distorted in a way that affects the experienced shape and size. Suppose that this is so, and that the external object that is really there is white and egg-shaped and substantially smaller than it appears to be. How in such a case could I be said to experience it *immediately*?

But, of course, it might also be the case that no such distortion is taking place, and that I am experiencing the external ball exactly as it really is. Even then, is it not obvious that the character of my immediate experience is a result, not just of the ball and its characteristics, but of all of these other kinds of factors, even though they do not in this case produce any alteration or distortion? The conclusion that has seemed to many philosophers to follow from considerations of these sorts is that the object or entity or whatever it is that is *immediately* experienced is not the external material object, but is instead the end result in my mind of this complicated causal process to which that external object, if it exists, is merely one out of many contributing factors, and a relatively remote one at that. This is a conclusion that is strikingly similar to that of the argument from illusion.[18]

Tentative Conclusion and Further Problems

We now have two different arguments in support of the thesis that what we immediately experience in actual and apparent sensory experience is not an external material object, but rather something else, something, as we have put it, that exists only in or in relation to the immediate experience in question. Philosophers have in fact differed widely as to whether the resulting case for this conclusion is strong enough to compel rational assent, with earlier philosophers mostly accepting the thesis in question on this basis and recent ones being predominantly inclined to reject it. For the moment, I propose to conclude only that the thesis in question is strongly enough supported to make it interesting and important to explore the consequences of accepting it, something that will occupy us for the rest of the present chapter and most of the next. Eventually, toward the end of the next chapter, when those consequences have become reasonably clear, we will reconsider whether there is a defensible way to avoid accepting such a thesis.

Before we get to that point, there are two main issues that need to be considered. One is the metaphysical nature of immediate experience and its objects—including, as we will see, the issue of whether they are even properly described as *objects* at all. In the balance of the present chapter, we will consider the two most widely held views on this question: the *sense-datum* theory and the *adverbial* theory. As we will eventually see, the issue between these two views may well make no real difference to the epistemological questions that are our primary concern, but this can hardly be decided until we have examined them. The second main issue is how and indeed whether it is possible to justify beliefs about external material objects on the basis of perceptual experiences whose immediately experienced objects (or entities or whatever they turn out to be) are, as we are assuming for the sake of the argument, quite distinct from such material objects. This will be the main topic of the next chapter.

The Sense-Datum Theory

The sense-datum (plural: sense-data) theory is the historically more prominent view, growing as it does more naturally out of the fuzzier talk of "ideas" or "impressions" to be found in philosophers like Locke, Berkeley, and Hume.[19] As the term itself suggests, sense-data are supposed to be the entities that are directly or immediately *given* (a variant term for immediately experienced[20]) in sense experience. But what exactly is the nature of such entities supposed to be?[21]

First, sense-data are supposed to be objects or entities that actually possess the very qualities that are immediate experienced. Indeed, much of the point of the notion is to *explain* why a material object that actually has one quality can lead to an experience of quite a different quality, or why, as in the rat hallucination case, qualities can be experienced when there is no material object having even approximately those qualities present at all. Thus, according to the sense-datum theory, if I experience a trapezoidal shape of a certain shade of dark reddish brown, then the immediate object of my experience is a sense-datum that actually is trapezoidal in shape and that shade of dark reddish brown in color. If I experience a bent shape in the stick case, then the sense-datum that I am immediately experiencing actually is bent in just that way. And when I hallucinate the pink rats, the sense-data that I am immediately experiencing actually are pink and rat-shaped. (Implicit here is the idea that while I can misperceive material objects, I cannot misperceive sense-data, for the sense-datum is precisely what has whatever qualities I am most immediately aware of, leaving no apparent logical room for misperception.)

Second, there is an important and difficult issue here as to whether sense-data are two- or three-dimensional as regards their spatial characteristics. The historically most standard view has been that they are two-dimensional, that the third dimension, though experienced in some sense, is actually a result of inference or suggestion, rather than being immediate experienced. Berkeley was the original philosopher to argue explicitly for this view, claiming that distance in the third dimension amounts to "a line turned endwise to the eye" and is thus incapable of being immediately seen.[22] Though a few philosophers have challenged this view, insisting that the third dimension is experienced as immediately as the others, we will mostly follow the more traditional view here.[23] There are also similar questions about whether sense-data are capable of having various other sorts of properties, though the underlying principle is always that they have *whatever* qualities are actually experienced immediately.

Third, it is clear that sense-data are supposed to be distinct from ordinary, external material objects.[24] It is also clear that they cannot be identified with entities (or processes) existing in the brain, since these also fail in general to possess all of the immediately experienced qualities, most obviously colors.[25] Sense-data seem, therefore, to be distinct from *anything* in the material world. They have sometimes been thought of as existing in the mind, but if the mind is thought of in a Cartesian way as a nonspatial substance, it is difficult to see how it can literally contain entities having shape and color, as the sense-data involved in visual experience would have to do. This in turn has sometimes led to the view that sense-data are *neither* physical nor mental in character, that they somehow exist in relation to the mind, but are not literally in it.[26]

Fourth, sense-data have often been thought of as *momentary* entities, incapable of persisting through time in the way that material objects and persons are commonsensically thought to do. In fact, there seems to be no clear reason why what is immediately experienced in a temporal passage of experience in which the immediately experienced qualities do not change could not be one and the same sense-datum (or set of sense-data) through the entire time in question. But since sense-data have been introduced solely as the bearers of immediately experienced qualities, there does not seem to be any easy way to make sense of their qualities changing over time, since there is no apparent basis on which to identify the sense-datum existing after a change in the immediately experienced qualities as the same one that existed before the change. And since changes of some sort or other are almost ubiquitous in immediate experience, this comes at least very close to securing the result that sense-data never persist through time.

Fifth, an obvious question to ask is how many sense-data are being immediately experienced at a particular moment, for example, as I look across my study and out the window, seeing the edge of my computer table, a reading chair, a floor lamp, the window frame itself, the edge of the house, a number of trees, and patches of cloudy sky. Are there distinct sense-data for each object or perhaps even for each distinguishable part of an object, or is there just one large and variegated sense-datum having all of the immediately experienced qualities involved in the whole visual array? In fact, proponents of sense-data have worried very little about this issue, seeming to suggest that any of these answers will do, in a way somewhat analogous to the way in which it seems to make no real difference whether I think of, for example, my television set as one material object or as a collection of smaller material objects, where the division into smaller objects could be done in a wide variety of ways. (Is there in fact any serious issue here?)

Sixth, two more puzzling questions that have sometimes been asked are (i) whether sense-data can exist at times when they are not being immediately experienced, and (ii) whether the same sense-datum could be experienced by more than one person. The most standard version of the sense-datum theory gives a negative answer to both of these questions, and virtually all proponents of sense-data have given a negative answer to (ii). But the rationale for these answers is less than fully clear, in part because the nature of the entities in question is so puzzling. (For present purposes, I will simply assume that the two negative answers are in fact correct.)

It should be clear that sense-data are at least puzzling entities, particularly as regards their apparently being neither physical nor mental in character. But before attempting a further assessment of the view, we will consider its main rival, a view not formulated until the twentieth century.

The Adverbial Theory

The sense-datum theory is often characterized as an *act-object* theory of the nature of immediate experience: it accounts for such experience by postulating both an *act* of awareness or apprehension and an *object* (the sense-datum) which that act apprehends or is aware of. The fundamental idea of the adverbial theory, in contrast, is that there is no need for such objects and the problems (such as whether they are physical or mental or somehow neither) that they bring with them. Instead, it is suggested, merely a mental act or mental state with its own intrinsic character is enough to account for immediate experience.

According to the adverbial theory, what happens when, for example, I immediately experience a dark reddish brown trapezoidal shape is that I am in a certain specific state of sensing or sensory awareness or of *being appeared to*: I sense in a certain manner or am appeared to in a certain way, and it is that specific manner of sensing or way of being appeared to that accounts for the specific content of my immediate experience. This content can be verbally indicated by attaching an *adverbial* modifier to the verb that expresses the act of sensing[27] (which is where the label for the view comes from). Thus in the example just mentioned, it might be said that I sense or am appeared to *dark-reddish-brown-trapezoid-ly*—where this rather artificial term is supposed to express the idea that the qualitative content that is treated by the sense-datum theory as involving features or properties of an object should instead be thought of as somehow just a matter of the specific manner in which I sense or the specific way in which I am appeared to. Similarly, when I hallucinate a pink rat, I sense or am appeared to *a-pink-rat-ly*—or, perhaps better, *a-pink-ratshape-ly*. And analogously for other examples of immediate experience.

The essential claim here is that when I sense or am appeared to dark-reddish-brown-trapezoid-ly, there need be nothing more going on than that I am in a certain distinctive sort of experiential state. In particular, there need be no object or entity of any sort that is literally dark reddish brown and trapezoidal—not in the material world, not in my mind, and not even in the netherworld of things that are neither physical nor mental.

Assessment of the Sense-Datum and Adverbial Theories

How might the choice between these two different accounts of the metaphysical nature of immediate experience be made? Each of the two views has fairly obvious virtues and equally obvious drawbacks. The sense-datum theory accounts much more straightforwardly for the character of immediate experience. I experience a dark reddish brown trapezoidal shape because an object or entity that literally has that color and shape is directly before my mind. But both the nature of these entities and (as we will see further below) the way in which they are related to the mind are difficult to understand. (One more specific question worth asking here is whether we really have a clear understanding of how *shape* in particular could be a property of a nonphysical entity.)

The adverbial theory, on the other hand, has the advantage of being metaphysically simpler and of avoiding difficult issues about the nature of sense-data.[28] The problem with it is that we seem to have no real understanding of the nature of the states in question or of how exactly they explain or account for the character of immediate experience. It is easy, with a little practice, to construct the adverbial modifiers: simply hyphenate the description of the apparent object of immediate experience and attach "ly" at the end. But it is doubtful that anyone has a very clear idea of the meaning of such an adverb, of what exactly it says about the character of the state—beyond saying merely, unhelpfully, that it is such as to *somehow* account for the specific character of the experience.

Here I will limit myself to a brief consideration of one further, less obvious argument on each side, and then to pointing out why the issue between these two views, though of great metaphysical significance, may not matter very much if at all for epistemological purposes. One major proponent of the sense-datum theory has advanced the argument that the adverbial theory cannot adequately describe cases in which we experience a number of different apparent objects having a variety of different properties in a way that keeps straight which object has which property.[29] Thus compare a case in which I am experiencing a red circle and a green square with one in which I am experiencing a green circle and a red square. In both cases, I might be said to be sensing or to be appeared to red-and-green-and-round-and-square-ly, thus apparently failing to capture the clear distinction between the two cases. And the suggestion is that only the sense-datum theory can successfully distinguish what is going on in such cases, by making explicit reference to each of the apparent objects.

But this objection seriously underestimates the resources available to the adverbial theory. In the case in question, the adverbialist can say that I sense red-circle-and-green-square-ly in the first case and green-circle-and-red-square-ly in the second case, thus capturing the difference. More generally, if it is possible to capture the content of a particular immediate experience adequately in sense-datum terms, as the sense-datum theorist must surely agree that it is, then the adverbialist can construct a description that is equally adequate insofar as the present issue is concerned by simply making the entire sense-datum description the basis for his adverbial modifier, that is, by saying that the person is sensing or being appeared to [such and such sense data]-ly, with the appropriate sense-datum description going into the brackets.

The additional argument in the opposite direction is, in my judgment, more telling. A sense-datum theorist needs some account of the relation between a person and a sense-datum when the former immediately experiences the latter. The natural thing to say is that the sense-datum somehow influences the internal state of the person (that is, of his or her mind) in a way that reflects the sense-datum's specific character. But the resulting state of mind would then be just the sort of state that the adverbial theory describes, one which is such that a person who is in it will thereby experience the properties in question. And there would then be no apparent reason why such a state could not be produced directly by whatever process is supposed to produce the sense-datum, with the latter thus becoming an unnecessary intermediary. Thus the sense-datum theorist must apparently say that the immediate experience of the sense-datum does not involve any internal state of the person that reflects its character, but is instead an essentially and irreducibly *relational* state of affairs. The person simply experiences the sense-datum, but without there being any corresponding change in his or her internal states that would adequately reflect the character of the supposed sense-datum and so make its existence unnecessary in the way suggested. But does this really make good metaphysical sense, and, more importantly, would it allow the person to grasp or apprehend the nature of the sense-datum in a way that could be the basis for further justification and knowledge? It is very hard to see how such a view is supposed to work.

Both views thus have serious problems, though, in light of the last argument, I would assess the problems of the sense-datum theory as the more serious. Fortunately, however, as already suggested, it does not seem necessary for strictly *epistemological* purposes to decide between these two views. The reason is that while they give very different accounts of what is ultimately going on in a situation of immediate experience, they make no difference with respect to the experienced content of that experience. And it is on that experienced content, not on the further metaphysical explanation of it, that the justificatory power, if any, of such an experience depends. Thus when we turn, in the next chapter, to the issue of whether and how immediate sensory experience can justify beliefs in external material objects, we may safely leave the issue between the sense-datum theory and the adverbial theory unresolved—though it will prove more convenient to talk as though the sense-datum theory is true, leaving the corresponding adverbial description of experience to be constructed by the reader in the way already indicated.

Notes

1. See George Berkeley, *Three Dialogues between Hylas and Philonous* (1713), in *Principles, Dialogues, and Philosophical Correspondence*, ed. C. M. Turbayne (Indianapolis, Ind.: Bobbs-Merrill, 1965), p. 145 (the first dialogue, toward the end) for a parallel example.

2. Of course, I could in a sense experience the scratching and bumping by hearing the noise, even if I failed entirely to realize that this was what I was experiencing, in which case the second part of the second mode of dependence would no longer obtain in relation to me. But in that case, at least from an internalist standpoint, my experiencing the scratching and bumping would have no epistemic or justificatory significance over and above that of my experiencing the noise.

3. Some philosophers have spoken at this point of an "unconscious inference," but this is a highly dubious notion, one that it is difficult to attach any very clear content to.

4. We will reconsider this issue, in a somewhat modified form, both at the end of chapter 7 and again, from rather different angles, in chapters 9 and 10.

5. Whether these "sensations" (which may not in the end be the best term) might still themselves be physical, something like processes in the brain, is an issue in the philosophy of mind that is mostly beyond the purview of this book. Descartes, being a dualist, would presumably have denied that they are in any sense physical or material. And other philosophers, as we will see, have seemed to say that what is immediately experienced in such cases is neither physical nor mental in nature.

6. See Bertrand Russell, *The Problems of Philosophy* (London: Oxford University Press, 1912), chapter 5.

7. Think here of the phenomenon of "phantom limbs": cases where people experience pain or kinesthetic sensations that seem to be located in limbs that have in fact been amputated.

8. In the first of his *Three Dialogues between Hylas and Philonous*.

9. Or, sometimes, "sensa" (singular: "sensum").

10. Not even in any straightforward way with parts or states of my brain, since none of those are pink and rat-shaped.

11. Notice carefully that neither this nor any of the previous versions of the argument in any way presupposes that I am actually *deceived* in any way about what is really there in the material world. If I am familiar with the kinds of phenomena in question, my judgments about the material world may still perfectly well be correct: I may judge that the stick is straight, that there are really no rats, and that the table is rectangular. What is at issue is only the qualities that are immediately experienced, no matter what judgments my overall cognitive state may lead me to make.

12. And not in any straightforward way a state or process in my brain either, for the reason explained in note 10.

13. Size is much trickier: from what distance, if any, do I experience the "true" size of the table?

14. And of course if, as Locke held, no material object ever has a "secondary quality" like color, there will be no cases where the immediately experienced color is genuine. This Lockean doctrine will be discussed further in the following chapter. (The basic line of argument in this paragraph was first offered by Berkeley in *Principles of Human Knowledge*, section 10.)

15. For a comprehensive but rather one-sided discussion of these and other responses to the argument from illusion, see J. L. Austin, *Sense and Sensibilia* (London: Oxford University Press, 1962).

16. Think about this point: If each of a set of separate arguments only make a conclusion probable, is there any way that together they could establish it conclusively (assuming that they are not connected in any further way)?

17. One odd thing about this second argument is that accepting its conclusion may very well lead to serious doubts about whether we really have the sorts of knowledge concerning the perceptual process that the argument is based on—or indeed whether we can even know that there is such a process at all. But I will set this problem aside for now.

18. In fact, it is not clear that the two arguments point to exactly the same conclusion. (Think about this.) I will assume, however, that the difference, if any, is not enough to make any real difference.

19. As noted earlier, some philosophers have preferred the term sensum (plural: sensa). Although it would be possible to distinguish in very subtle ways between the exact usage and implications of these two terms, I will not attempt to do so here. There are also other, less widely adopted terminological variants.

20. Suggesting again that sense-data are simply and unproblematically presented to the mind, with no need for anything like inference or interpretation.

21. One of those who introduced the term, namely the British philosopher G. E. Moore, defines sense-data as *whatever* is immediately experienced, leaving it open that sense-data might turn out, at least in some cases, to simply be external material objects. See Moore, *Some Main Problems of Philosophy* (London: Allen & Unwin, 1953), chapter 2. Most of those who have used the term, however, have used it to refer to the distinct objects of immediate experience whose existence is allegedly established by the argument from illusion and the causal or scientific argument, as discussed above, and that is the way in which the term will be employed here. There are also other divergences between different philosophers as to the nature of sense-data and/or the precise meaning of the term, some but not all of which will be mentioned in our discussion.

22. See the first of the "Three Dialogues between Hylas and Philonous," in Berkeley, *Principles, Dialogues, and Philosophical Correspondence*, ed. C. M. Turbayne (Indianapolis, Ind.: Bobbs-Merrill, 1965), p. 143; and Berkeley, *An Essay Towards a New Theory of Vision* (1709).

23. But here is another issue for you to think about on your own. For an extended defense of the three-dimensional view, see H. H. Price, *Perception* (London: Methuen, 1932; 2nd ed., 1950).

24. Aside from Moore's variant usage, as discussed in note 21.

25. Such a conclusion seems to go beyond what would follow from the causal or scientific argument alone, which would apparently be satisfied by brain processes or entities that did not actually have the immediately experienced qualities, as long as they could account somehow for the character of immediate experience—as materialist theories of mind have claimed to do. Thus in relation to this issue, the argument from illusion is the more fundamental of the two arguments.

26. Thus G. E. Moore once famously argued that the very fact that sense-data are experienced is enough to show that idealism, the view that everything that exists is reducible to minds and their states, is false. See his "A Refutation of Idealism," in Moore, *Philosophical Studies* (London: Routledge & Kegan Paul, 1922), pp. 1–30.

27. Grammatically, adverbs ("quickly," "rashly," "surprisingly," etc.) indicate the way or manner in which something is done or occurs.

28. A further advantage often claimed for the adverbial theory is that it is compatible with materialist views of the mind: while it is clear that the brain does not contain entities having the properties ascribed to sense-data and at best obscure how it could stand in a relation of apprehension to such entities, there is no clear reason why a state of being appeared to *dark-reddish-brown-trapezoid-ly* could not just be a brain state. (To which it might be responded: (i) that we have no real understanding of how it could be a brain state either, of what features of a brain state would make it a state of thus being appeared to; and (ii) that the absence of any clear difficulty here is simply a reflection of the obscurity of the nature of the supposed adverbial state.)

29. Frank Jackson, *Perception: A Representative Theory* (Cambridge: Cambridge University Press, 1977), pp. 64–68.

CHAPTER SEVEN

∿

Knowledge of the External World

We have so far tentatively accepted the conclusion that the *immediate* object of awareness in perceptual experience is never an external material object, but is instead something of a quite different sort: either a sense-datum or else the content of a state of sensing or being appeared to (in the latter case there is of course, strictly speaking, no *object* at all). It will be useful to have a brief label for this disjunctive result, and I will refer to it here as *perceptual subjectivism*.[1] We have not tried to decide in any firm way between these two views, which, I have suggested, are in fact more or less equivalent in their epistemological (though obviously not their metaphysical) implications. In the present chapter, however, it will be convenient, for reasons of simplicity, to couch our discussion mainly in terms of sense-data, leaving the alternative adverbial version to be supplied by the reader.

We have now to consider the implications of perceptual subjectivism for the epistemological issue upon which it bears most directly, which is also arguably the most central issue of the modern period of epistemology, which began with Descartes: the issue of whether and, if so, how beliefs concerning the external material world and the objects that it allegedly contains can be justified on the basis of our immediate sensory experience, thus understood. We have already looked briefly at Descartes's rather unsatisfactory theological response to this problem. In this chapter, we will first look at the views of Descartes's immediate successors, the so-called British Empiricists Locke, Berkeley, and Hume, whose arguments played a major role in shaping the subsequent discussion. We will then examine the two main alternative accounts of "knowledge of the external world" (on the assumption that perceptual sub-jectivism or something like it is indeed true) that have subsequently emerged, mainly in the forms that they have taken in the twentieth century: *phenome-nalism* and *representationalism*. Difficulties with these views will then prompt, in the last part of the chapter, a reconsideration of whether rejecting percep-tual subjectivism might make available a further, more promising alternative.

Locke, Berkeley, and Hume on Perception and the External World

As noted earlier, Locke and Berkeley speak not of sense-data or adverbial contents, but of "ideas" or "ideas of sense"—with the former term being ap-plied also to contents of thought and indeed apparently to conscious con-tents of any kind. The way that they use these rather slippery terms suggests in many places something like a sense-datum theory of the immediate objects of sensory experience.[2] For our purposes, however, it will suffice to take the term "idea" merely to refer to conscious contents of any sort, and "ideas of sense" to the distinctive contents of sensory experience, without supposing these terms to indicate any definite metaphysical picture of the nature of such contents.

Locke's view is clearly that our beliefs or opinions about material objects existing outside of our minds are justified by our ideas of sense.[3] But his dis-cussion of this point is both rather uncertain and quite guarded. He says that our assurance on this basis concerning material objects "deserves the name of knowledge" [631], thus seeming to suggest that it is not knowledge simply and with no qualification. He also questions whether anyone can be gen-uinely skeptical about the existence of the things that he sees and feels, and speaks rather vaguely of "the assurance we have from our senses themselves, that they do not err in the information they give us" [631–32].

But the closest that Locke comes to explaining *how* such beliefs are justi-fied by sensory experience is his citing of four "concurrent reasons" that are supposed to further confirm the assurance derived from the senses: First, we can know that sensory ideas are "produced in us by exterior causes" by ob-serving that those lacking a particular sense organ can never have the corre-sponding sensory ideas [632]. (Thus, for example, a blind man can never have immediate sensory experiences of visual qualities such as color.) Sec-ond, another reason for thinking that our sensory ideas result from external causes is their *involuntary* character, as contrasted with imagination and, to a lesser extent, memory [632]. (Thus if I have my eyes open and am facing in a particular direction, I have no choice as to what apparent objects or properties I will experience, that is, in Locke's view, what ideas of vision I will experience—as I look out my study window, I cannot help being aware of a mass of variegated green and brown that I take to be a perception of trees, branches, and leaves.) Third, another difference between our immediate sensory experiences and other sorts of ideas, such as those of imagination and memory, is that sensory ideas of certain kinds are accompanied by *pain*, whereas the corresponding ideas of imagination and memory are not [633]. (For example, if I have the immediate sensory experience of apparently hitting my hand with a hammer while attempting to drive a nail, I will usually experience pain along with it; but if I merely imagine or remember such an experience, there is no pain.[4]) Fourth, "our senses, in many cases, bear witness to the truth of each other's report, concerning the existence of sensible things without us" [633]. (For example, my visual experience of the appearance of a fire close to my body is normally accompanied by tactile experiences of heat, apparent smells of burning, the apparent hearing of cracklings or other distinctive firelike sounds, etc.—think here of other examples of your own.) But Locke has little to say as to just *how* these "concurrent reasons" are supposed to show that our beliefs concerning material objects that are arrived on the basis of our immediate sensory experiences are justified by those experiences. Does such a conclusion really follow, and, if so, how and why? (Stop and think about this question on your own before reading further. How much force in this direction, if any, does each "reason" have and why? Do they support the desired conclusion separately, or is there perhaps some way that some or all of them work together?)

In fact, Locke's supposed reasons are of very unequal weight. The first one is totally worthless, because it begs the very question at issue and also would require a prior solution of another, related epistemological problem. Until the problem of justifying belief in external objects on the basis of his sensory experience has been solved, Locke is obviously not in a position to appeal to supposed facts about other people's sense organs, since sense organs are physical structures and so beliefs about them would have to be justified in just the way that is in question. Moreover, to invoke this first reason, he would also have to have justified beliefs about the mental states of other people, specifically concerning whether they do or do not have sensory ideas of the relevant sort. How this latter sort of knowledge is possible is a serious problem in itself (the "problem of other minds"—considered briefly in the next chapter). But it is pretty clear on reflection (think about this) that knowledge of other people's mental states normally depends on *prior* knowledge of the behavior and condition of their physical bodies, thus again presupposing the very knowledge of the material world that has not yet been accounted for.

(This obviously assumes that we have no other way of justifying beliefs about the material world and about other minds.)

Locke's second reason is at least a bit better. The involuntary or sponta-neous character of my sensory experience does at least distinguish it from other sorts of mental states and experience (albeit perhaps not in a com-pletely sharp way—aren't many memories and even some imaginings simi-larly involuntary?). But this fact does not by itself seem to establish that im-mediate sensory experiences are, as he claims, caused by something external to the person who has them. Why couldn't my involuntary sensory experi-ences result instead from some subconscious or unconscious faculty of my own mind that is outside my voluntary control? And, even more obviously, that the ideas are involuntary tells us nothing at all about whether the ex-ternal cause, if there is one, has the specific properties that my sensory expe-rience seems to portray (whether it "resembles my ideas," as Locke would put it). Why couldn't the external cause of my idea of a green tree, again if there is one, neither be green nor have the other properties of a tree? Indeed, why couldn't it, as Berkeley will suggest, be something utterly different from a ma-terial object? And the third reason, while again perhaps showing that sensory experiences are importantly different from many other mental phenomena, also does not support in any clear way a conclusion about what is responsible for this difference.

What about the fourth reason? Surely it is a striking fact that my various sensory experiences fit together in an extremely orderly and coherent fash-ion to depict an ongoing world that is both extremely complicated and highly regular or law-governed. The information or apparent information de-rived at a given time from one sense agrees to a very great degree with both that derived at that time from other senses and also with that derived from both the same sense and others at other times—allowing, of course, for the ongoing change and development of the world, which is also something that is reflected in regularities within our sensory experience. Thus if I seem to see a chair, I can normally also have the experience of touching it, given that I also have the experience of moving my body in the right direction and far enough. And the experiences that I have of the furniture and contents of my office before leaving for a class agree very well with the similar experiences that I have after I have apparently returned—allowing, in some cases, for the actions of the janitor or my dog (who is sometimes left there) or my wife (who has a key). (You should try to spell out some further, more detailed ex-amples of this general order and coherence of experience on your own.)

But how exactly is this admittedly striking fact supposed to support Locke's intended conclusion, namely that there is good reason or justification for thinking that the beliefs about the material world that we arrive at on the basis of our immediate sensory experience are likely to be true? On this obviously crucial question, Locke has very little to say. (Can you see how an answer might go, given what has been said so far?—think about this question before proceeding.)

In fact, if you think carefully about it, the order of my immediate sensory experience and the seeming agreement between experiences apparently produced by different senses would not be striking, or at least not nearly so striking, if those ideas were under my voluntary control—for then I could deliberately imagine an orderly world, in something like the way in which this is done by an artist or novelist. What makes the order so noteworthy is precisely that it is not voluntarily created, but just occurs spontaneously and, in many of its details, unexpectedly. Thus we see that Locke's fourth "concurrent reason" needs to be supplemented by his second, and that it is these two *together* that might provide at least the beginnings of a real argument. Experience that was involuntary but chaotic would show very little, and neither would experience that was orderly but voluntarily controlled. It is experience that is *both* involuntary and highly orderly that seems to demand some sort of further *explanation*: what is it that produces and sustains the order? Thus it is natural to interpret Locke as arguing, admittedly without formulating the point very clearly or explicitly, that the *best explanation* of his involuntary but orderly experience is that it is systematically caused by a world of independent material objects which it depicts with at least approximate accuracy.[5] (The main way in which the depiction is only approximately accurate is that, according to Locke, material objects have only *primary qualities* like size, shape, and motion,[6] but not *secondary qualities* like color, smell, taste, and temperature (as felt).)

Does this argument really show that our beliefs about the material world that are arrived at on the basis of our involuntary sensory experience are likely to be true and hence justified? It seems reasonable to think that there must be *some* explanation for these features of our sensory ideas, which is just to say that the sort of order that they exhibit is extremely unlikely to result from mere chance.[7] But is Locke's proposed explanation the right one?

Berkeley, while appealing to essentially the same features of our sensory ideas (their being independent of our will and their being orderly and coherent[8]), offers a quite different and in his view superior explanation: that our sensory ideas are produced in our minds by God, who determines and controls their orderly character, so that there is thus no need or justification for supposing that the independent material realm advocated by Locke really exists. Berkeley's God obviously bears a striking resemblance to Descartes's evil genius, with the crucial difference that whereas Descartes assumes that the evil genius would be *deceiving* us, Berkeley's view is in effect that having sensory ideas systematically produced in us by God (presumably reflecting God's ideally complete picture of the world thus depicted) is *just what it is* for a world of ordinary objects to exist.[9] Thus we have at least two competing explanations for the same facts concerning our sensory experience, and the question is how we should decide between such explanations.

Assuming, that is, that we can rationally decide at all. Hume's response to the problem is to deny that *any* such attempt to explain our experience by appeal to objects or entities existing outside of that experience could ever be justified. An essential ingredient of both Locke's and Berkeley's proposed explanations is the claim that our immediately experienced sensory ideas (or "impressions," as Hume calls them, in order to distinguish them from other kinds of ideas) are *caused* by the external entities that those explanations invoke—by material objects, according to Locke's explanation, and by God, according to Berkeley's. Moreover, it seems obvious that any similar attempt to explain experience by appeal to something existing outside experience (even the person's own unconscious mind) will require a similar causal claim (for how else would the explanation work?). But, argues Hume, causal relations can be known only by *experiencing* the regular sequence of cause and effect, something that is impossible in the case of an alleged causal relation between something outside immediate experience and that experience itself.[10] In relation to Locke's explanation specifically, the point is that I cannot immediately experience material bodies causing my sensory ideas because I have no immediate experience of such bodies at all; and the claim that I *indirectly* perceive material bodies presupposes for its justification an explanation relying on the very causal relation in question and so cannot be used to establish that such a causal relation exists.

Hume's further discussion of the issue of the external world[11] is characteristically muddled by his general tendency to conflate and confuse issues concerning justification with issues having to do with the psychological causation or genesis of the beliefs in question. Thus he mainly tries to explain how the belief in a mind-transcendent material world could have arisen psychologically. His rather implausible suggestion is that we confusedly take the immediate objects of our experience, our impressions of sense, to *be* mind-transcendent objects. But it is nonetheless easy to see how a Hume who was clearer about the distinction between psychological explanation and epistemic justification might have argued that the content of our claims about material objects, to the extent that this is justified, must have to do *solely* with features and patterns of our sensory experience, rather than with genuinely mind-transcendent objects. (This is an extremely puzzling and com-monsensically implausible view, one that you will very likely not be able to fully understand until we have discussed it further.)

Thus we have initial adumbrations of the two main views that we will now proceed to discuss more systematically. Locke's view, according to which our subjective sensory experience and the beliefs that we adopt on the basis of it constitute a *representation* of the external material world, one that is caused by that world and that we are justified in thinking to be at least approximately ac-curate, is a version of the more general position known as *representationalism* or *representative realism.*[12] (So also is Descartes's view.) The second main view, which Hume's discussion suggests but never quite arrives at, is that (i) we can have no knowledge (or perhaps even no intelligible conception) of a realm of external causes of our experience, but also (ii) that our beliefs about the ma-terial world can still be in general justified and true because their content in fact has to do only with the features and order of our subjective experience. This is the view that has come to be known as *phenomenalism*, a version of ide-alism. (Contrary to what is often suggested, Berkeley's "idealist" view is not in fact in any clear way an anticipation of phenomenalism, but rather in effect a curious version of representationalism, in which our perceptual ideas consti-tute partial representations of the much more complete picture of the material world constituted by God's much more complete ideas; to take Berkeley to be a proto-phenomenalist is to ignore the central role of God in his view.) Yet a third possibility would be the essentially skeptical view that we can know that our experiences are externally caused in *some* way, but can know nothing fur-ther about the nature of those causes.[13] Such a skeptical view would, of course, not be a *solution* to the problem of the external world, but rather a confession that there is no solution; it is thus a view to be adopted only after the other two possibilities have clearly failed.

Historically, the objections to the representationalism of Descartes and Locke, especially the Humean one discussed above, were widely taken to be decisive, with positions in the direction of phenomenalism being viewed as the main nonskeptical alternative, especially in the first two-thirds or so of the twentieth century.[14] Thus we will begin our more systematic discussion with a consideration of phenomenalism, and then return later to the consid-eration of representationalism that was begun in the discussion of Locke.

Phenomenalism

As just briefly formulated, the phenomenalist view is that the content of propo-sitions about material objects and the material world is *entirely* concerned with features and relations of the immediate objects of our perceptual experience, that is, the features and relations of our sense-data.[15] According to the phenomenalist, to believe that a physical or material object of a certain sort exists just *is* to believe that sense-data of various sorts have been experienced, are being experienced, will be experienced, and/or would be experienced under certain specifiable conditions. Thus, for example, to believe that there is a large brown table in a certain room in the University of Washington Library is to believe, roughly, (i) that the sorts of sense-data that seem from a commonsense standpoint to reflect the presence of such a table either have been, are presently, or will in the future be experienced in the context of other sense-data, themselves experienced concurrently or immediately before or after, that reflect the location as the room in question; and in addition—or instead, if the table has never in fact been perceived and never in fact will be perceived—(ii) that such sense-data *would* be experienced *if* other sense-data that reflect the perceiver's going to the library and to that room were experienced. (This is quite a complicated specification, and you will have to think very carefully about what it is saying.)[16]

In a fairly standard formula, to believe that such a material object exists is, according to the phenomenalist, to believe nothing more than that sense-data of the appropriate sort are actual (in the past, present, or future) and/or possible—where to say that certain sense-data are *possible* is to say, not just that it is logically possible for them to be experienced (which would apparently always be so as long as the description of them is not contradictory), but that they *would* in fact actually be experienced under certain specifiable circumstances (specifiable in sense-datum terms); thus it would be somewhat clearer to speak of actual and *obtainable* sense-data. The British philosopher John Stuart Mill put this point by saying that material objects are nothing but "permanent possibilities of sensation,"[17] that is, of sense-data—where, of course, the possibilities in question are only *relatively* permanent, since objects can change or be destroyed. The crucial thing to see is that what Mill and the other phenomenalists are saying is that there are no independently existing objects that are responsible for the possibilities of sensation or the obtainability of sense-data; the actuality and obtainability of sense-data are *all there is* to the physical or material world.

Phenomenalism is in fact one of those occasional (some would say more than occasional) philosophical views that is *so* monumentally bizarre and implausible, at least from anything close to a commonsense standpoint, as to perhaps make it difficult for some of you to believe that it really says what it does—and even more difficult to believe that such a view has in fact sometimes been widely advocated and (apparently) believed, indeed that it was arguably the dominant view concerning the problem of the external world for a good portion of the twentieth century. The first and most important thing to say about this situation is that you must not, as sometimes happens, allow it to cause you to fail to understand what the view is saying by trying to make it more reasonable than it is. The phenomenalist really is saying that there is *nothing more* to the material world (including, of course, our own physical bodies!—think carefully about that) than our subjective sensory experiences and the possibility, in the sense explained, of further such experiences (though there is, as we will eventually see, a serious problem about the "our").

But why should such an obviously implausible view be taken seriously, even for a moment? We have already in fact encountered the essential ingredients of the main argument for phenomenalism, but it will be helpful to reiterate them in a somewhat more explicit fashion. One main premise of the argument is the Humean thesis that causal relations can be known only via experience of the causal sequence, so that, as already explained, there is no way in which a causal relation between the immediate content of experience and something outside that immediate content could be known, and hence no way to justifiably invoke such external causes as explanations of that experience. This thesis has a good deal of initial plausibility, and can be rebutted only by offering some other account of how causal relations can be known. The other main premise is simply the commonsense conviction that skepticism is false, that we do *obviously* have justified beliefs and knowledge concerning ordinary objects like trees and rocks and buildings and about the material world in which they exist. And the argument is then just that the only way that such justified beliefs and knowledge are possible, given that no causal or explanatory inference from immediate experience to material objects that are genuinely external to that experience could ever even in principle be justified, is if the content of our beliefs about the material world does not really have to do with objects existing outside our immediate experience, but instead pertains just to the objects of that experience and the order that they manifest. Most phenomenalists will admit that this seems initially very implausible, but will try to argue that this apparent implausibility is in some way an illusion, one that can be explained away once the phenomenalist view and the considerations in favor of it have been fully understood.[18]

Objections to Phenomenalism

The foregoing argument, like most arguments for implausible philosophical views that are nonetheless widely held, is a serious argument, one not easily dismissed. Neither premise is easy to rebut, and the conclusion does seem to follow from these premises. But it is, of course, still abundantly obvious that this conclusion cannot be correct, and so that something must have gone wrong.[19] For it is obvious upon even the slightest unbiased reflection that the content of propositions about physical or material objects does pertain, whether justifiably or not, to a realm of entities that, if genuine, exist outside of our minds and experiences in an independent physical realm.

This basic insight seems in fact to constitute by itself a more than adequate reason to reject phenomenalism. But since it nevertheless amounts to little more than a direct, unargued denial of the view, it will be useful to see if we can find further objections and problems of a more articulated sort pertaining to phenomenalism. (Considering such objections and the responses available to the phenomenalist will also help you to better understand the view.) In fact, there are many such objections and problems that have been advanced. Here we will be content with a few of the most interesting ones.

Consider, first, what is perhaps the most obvious question about the phenomenalist view: *Why*, according to the phenomenalist, are the orderly sense-data in question obtainable or "permanently possible"? What is the *explanation* for the pattern of actual and obtainable sense experiences that allegedly constitutes the existence of a material object or of the material world as a whole, if this is not to be explained by appeal to genuinely external objects? The only possible phenomenalist response to this question is to say that the fact that sensory experience reflects this sort of order is simply the most fundamental fact about reality, not further explainable in terms of anything else. For *any* attempted further explanation, since it would obviously have to appeal to something outside of that experience, would be (for the reasons already discussed) unjustified and unknowable.[20] The phenomenalist will add that it is obvious anyway that not everything can be explained, since each explanation just introduces some further fact for which an explanation might be demanded.

But while this last point seems correct (doesn't it?), it seems quite implausible to suppose that something as large and complicated as the total order of our immediate experience has no explanation at all—and also very obvious that common sense (at least if it accepted perceptual subjectivism) would regard claims about material objects as providing such an explanation, rather than as just a redescription of the experiential order itself (as the phenomenalist claims them to be). Perhaps, for all we have seen so far, the phenomenalist is right that we cannot ever know that any such explanation is correct, but this, if so, is an argument for *skepticism* about the material world, not a justification for perversely reinterpreting the meaning or content of claims about material objects. (Here it is important to be very clear that phenomenalism is *not* supposed to be a skeptical view, but rather an account of how beliefs about material objects are indeed justified and do constitute knowledge—given the phenomenalist account of the content of such beliefs.)

A second problem (or rather a set of related problems) has to do with the specification of the *conditions* under which the various sense-data that (according to phenomenalism) are what a material-object proposition is about either are or would be experienced. It is clear that such conditions must be specified to have even a hope of capturing the content of at least most such propositions in sense-datum terms. To recur to our earlier example, to say merely that the sense-data that are characteristic of a brown table are actual or obtainable in some circumstances or other may perhaps capture the content of the claim that the world contains at least one brown table (though even that is doubtful), but surely not of any more specific claim, such as the one about such a table being in a particular room in the University of Washington Library. For that, as we saw briefly, conditions must be specified that say, as it were, that it is in relation to that particular room that the sense-data are or would be experienced. (But remember here that for the phenomenalist, the room does not exist as a mind-external place; talk of a room or of any physical location is to be understood merely as a way of indicating one aspect of the order of immediate experience, namely that the various sense-data that reflect the various features ascribed to the room tend to be experienced together or in close succession, with this whole "cluster" of sense-data standing in similar relations to the further sense-data that pertain to the surrounding area.)

What makes this problem extremely difficult at best is that for phenomenalism to be a viable position, the conditions under which sense-data are experienced or obtainable must themselves (as just in effect indicated) be specifiable in terms of *other sense-data*, not in terms of material objects and structures such as the library or room in question. For the essential claim of phenomenalism is that the content of propositions about material objects can be *entirely* given in terms of sense-data. If in specifying the conditions under which the actual and obtainable sense-data relevant to one material-object proposition would occur, it were necessary to make reference to other material objects, then the account of the content of the first proposition would not yet be completely in sense-datum terms. And if in specifying the conditions relevant to claims about those other material objects, still other material objects would have to be mentioned, and so on, then the phenomenalist account would never be complete. If the content of propositions about material objects cannot be given *entirely* in terms of sense-data, if that content involves essential and ineliminable reference to further such objects, then phenomenalism fails.)

There are in fact many problems here, but we may continue to focus on the one suggested by the example of the table in the library room. How can the idea that sense-data are or would be observed in a certain location be adequately captured in purely sense-datum terms? The natural response, which was in effect invoked when the example was originally discussed, is to appeal to the idea of a *sensory route*: a series of juxtaposed and often overlapping sense-data that would be experienced in what we think of intuitively as moving to the location in question. (But, to reiterate, there is not supposed to be any real mind-external location or bodily movement; according to the phenomenalist, claims about this sort of experienced movement have to do *only* with sequences of sense-data that are experienced or could be experienced—including those that we think of intuitively as the feelings associated with bodily movements like walking.)

There are at least two serious problems pertaining to this answer, however. One is that there are normally many *different* sensory routes to a given location, depending on where one starts and how one approaches it; and if the starting location is itself determined by a previous sensory route, then a regress threatens, in which the sensory conditions must go further and further back in time without ever reaching a place from which they can begin. A second problem is that it seems clear that we can often understand the claim that a certain material object or set of objects exists at a certain physical location without having any clear idea of the relevant sensory route: for example, I understand the claim that there are penguins at the South Pole, but have no clear idea of the sensory route that I would have to follow to guarantee or even make it likely that I have reached the South Pole. (Note that it is a *guarantee* that is actually required, for otherwise the content of the claim in question as not been fully captured.)[21]

An alternative possibility[22] is that the relevant location can be adequately identified in sensory terms by specifying other sense-data that would, as it were, be experienced there, rather than by a sensory route: by those pertaining to the local scenery or landmarks or reflecting locating measurements of some kind. Perhaps there are some locations where this would work (though one must remember such things as movie sets and amusement parks and, before long, virtual reality devices). But we must remember that it is the content of the original material object proposition that is supposed to be reflected in these specifications, and it seems abundantly clear (but this is again something to think about carefully and in detail) that there are many, many propositions about material objects in various locations that I can understand perfectly well without having in mind any adequate way of identifying that location in purely sensory terms—or, to bring in the other possibility, a way of specifying a sensory route from some location that I can thus identify.

And there is also the related, but still much more difficult problem of what the phenomenalist can say about the content of propositions about material objects and events in the *past*, perhaps the very distant past. Consider this one carefully on your own, focusing on the most difficult case: past events that were not observed by anyone at the time in question. Under what sensory conditions would sense-data of a tree have to have been obtainable to make it true that there was a pine tree in the place now occupied by my house in 1000 B.C.? It is thus very doubtful that the sort of specification of conditions that the phenomenalist needs is possible in general.

A generalization of this objection is offered by the American epistemologist Roderick Chisholm.[23] Chisholm argues that there is in fact *no* conditional proposition in sense-datum terms, however long and complicated the set of conditions in the "if" part, that is *ever* even part of the content of a material-object proposition. This is shown, he claims, by the fact that for any such sense-datum proposition, it is *always* possible to describe conditions of observation (including conditions having to do with the state of the observer) under which the sense-datum proposition would be false, but the material-object proposition might still be true. The idea here is to describe various sorts of abnormalities pertaining to the conditions or the observer: for example, having followed the sensory route to the room in the library, I am suddenly struck blind or knocked unconscious or injected with a mind-altering drug at just the instant before I would experience the distinctive table sense-data, which thus are not experienced (or the lighting is so altered as to make it impossible to see the table or to make it look very different in color; or the table is dropped through a trap door in the floor, to be restored only after I leave;[24] etc.). Chisholm's suggestion, which you should think about more fully by imagining many more examples of your own, is that the only way to guarantee that the sense-data that are experienced reflect the object that is actually there is to specify the conditions in *material* terms. But in that case, for the reason already discussed, the phenomenalist project cannot succeed.

A third, somewhat related, but deeper problem arises by reflecting that it is apparently a condition for the success of phenomenalism that the realm of sense-data have an intrinsic order of its own, one that can be recognized and described solely in terms of the sense-data themselves. For how could we (without invoking independent material objects) have any justification for thinking that further sense-data will, under various conditions, occur, except by finding regularities in those we actually experience and reasoning inductively? But does such an intrinsic order of sense-data really exist? It is obvious that our sense-data are not completely chaotic, but far less obvious that they have an order that can be captured without making reference to material objects. And this is not something that the phenomenalist can just assume, for it is utterly essential to his whole position.

One way of thinking about this issue is in fact suggested by Mill, a proponent of phenomenalism, who speaks of sense-data (his term, as we have seen, is "sensations") falling into "groups," intuitively those that are all perceptions of the same material object or perhaps of the same general kind of material object (think of all the different sense-data, mainly those of vision and touch, that would be experiences of a particular table or of tables in general). He then remarks that in "almost all" cases, the regular sequences that are to be found in our experience pertain not to specific sense-data, but to these groups: for example, that sense-data belonging to the mailman group are regularly followed by sense-data belonging to the letters in the mailbox group; that sense-data belonging to the opening-the-door-of-the-departmental-office group are for me regularly followed by sense-data of the departmental-staff-and-other-colleagues group or groups; etc.[25] But if the regularities pertaining to sense-data are mostly or entirely of this sort, then the phenomenalist seems to have a severe problem. For if (i) the justification for his conditional claims that certain sense-data are or would be experienced if other sense-data are or were experienced depends on identifying regularities in the occurrence of sense-data, and if (ii) most or all of the regularities to be found depend on viewing sense-data as members of such groups, and if (iii) the only justification for lumping very different sense-data into such groups is the observed regularities themselves, then it becomes hard to see how the whole project can ever get started. There would have to be observed regularities prior to justified grouping, but also justified grouping prior to being able to justify most or all claims about regularities. (This is perhaps the most difficult issue and line of argument in this entire book, one that I bring in only because it is relevant both to the essential core of the phenomenalist view and, in a way to be discussed later, to the prospects for representationalism. To assess it, you need to think carefully about all three of the "if" claims in the statement of the argument, with examples, as usual, being extremely helpful.)

A fourth and final objection to phenomenalism, one that is, thankfully, much simpler and more straightforward, concerns what the phenomenalist must apparently say about the knowledge of the mental states of people other than myself (or other than whoever is thinking about the issue—for reasons that will become clear, each of you will have to formulate this issue for yourselves). The whole thrust of the phenomenalist position, as we have seen, is that *any* inference beyond immediate experience is impossible, that claims that might seem to be about things outside of experience must, if they are to be justified and knowable,[26] be understood as pertaining only to features and orderly patterns of that experience. But the mental states of *other* people, their experiences and feelings and conscious thoughts, are surely outside of *my* immediate experience. Indeed, to reach justified conclusions about what people distinct from me are genuinely thinking and experiencing would apparently require *two* inferences: first, an inference from my immediate experience of sense-data pertaining to their physical bodies to conclusions about those bodies; and then, second, an inference from the facts about those bodies thus arrived at to further conclusions about the minds and mental states of the people in question. *Both* of these inferences depend on causal relations that are, according to the phenomenalist, unknowable, because we cannot experience both sides, or in the second case even one side, of the relation; and thus neither inference, construed in that way, is justified according to the basic phenomenalist outlook.

What phenomenalism must apparently say here, in order to be consistent, is (i) that the content of propositions about the conditions and behavior of other people's bodies (like that of all other material object propositions) pertains only to facts about *my* immediate experience; and (ii) that the content of further claims about the mental states associated with those bodies is only a further, more complicated and less direct description of, once again, *my* experience. Though the phenomenalist would perhaps resist putting it this way, the upshot is that *my* mind and mental states, including my immediate experience, is the only mind and the only collection of mental states that genuinely exist, with claims that are apparently about other minds amounting only to further descriptions of this one mind and its experiences. This is the view known as *solipsism*—which each of you must obviously formulate for yourselves (assuming that any of you are really out there!). It seems clearly to be an absurd consequence, thus yielding a really decisive objection, if one were still needed, to phenomenalism.[27]

Back to Representationalism

If phenomenalism is indeed untenable, and assuming that we continue to accept perceptual subjectivism, then the only nonskeptical alternative apparently left is *representationalism*: the view, restating it a bit, that our immediately experienced sense-data, together with the further beliefs that we arrive at on the basis of them, constitute a *representation* or depiction of an independent realm of material objects—one that we are in general, according to the representationalist, justified in believing to be true.

Defenses of representationalism have taken a variety of forms, but I will assume here that the best sort of defense for such a view is one along the general lines that we found to be suggested, albeit not very explicitly, in Locke (and indeed also, though even less explicitly, in Descartes). The central idea is, first, that (contrary to the claim of the phenomenalist) some *explanation* is needed for the complicated and intricate order that we find in our involuntarily experienced sense-data (or adverbial contents); and, second, that the *best* explanation, that is, the one most likely to be correct, is that those experiences are caused by and, with certain qualifications, systematically reflect the character of a world of genuinely independent material objects, which we accordingly have good reasons for believing to exist.

I have already remarked that representationalism was widely repudiated as untenable during most of the period between Locke and recent times, with the main argument being the one that we found in Hume about the unknowability of any causal relation between something outside experience and experience itself. We will begin by looking further at that argument and considering in a general way how it might be answered. Having argued that representationalism cannot be simply ruled out as impossible in the way that Hume tries to do, we will then consider the further issue of whether and how the specific explanation of experience that the representationalist proposes can be defended against other alternatives, such as Berkeley's. Finally, we will look at the significant qualification, already briefly mentioned, advocated by Descartes, Locke, and many others with regard to the accuracy with which our experience represents the true character of material objects: the one having to do with the distinction between *primary* and *secondary* qualities.

A Response to Hume's Argument: Theoretical or Explanatory Inference

To recall, Hume's objection to representationalism rests on the premise that causal relations can be known only by experiencing the regular sequence between cause and effect, which requires experiencing both sides of the causal relation. This, he argues, is impossible for an alleged causal relation between something outside of direct experience and the experience itself, so that the claim that such a causal relation exists can never be justified or known.[28] And therefore, he concludes, neither can the representationalist's proposed explanation of the order of our experience, since that depends essentially on such an unknowable and unjustifiable causal claim.

If Hume's initial premise is accepted, then the rest of his argument seems to follow. But should that premise be accepted? One way to approach this issue is to consider examples where we seem to reason in ways that conflict with that premise but which still seem intuitively cogent. Here I will consider two examples of this kind, the first having to do with the knowledge of other minds (discussed further in the next chapter) and the other having to do with knowledge concerning unobservable entities and events, such as electrons or quarks or radioactivity, in theoretical physics. In both of these cases, we seem intuitively to have justified belief and knowledge pertaining to causal relations that could not be arrived at in the way that Hume's premise, if correct, would require. (In considering both of these examples, we adopt the standpoint of common sense, thus assuming that the problem of the external world has—somehow—been solved.)

In the other minds case, the relevant causal relation is that between another person's conscious mental states or events and the behavior (including, importantly, the verbal behavior) of his or her body. I certainly *seem* to have knowledge of a wide variety of causal relations of this kind (that pain causes wincing or moaning, that fear causes various sorts of defensive or avoidance behavior, that having the belief that it is raining tends to cause one to answer "yes" when asked if it is raining, etc.), but the mental states or events that are the alleged cause are almost entirely outside of my immediate experience; and so also, analogously, for anyone else who might have such knowledge. To be sure, for each person, there is one set of such supposed causes, the ones occurring in his or her mind, that *can* be immediately experienced. But an inductive argument from the cases where this is possible seems obviously too weak, being based on such a small and possibly unrepresentative set of cases, to justify the general causal knowledge that each of us seems commonsensically to have in this area. The issue of how such knowledge might actually be justified will be considered further in the next chapter. The point for the moment is just that here is an example of apparent causal knowledge that does not seem to conform to Hume's premise.

The case of unobservable scientific entities and events is even clearer. Here we seem to have justified belief and knowledge concerning causal relations among such entities and events and between them and various sorts of observable results, even though the entities and events themselves cannot be experienced in even the indirect sense: knowledge, for example, that radioactivity results from the splitting or decay of various sorts of atoms and that it produces a crackling sound in a Geiger counter. Obviously beliefs concerning relations of these kinds cannot be justified by experiencing both sides of the causal relation in the way that Hume's premise would require.

Notice carefully that the claim so far is *not* that these alleged cases of causal knowledge are genuine, so that Hume's premise would have to be mistaken. It is possible for a proponent of Hume's view to respond by claiming either that we do not really have the causal knowledge in question (or possibly, though this seems even more difficult to defend, that it can in fact be somehow accounted for in a way that is compatible with the Humean claim). Thus defenders of Hume's view have often also been advocates of *behaviorism* (the view that there is nothing more to mental states than patterns of observable behavior) and of *fictionalism* (the view that seemingly unobservable scientific entities do not really exist, but only reflect ways of talking that help to systematically describe observations).[29] But these views both seem desperately implausible, so that if a reasonably plausible general account can be given of how such causal knowledge can be justifiably arrived at, this would be enough to warrant the rejection of Hume's premise and the argument that results from it.

The account that has been offered, by a series of philosophers of whom the first was probably the American philosopher Charles Sanders Peirce, holds that knowledge of the sort in question depends on a fundamental and sometimes unrecognized mode of reasoning, one that is quite distinct from both deductive reasoning and the inductive reasoning that was considered in chapter 4. Peirce called it "abductive reasoning," but it is perhaps more perspicuously characterized as *theoretical* or *explanatory* reasoning. In reasoning of this sort, a hypothesis is advanced to explain some relevant set of data and is justified simply on the basis of being the *best explanation* of the data in question.[30] Exactly what makes an explanation the *best* is a difficult and complicated issue, as we will see to some extent below, but the point for the moment is that *if* such an assessment can be defended, then it allegedly becomes justifiable to accept the entire explanatory hypothesis, *including any causal claims that it may involve*, on that basis—without any requirement that there be experiential evidence of the sort that Hume's premise would require for those causal claims by themselves. Thus for example when the entire physical theory of radioactive isotopes and their decay into other kinds of atoms is justified as the best explanation of a variety of observed phenomena, including the fogging of photographic film, changes in the composition of samples, tracks in cloud chambers, etc., the causal relations between the various kinds of atoms and particles and also between these unobservable entities and processes and their observable manifestations are justified as part of the total package, with accordingly no need for them to be justified separately.[31]

A full defense of the idea of theoretical or explanatory reasoning is obviously not possible in the present book. The suggestion for the moment is only that the idea is plausible enough, especially in light of examples like those given, to make it reasonable to reject Hume's thesis about knowledge of causal relations, at least tentatively, thus opening the door to the possibility that the representationalist position on the problem of the external world might be defensible after all.

The Representationalist Explanation

But this only opens the door. We still need to worry about whether the representationalist's proposed explanation of our experience is really the *best* one. And before we can do that, we need to consider in substantially more detail what the rationale for that explanation might be and how it is supposed to work.

The place to start is to ask what it is about the character of our immediate sensory experience that points to or perhaps even seems to demand such an explanation. As we saw earlier, Locke points to two features of our experience in this connection: its involuntary character and its systematic order. But while these features may indeed demand *some* sort of explanation, they do not, at least when described at that level of abstraction, seem to point at all clearly at the specific one that the representationalist favors (which is why the door is seemingly open to Berkeley's alternative). If anything about experience does this, it will thus have to be, I would suggest, more specific features than any that Locke explicitly mentions.

Here is a question for you to think hard about, preferably before reading beyond this paragraph—one that is both historically and substantively as fundamental as any in the whole field of epistemology. Think as carefully as you can about your immediate sensory experience: your experience of qualities like colors and shapes and apparent spatial relations and apparent sounds and tactile qualities and so on. You are presently experiencing patterns of black and white marks that according to the representationalist are caused by and represent the pages of this book, along with other colors reflecting the immediate surrounding environment; your auditory sensations might be those allegedly reflecting the steps of people in the library or the music that you listen to while you read; you have tactile sensations allegedly reflecting things like the book in your hand, the chair or couch you are sitting on, and so on; perhaps there is an odd smell of some sort as well. What, if anything, about those experienced qualities *taken in themselves* suggests that their source or cause is an independent realm of material objects of the sort that the representationalist advocates? Why, apart from mere familiarity, does such an explanation of experience seem so natural and compelling?

My suggestion is that the answer to this question has two main parts. The first points to the presence in immediate experience of repeatable *sequences* of experienced qualities, qualities that overlap and often shade gradually into one another. Here I have in mind something like the "sensory routes" that are, as discussed earlier, invoked by the phenomenalist. While these "sensory routes" cannot ultimately do the job that the phenomenalist needs them to do, for the reasons given there, they are nonetheless very real and pervasive. Think of the ways in which such "sensory routes" can be experienced in opposite orders (imagine here what common sense would regard as walking from one place to another and then returning to the first place by the same route—perhaps even walking backwards, so as to make the two sequences as similar as possible). Think of the ways in which such "sensory routes" intersect with each other, thus, for example, allowing one to get from one end to the other without going through the "route" itself, thereby delineating a sensory loop. Think of the resulting structure of a whole set of overlapping and intersecting "sensory routes."[32]

Here it may be helpful, as a kind of analogy, to think from a commonsense standpoint of how you would go about programming a computer game to simulate a "space" containing "objects" through which the computer character can move. You would program successive "screens" of visually observable colors and shapes in such a way as to mimic the appearance of objects that are gradually approached and passed, perhaps with concomitant sound qualities that get louder and then softer and imaginably even other systematically varying qualities like smells or temperatures. (Perhaps the game is played in an enclosed booth that can be heated or cooled.) You would also include some controllable way in which the character can be made to face in different directions, move at different rates, and stand still. In these terms, my suggestion is that our actual immediate experience has more or less exactly the features that an ideal program of this sort would create. (Again, you will have to ponder this point, "chew on" it, in relation to a range of your own examples, in order to fully understand it.)

The idea is then that at least the most obvious and natural explanation of these features of our experience is that we are located in a spatial realm of objects through which we move and of which we can perceive at any given moment only the limited portion that is close enough to be accessible to our various senses (what this requires differs from sense to sense)—a kind of experiential "tunnel." Our experience reflects both the qualities of these objects and the different perspectives from which they are perceived as we gradually approach them from different directions, at different speeds, under different conditions of perception, etc. Thus the relatively permanent structure of this spatial array of objects is partially reflected in the much more temporary and variable, but broadly repeatable features of our immediate experience. (Are we being misled by mere familiarity here? Can you think of another explanation of these features of experience that is equally "natural" or reasonable?)

The second part of the answer to the question of what it is about the character of immediate experience that points to the representationalist explanation cites the fact, already noticed in our discussion of phenomenalism, that the experiential order just described, though undeniably impressive, is in fact *incomplete* or *fragmentary* in a number of related ways. The easiest way to indicate these is by reference to the sorts of situations that, from a commonsense standpoint, produce and explain them (though the representationalist cannot, of course, assume at this stage, without begging the question, that these things are what is actually going on). Imagine then traversing a "sensory route" of the sort just indicated, but doing so (i) with one's eyes closed (or one's ears plugged, etc.) during some of the time required, or perhaps while asleep during part of the time (traveling in a car or train); or (ii) while the conditions of perception, including those pertaining to the functioning of your sense-organs and to your mental "processing," are changing or being varied (involving such things as changing lighting, including complete darkness; jaundice and similar diseases that affect perception; objects and conditions that temporarily block or interfere with perception; even something as simple as turning one's head in a different direction, blinking, or wiping one's eyes). If you think about it carefully, you will see that interfering factors of these various kinds make the sensory sequences that define the various "routes" far less regular and dependable than they might at first seem. (The more time you spend thinking carefully about specific examples, the better you will understand and be able to evaluate this point.)

Thus the basic claim is that the realm of immediate sensory experience, of sense-data (or adverbial contents), is both *too orderly* not to demand an explanation and *not orderly enough* for that explanation to be that the sense-data have an intrinsic order of their own. What this strongly suggests, the representationalist will argue, is an independent realm of objects outside our experience, one that has its own patterns of (mainly spatial) order, with the partial and fragmentary order of our experience resulting from our partial and intermittent perceptual contact with that larger and more stable realm.

The discussion so far provides only an initial and highly schematic picture of the representationalist's proposed explanation. It would have to be filled out in a number of ways in order to be even approximately complete. Here I will be content with three further points. First, the main focus of the discussion so far has been on *spatial* properties of material objects and the features of immediate experience that seem to suggest them. Thus the result to this point is at best only a kind of skeletal picture of the material world, one that would have to be "fleshed out" in various ways in order to even approximate the commonsense picture of the world. In fact, it is useful to think of the representationalist explanation as starting with spatial properties as a first and most fundamental stage and then adding further refinements to that starting point.

Second, the main addition to this initial spatial picture of the world would be various sorts of *causal* relations among material objects and between such objects and perceivers, together with the causal and dispositional properties of objects (flammability, solubility, malleability, brittleness, toxicity, etc.) that underlie such relations. These are, from the representationalist standpoint, basically added in order to explain apparent changes in material objects that are reflected in relatively permanent changes in the otherwise stable "sensory routes." Here it is important to note that like the stable spatial order, the causal regularities that pertain to material objects are only intermittently and fragmentarily reflected in immediate experience, partially for the reasons already considered, but also because any given perceiver may simply not be in the right position to observe the beginning or end or some intermediate part of a given causal sequence, even though other parts are experienced. Simple examples would include throwing a rock into the air without seeing or hearing it land, pulling on a string without observing the movement of an object at the other end (or seeing the object move but without observing the movement of part of the intervening string), or planting a seed and returning later to find a well-developed plant.[33]

Third, there is the issue of primary and secondary qualities. As already noted, Locke's view is that material objects have *primary* qualities like size, shape, and motion through space, but not *secondary* qualities like color, smell, taste, and felt temperature, a view with which most other representationalists have tended to agree. Here it will suffice to focus on color, surely the most apparently pervasive and interesting of the secondary qualities.[34] Clearly to deny that material objects are genuinely colored complicates the representationalist's proposed explanation by making the relation between material objects and our immediate experiences much less straightforward than it would otherwise be: according to such a view, whereas our immediate experiences of spatial properties are caused more or less directly by closely related spatial properties of objects (allowing, importantly, for perspective), our immediate experiences of color properties are caused by utterly different properties of material objects, primarily by how their surfaces differentially reflect wavelengths of light.

Locke offers little real argument for this view, but the argument he seems to have in mind[35] is that as the causal account of the material world develops, it turns out that ascribing a property like color (construed as the "sensuous" property that is present in immediate visual experience) to material objects is in fact quite useless for explaining our experiences of colors. What colors we experience depend on the properties of the light that strikes our eyes and this in turn, in the most standard cases, depend on how material objects reflect and absorb light, which yet in turn depends on the structure of their surfaces as constituted by primary and causal properties. I think that this is correct as a matter of science, but the important point for the moment is that *if* it is correct, then the denial that material objects are really colored simply follows from the basic logic of the representationalist position: according to representationalism, the only justification for ascribing *any* property to the material world is that it best explains some aspect of our immediate experience, so that the ascription of properties that do not figure in such explanations is automatically unjustified.[36]

Alternatives to the Representationalist Explanation

The discussion so far has perhaps made a reasonable case, though of course nothing like a conclusive one, first, that the representationalist's proposed explanation of the order of our immediate experience cannot be ruled out on Humean grounds; and, second, that this explanation has a good deal of plausibility in relation to that experience. But this is still not enough to show that it is the *best* explanation and hence the one, even assuming the general acceptability of theoretical reasoning, whose acceptance is thereby justified. Here we are essentially back to the question posed very early on in this chapter: why, if at all, should the explanation of our experience that invokes external, mind-independent material objects be preferred to other possible explanations such as Berkeley's (or the very similar if not identical one that appeals to Descartes's evil genius)?

It should be obvious that Berkeley's explanatory hypothesis is capable of explaining the very same features of immediate experience that the representationalist appeals to. All that is needed, as suggested earlier, is for God to have an ideally complete conception or picture of the representationalist's material world and then to systematically cause experiences in perceivers that reflect their apparent location in and movement through such a world.

(This assumes that God can recognize intentions to "move" in various directions and adjust the person's perceptions accordingly; of course, no genuine
movement really takes place, nor does the perceiver really have a physical location.[37]) A different, but essentially parallel explanatory hypothesis, is provided by a science fiction scenario: the perceiver is a disembodied brain float-
ing in a vat of brain nutrients and receiving electrical impulses from a
computer that again contains an ideally complete model or representation of
a material world and generates the impulses accordingly, taking account of
motor impulses received from the brain that reflect the person's intended
movements. And further explanatory hypotheses can be generated according
to the same basic formula: there must be some sort of a representation or
model of a material world together with some sort of mechanism (which
need not be mechanical in the ordinary sense) that systematically produces
experience in perceivers, allowing for their subjectively intended movements. Any pattern of immediate experience that can be explained by the
representationalist's explanatory hypothesis can thus automatically be also
explained by explanatory hypotheses of this latter sort, probably indefinitely
many of them, with no possible experiential basis for deciding between them
or between any one of them and the representationalist hypothesis.

If there is to be a reason for favoring the representationalist hypothesis,
therefore, it will have to be a priori in character, and it is more than a little
difficult to see what it might be. Here I will limit myself to one fairly tentative suggestion, before leaving the issue for you to think further about.

One striking contrast between the representationalist's explanatory hypothesis and the others we have looked at is that under the representationalist view there is a clear intuitive sense in which the qualities of the objects
that explain our immediate experience are directly reflected in the character
of that experience itself, so that the latter can be said to be, allowing for perspective and perhaps other sorts of distortion, experiences of the former, albeit indirect ones. Once again this applies most straightforwardly to spatial
properties: thus, for example, the rectangular or trapezoidal shape that is immediately experienced can be said to be an indirect perception of a rectangular face of the material object that causes that experience. In contrast, the
features of the elements in the other explanatory hypotheses that are responsible for the various features of our experience are not directly reflected
in that experience. For example, what is responsible in these other hypotheses for the rectangular or trapezoidal shape in my immediate experience is
one aspect of God's total picture or conception of a material world, or perhaps one aspect of a representation of such a world stored in a computer. This
aspect has in itself no shape of any sort (or at least, in the case of the com-

puter, none that is at all relevant to the shape that I experience); it is merely a *representation* of a related shape, according to some system of representation or coding. Thus its relation to the character of the experience that it is supposed to explain is inherently less direct, more convoluted than in the case of the representationalist's explanation.

My suggestion is that the inherently less direct, more convoluted character of the way that these competing explanatory hypotheses account for the features of our immediate experience may yield a reason for preferring the more direct and thus in an sense simpler representationalist explanatory hypothesis, for regarding it as more likely to be true. But how, exactly?[38] The idea is that an explanatory hypothesis like Berkeley's, at least as we have construed it, depends for its explanatory success on the truth of two equally essential claims: first, the claim that a material world of the sort postulated by the representationalist *could* account for the features of our experience, for it is precisely by emulating or mimicking the action of such a world that God (or the computer) decides just what experiences to produce in us; and, second, that God (or the computer) can indeed successfully produce the required emulation. But the representationalist view requires only the truth of the first of these two claims. It is thus, I suggest, inherently less vulnerable to problems and challenges and so more likely to be true. And this is an apparent reason for regarding the representationalist's explanatory hypothesis as providing the best of these competing explanations.[39] (An approximate analogy:[40] Suppose that I come home to find my truck, to which only my wife has the key, gone from my driveway. One explanatory hypothesis is that she has driven it somewhere on her own. A second explanatory hypothesis is that an intruder has kidnapped her and forced her to drive somewhere. Assuming that there is no further evidence that also requires explanation, such as a broken door or window, the first explanatory hypothesis is more likely to be true than the second simply because the second one requires both the essential ingredient invoked in the first explanatory hypothesis (my wife using her key to drive the truck away) and a further, separate ingredient (the intruder, who forces her to do so). Because it requires both of these ingredients, the second explanatory hypothesis is less likely to be true than the first, which requires only one of them.[41])

Is this a successful argument for representationalism? There are at least two questions about it that need to be considered. First, the argument assumes that the competitors to representationalism are all parasitic upon the representationalist explanatory hypothesis in the way indicated, and it is worth asking whether this is really so. Is there an explanation of our immediate experience that does not in this way rely on an emulation of the way in which a material world would produce that experience? It will not do to say simply that God causes our experience without saying how and why it produces the specific results that he does, for that is not really to give a complete explanation. But is there some other way of filling out Berkeley's explanatory hypothesis or one of the parallel ones that does not invoke a conception or model of a material world? Second, even if the argument succeeds to a degree, *how* probable or likely does it make the material world hypothesis in comparison to these others? Is the resulting degree of probability or likelihood high enough to agree approximately with our commonsense convictions in this regard (or to yield knowledge, assuming that some version of the weak conception of knowledge is correct[42])? I will leave these further difficult questions for you to think about.

Is There a Better Alternative?: Direct Realism

The upshot of our discussion so far is that phenomenalism appears entirely untenable, and that at least a better defense than many have supposed possible can be offered for representationalism. Many recent philosophers, however, have thought that there is a *third* alternative that is superior to either of these: one usually referred to as *direct realism*. The central idea of direct realism is that the view we have called perceptual subjectivism is false, that is, that instead of immediately experiencing either sense-data or adverbial contents, we instead *directly* experience external material objects, without the mediation of these other sorts of entities or states. And the suggestion often seems to be, though this is usually not explained very fully, that such a view can simply bypass the representationalist's problem of justifying an inference from immediate experience to the material world and do so without having to advocate anything as outlandish as phenomenalism.[43]

For anyone who has struggled with the idea of sense-data (or the adverbial alternative) and with the difficulties and complexities of representationalism and phenomenalism, the apparent simplicity of direct realism, the way in which it seems to make extremely difficult or even intractable problems simply vanish, may be difficult to resist. We must be cautious, however. What does such a view amount to, and can it really deliver the results that it promises?

We may begin with a point that is often advanced in arguments for direct realism, one that, while correct as far as it goes, turns out in fact to be of much less help than has sometimes been thought in either defending or even explaining the view. Think about an ordinary example of perceptual experience: standing in my back yard, I watch my dogs chasing each other in a large circle around some bushes, weaving in and out of the sunshine and shadows, as a car drives by on the street. The direct realist's claim is that in such a case (assuming that I am in a normal, nonphilosophical frame of mind), the picture that it is easy to find in or read into some representationalists, according to which I *first* have thoughts or occurrent beliefs about the character of my experience (whether understood in sense-datum or in adverbial content terms) and *then* infer explicitly from these to thoughts or beliefs about material objects is simply and flatly wrong as a description of my actual conscious state. In fact, the only things that I think about at all *directly* and explicitly in such a case are things like dogs and bushes and cars and sunlight, not anything as subtle and abstruse as sense-data or adverbial contents. The direct realist need not deny (though some have seemed to) that my sensory experience somehow involves the various qualities, such as complicated patterns of shape and color, that these other views have spoken of, or even that I am in *some* way aware or conscious of these. His point is that whatever may be said about these other matters, from an intuitive standpoint it is material objects and nothing else that are "directly before my mind"—and that any view that denies this obvious truth is simply mistaken about the facts.

I have already said that I think that the direct realist is at least mostly right about this. What happens most centrally in perceptual experience is that we have explicit thoughts or "perceptual judgments" about what we are perceiving; and in normal cases (apart from very special artistic or perhaps philosophical contexts), these perceptual judgments are directly and entirely about things (and processes and qualities) in the external material world. Philosophers speak of that which a propositional state of mind is directly about as its *intentional object*, and we can accordingly say that the intentional objects of our basic perceptual judgments are normally alleged or apparent material objects. In this way, the relation of such judgments to material objects is, it might be said, *intentionally* direct.

But what bearing, if any, does this intentional directness have on the central epistemological question of what reason or justification we have for thinking that such perceptual judgments about the material world are *true*? Perhaps the sort of direct presence to the mind that is involved in the idea of immediate experience (see the discussion in the previous chapter) yields the result that one's beliefs or awarenesses concerning the objects of such experience are automatically justified, simply because there is no room for error to creep in.[44] But is there any way in which it follows from the mere fact that perceptual judgments about material objects are *intentionally* direct that they are also *justified*? It still seems obvious that both a perceptual judgment and the total state of mind of which it is a part are quite distinct from the material object, if any, that is its intentionally direct object. This is shown by the fact that in cases like hallucination, the object in question need not exist at all, but it would be clear enough even without such cases—phenomenalist views having been rejected, the material object does not somehow literally enter the mind. Thus even though perceptual judgments are directly about such objects in the intentional sense, the question of whether they represent them *correctly* still arises in exactly the same way that it does for the representationalist. And this question must apparently still be answered, if at all, by appeal to the immediately experienced features involved in the perceiver's state of mind, with the specific character of the sensory experience being the only obvious thing to invoke.

Thus while the idea of intentional directness can be used to present a somewhat more accurate picture of a normal perceiver's state of mind, the view that results is still fundamentally a version of representationalism in that it faces the same essential problem of justifying the transition (whether it is an explicit inference or not) from the character of the person's experience to beliefs or judgments about the material world. If this is all that direct realism amounts to, then it is not a genuinely distinct third alternative with regard to the basic issue of how perceptual beliefs or judgments are justified.

Is there any further way to make sense of the "directness" to which direct realist appeals, one that might yield more interesting epistemological results? It is far from obvious what it would be. Some proponents of this supposed view have tried to deny that we have any awareness of the character of our immediate experience that is both distinct from our judgmental awareness of material objects and of the sort that could provide the basis for the justification of material object claims. Such a challenge raises subtle and difficult issues about different kinds of awareness, but it is hard to see how it could really be correct. Moreover, the correctness of this challenge, while it would surely constitute a serious or perhaps even conclusive objection to representationalism, would not in any way yield a positive direct realist account of how beliefs about the material world are justified, if not in the representationalist way.

My tentative conclusion (which some of you may want to investigate further by consulting some of the recent literature on direct realism[45]) is that the idea that direct realism represents a further alternative on the present issue is a chimera. Thus, once phenomenalism is rejected as hopeless, the only alternatives with regard to knowledge of the external world appear to be skepticism and some version of representationalism, perhaps one that recognizes and incorporates the view that perceptual judgments about the material world are intentionally direct.[46]

Notes

1. Because on these views, what we are immediately aware of in perceptual experience is something subjective: either a kind of object that arguably exists only in relation to the experience of a particular person or else the content of a mental act of sensing or being appeared to. This label is my own coinage, there being no standardly accepted term or phrase that is quite appropriate.

2. Perhaps accompanied by the view that the contents of nonperceptual thoughts are constituted by mental *images*. (Think carefully about whether this is a plausible view of thought content.)

3. Locke, *Essay concerning Human Understanding*, Book IV, ch. 11. Subsequent page references in the text are to the edition edited by P. H. Nidditch (Oxford: Oxford University Press, 1975). I have amended the quotations to reflect modern standards of capitalization.

4. There may of course be *imagined* or *remembered* pain, but that is obviously not the same thing as really experienced pain.

5. For an interpretation of Locke's argument along these general lines, see J. L. Mackie, *Problems from Locke* (Oxford: Oxford University Press, 1976), ch. 2.

6. Locke adds *solidity*, but this does not fit at all well with the other primary qualities. I will have a little more to say about the primary-secondary distinction later in the chapter.

7. Compare the analogous point about regularities in our observations captured by a standard inductive premise, as discussed in chapter 4.

8. Berkeley, *Principles of Human Knowledge*, sections 29 and 30.

9. In addition to the claim that his view provides a better explanation of our experience than Locke's (mainly because of the alleged difficulty of understanding how Lockean material objects could causally affect the mind—see *Principles*, section 19), Berkeley has a number of other objections to Locke's view. These are interesting but ultimately uncompelling, and so will not be discussed here. You may, however, find it interesting to look them up in Berkeley's *Principles* or *Three Dialogues between Hylas and Philonous*—especially since Berkeley is one of the clearest and most engaging of all philosophical writers.

10. This point is clearest in Hume, *An Inquiry Concerning Human Understanding*, Section XII, Part I; but it is also implicit in the discussion in Hume, *A Treatise of Human Nature*, Book I, Part IV, Section 2 ("Of skepticism with regard to the senses"). This argument is sometimes attributed to Berkeley (for example by Jonathan Bennett, *Locke, Berkeley, Hume* [Oxford: Oxford University Press, 1971], pp. 125–26), but this ignores the fact that such an argument would undercut Berkeley's own view just as much as Locke's.

11. Mainly in the *Treatise of Human Nature*.

12. Also sometimes referred to as indirect realism or the causal theory of perception.

13. This third possibility bears some resemblance to Immanuel Kant's view (in the *Critique of Pure Reason*), which is, confusingly, also sometimes referred to with the term "phenomenalism." But Kant attempts, futilely in my judgment, to avoid the impression of skepticism by claiming that although we cannot have knowledge of the external world

that is what is ultimately real, we can have knowledge of a kind of ersatz world that is somehow constituted by our experience. (See also the discussion of Kant in note 10 of chapter 3.)

14. This is somewhat oversimplified. There were also "absolute idealist" views, stemming from Kant and especially from the later German philosopher G. W. F. Hegel, that represent an odd combination of something like phenomenalism with something like Berkeley's appeal to a God. But sorting out and making sense of these views, which are now mainly of historical interest, is too large and difficult a task to be undertaken here.

15. Or the features reflected in immediately experienced adverbial contents. But, as noted above, I will mostly leave this alternative possibility to be supplied by the reader.

16. This specification and those that follow seem on the surface to suggest that any person who has beliefs about physical objects must be thinking explicitly in terms of sense-data (and so must possess the concept of a sense-datum), something that is extremely implausible (think about it). Phenomenalists have not in fact generally wanted to make such a claim, and have attempted to avoid it by saying that the sense-datum formulation is what the content of the beliefs "really amounts to" or is how it is correctly to be "philosophically analyzed." Whether the ideas involved in such formulations really succeed in solving this apparent problem is an issue that I cannot pursue further here—though some of you may want to think further about it on your own, perhaps by investigating the idea of "philosophical analysis."

17. Mill, *An Examination of Sir William Hamilton's Philosophy* (1865); the relevant passage is reprinted in *Readings in the Theory of Knowledge*, ed. John V. Canfield and Franklin H. Donnell (New York: Appleton-Century-Crofts, 1964), pp. 456–57.

18. There is also a second fairly widely advocated argument for phenomenalism, one that starts from the premise that all intelligible ideas or concepts are derived by "abstraction" from immediate experience, so that we arguably could not even *understand* the idea of objects existing outside of that experience. If this were so, and if (as again seems obvious) we do understand the idea or concept of a physical or material object, then it would follow that this idea or concept is not about transexperiential objects, and so apparently can only be about some feature or aspect of experience itself. The problem with this argument is that the initial premise about the derivation of concepts is far less obviously correct than is the claim that we do in fact obviously have ideas or concepts, indeed lots of them, that are about things outside immediate experience, making it far more reasonable to reject the conclusion than to accept the premise.

19. Eventually I will suggest that it is, not surprisingly, the first of the two premises that should be rejected.

20. And perhaps also unintelligible—see note 17, above.

21. See A. J. Ayer, "Phenomenalism," *Proceedings of the Aristotelian Society*, vol. 47 (1946–47), pp. 189–91, for a discussion of this example.

22. Suggested by Ayer, *ibid*.

23. Chisholm, *Perceiving* (Ithaca, N.Y.: Cornell University Press, 1957), Appendix.

24. This is a little tricky. In this case, the claim that there is a table in the room at the moment I am there is false. But it can still be true that there was a table there at an ear-

lier time, even though it was not true at that time that if I experienced the sense-data of going to that room, I would experience the table sense-data—since the table is always removed whenever I do that.

25. Mill, reprinted in Canfield and Donnell (see note 17), pp. 457–58.

26. And perhaps even if they are to be intelligible.

27. A woman once allegedly wrote to Bertrand Russell that she found solipsism to be so obviously a correct view that she couldn't understand why it wasn't more widely accepted. (Think about it!)

28. Notice that Hume's thesis would *not* rule out the experiential justification of claims about a causal relation between two material objects or events, as long as we are assuming that the problem presently under discussion, the problem of the external world, has been somehow solved. For then both of the relevant objects or events could be claimed to be *indirectly* experienced by experiencing the relevant sense-data. But this notion of indirectly experiencing something obviously cannot be invoked in this way where it is exactly the justification of the transition from immediately experienced sense-data to indirectly experienced material objects that is in question.

29. Both of these views are in fact strongly analogous to phenomenalism. Think about just how this is so.

30. Thus the sort of reasoning in question is also sometimes referred to as "inference to the best explanation."

31. In fact, reasoning of this general sort was already employed in the *a priori* justification of induction that was offered at the end of chapter 4, though without identifying it as such or discussing the underlying rationale. It is instructive to compare that case with these others and with the main representationalist argument.

32. For a much more extensive elaboration of this general sort of point, see H. H. Price, *Perception* (London: Methuen, 1932; 2nd ed., 1950). A very condensed summary of Price's account is contained in my paper "Foundationalism and the External World," in James Tomberlin (ed.), *Philosophical Perspectives*, vol. 13 (2000), pp. 229–49.

33. For a good discussion of the general representationalist argument, especially with reference to the causal regularities in the material world, see C. H. Whiteley, "Physical Objects," *Philosophy*, vol. 34 (1959), pp. 142–49. Whiteley, however, eventually arrives at a more extreme view according to which material objects explain our experience but cannot be known to have *any* of the properties actually manifested in that experience.

34. There are at least two further related questions lurking in the vicinity, which there is no space to adequately consider here. One concerns the way in which the two groups of qualities are distinguished. Primary qualities are predominantly spatial or geometrical in character. As noted earlier, however, Locke adds *solidity* to the list of primary qualities. What he has in mind by this is not entirely clear, but solidity seems to be *either* the feeling of resistance that a rigid object produces when touched (in which case, it seems to belong with the secondary qualities) or else the causal capacity of preventing other objects from occupying the same space (in which case it is a causal property, what Locke calls a "power," and again not a primary quality on a par with the others, all of which are directly reflected in experience). The other issue concerns Locke's apparent view that all genuine

qualities of material objects amount in the end to primary qualities or patterns of primary qualities. This would include all "powers" or causal capacities, including the causal capacities that are responsible for producing experiences of color and other secondary qualities in human perceivers. But this cannot be right if the primary qualities are the merely spatial or geometrical ones: a real object cannot have only properties of these sorts, since it would otherwise be indistinguishable from a geometrically specified region of empty space.

35. Originally put forth by his friend Robert Boyle (the discoverer of the law pertaining to the behavior of gases that bears his name).

36. This point about secondary qualities reveals something important about the nature of the representationalist argument. The initial argument *from* the empirical description of the characteristics of immediate sensory experience *to* at least a schematic picture of the material world—that is, the justification of the conditional claim that *if* experience has those features, then it is likely that there is a material world of a specified sort—must seemingly be entirely *a priori* in character. The reason here is just the one given in Hume's argument: it is because we can have no experience of the relation between external objects and our experience that only an *a priori* argument is possible. (Hume's mistake was not taking seriously enough the possibility of such an *a priori* argument.) But the discussion of secondary qualities suggests that at later stages, after the claim about the existence of the material world has been justified to some substantial degree, that claim can then be refined by appeal to further empirical and eventually scientific information. While this picture is appealing, more would have to be said about how it works and about when and how the transition from the purely *a priori* stage to later stages is made. (For a useful discussion of this point, see R. J. Hirst, "The Representative Theory of Perception," in *The Problems of Perception*, ed. Hirst et al. (London: Allen & Unwin, 1959), pp. 145–80.)

37. Here again a computer game provides a helpful analogy. In playing many such games, you control the "movement" of a computer character through the "world," often in a fairly realistic way, even though there is really no movement of that sort nor any world of that sort in which it might take place. In Berkeley's explanatory hypothesis, God plays the role of the computer.

38. Sometimes philosophers appeal in such discussions to a general standard of simplicity, according to which it is just a fundamental principle that the simpler explanation is more likely to be true. The problem with this is twofold: first, the justification or rationale for the principle in question is anything but clear; and, second, the way in which it would apply to the case with which we are concerned is at least debatable, since Berkeley's explanation, for example, might be claimed to be simpler, in a different way from the one just discussed, on the grounds that it invokes only one entity, albeit an extremely complicated one, rather than the many objects that make up a material world.

39. As some of you will know, it is a fact of probability theory that the probability of the conjunction of two propositions is equal to the product of their separate probabilities, so that where each of them has a separate probability less than one (that is, is not a necessary truth), the probability of the conjunction is automatically smaller than either of the separate probabilities. I have not formulated the foregoing argument in this form because

it could be argued that the second claim, at least the version that pertains to God, is a necessary truth. I am not convinced that this is right, but the issues involved cannot be discussed here.

40. Suggested to me by Ann Baker.

41. There are, of course, other possible explanations of the missing truck, for example, that a teenager has hotwired it and driven it away while my wife is out walking the dog. But the relevant point concerns only the relative likelihood of the two discussed in the text. (The point would be a bit clearer if we imagine a technological advance in which cars can be started and driven only by someone having the right thumbprint or voice or whatever, so that the intruder couldn't take the key from my wife and drive away alone.)

42. See chapter 3.

43. In earlier discussions of these issues, views in the general direction of direct realism were often referred to as "naïve realism" and ascribed to unsophisticated common sense.

44. Though this has been questioned, and we will reconsider the issue in chapter 9.

45. A good place to start is Michael Huemer, *Skepticism and the Veil of Perception* (Lanham, Md.: Rowman & Littlefield, 2001).

46. As we will see, some of the more recent views to be considered in chapters 9, 10, and 11 are in a way alternatives to representationalism. But this is because they repudiate, in different ways, the entire problem with which the representationalist is attempting to deal, not because they constitute alternative solutions to that problem.

CHAPTER EIGHT

~

Other Minds, Testimony, and Memory

We have now completed our discussion of the most obvious and widely discussed problems that arise within or grow fairly directly out of Descartes's basic epistemological outlook. In this chapter, I want to look somewhat more briefly and tentatively at three further, less widely discussed and perhaps somewhat less obvious problems, still approaching them from the broadly Cartesian standpoint that we have adopted so far. That these problems have on the whole received substantially less attention from epistemologists is the main justification for treating them in this more cursory way, even though they are in my judgment still far too important to neglect entirely. Partly for reasons of space, but also to give you some more restricted problems to think further about, I have left the discussion in each case in an even more tentative and unfinished state than in the earlier chapters.

The Problem of Other Minds

The problem of other minds, which was already briefly noticed at several points in the previous chapter, has to do with whether and, if so, how beliefs concerning the minds and mental states of people other than the person who has the beliefs in question are justified. From the standpoint of common sense, it seems obvious that we do often have justified beliefs (and knowledge) of this sort, that we often believe with justification that other people are experiencing pain or coldness or redness, feeling fearful or angry or happy, or believing or wondering or doubting various things. (To be sure, there are also plenty of cases in which we may be uncertain just what is going on in the mind of another and even, more rarely, cases where even the presence of a functioning mind is in serious doubt.)

Discussions of this problem have tended to focus on the conscious aspects of the mental states in question. It is important to emphasize, however, that one central ingredient of at least many of the states ordinarily classified as "mental" is the presence of distinctive sorts of *behavior* or *dispositions* toward such behavior: one who has no tendency at all to "fight or flee" cannot intelligibly be regarded as being afraid; and one who has the ability to speak (and who wants to be helpful), but has no disposition at all to say "yes" upon being asked whether it is raining, cannot intelligibly be said to believe that it is raining. (Notice in this second example how the behavioral disposition depends on the presence of a second mental state—the desire to be helpful—as well as the one in question.) But the core of the problem is still the justification of the part of the content of beliefs about other minds that has to do with conscious aspects, and it is this part of the issue upon which we will mainly focus here.

Consider then a relatively clear, though somewhat unpleasant example: You are a witness as a teenaged boy, who has been riding his bicycle somewhat carelessly, is brushed by a car and falls heavily off the bicycle, apparently injuring his leg. The leg is bleeding and the boy is grasping it, crying and moaning, and pleading for help. Stepping quickly to the nearby phone to summon help, you believe with the strongest possible conviction that the boy is experiencing quite severe pain and also that he is distressed and frightened, that he believes that he is injured, and that he desires help. And, at least from the standpoint of common sense, there is little doubt that these beliefs are strongly justified and indeed that they constitute clear examples of knowledge.

But why exactly is this so? What is your *reason* or *justification* in this sort of case for thinking that the beliefs in question are true? Clearly *part* of the answer is your observations of the boy's *behavior* (the seemingly agonized grasping and crying and moaning and apparent[1] pleading), together with the collateral circumstances (the force of the fall, the way that the boy landed, and the bleeding)—circumstances that are often included in a kind of expanded use of the term "behavior," a convenient usage that will be adopted here.[2] But how and why do these observed facts about behavior constitute a reason or justification for beliefs of the sort indicated concerning what is going on in the boy's mind? This is a question that would be very hard to take seriously for even a moment if you were actually in the circumstances described, but nonetheless one to which the answer is not at all obvious on reflection.

Logical Behaviorism

There is one answer to this question that is historically important enough to require mention here, but which is nonetheless too implausible, in my judgment, to be even a minimally serious candidate for being correct. For a substantial period in the early to middle part of the twentieth century, a number of philosophers adopted a view called *behaviorism* or, more accurately, *logical* (or *analytical*) *behaviorism*.[3] According to logical behaviorism, the content of propositions concerning minds and mental states is *entirely* captured by propositions about behavior and dispositions to behave. Thus on this view, for it to be true that the boy is experiencing severe pain in his leg is *nothing more* than for him to be behaving in ways like those described and others of the same general sort and/or for him to be disposed to behave (or continue to behave) in those ways. Though adopting logical behaviorism does not completely solve the problem of justifying beliefs concerning the minds and mental states of others (since there is still an inference from presently observed behavior to future behavior and dispositions to behave that requires justification of some sort, presumably inductive), it greatly reduces the difficulty by eliminating the need for an inferential transition from behavioral facts to facts of an apparently entirely different kind.[4]

But despite this advantage (which was, not surprisingly, the main reason for the popularity of the view), it seems obvious that logical behaviorism is *extremely* implausible—so much so that (as with phenomenalism) it is nearly impossible to believe that anyone ever really accepted it. Though there are extensive discussions and more complicated arguments to be found in the literature,[5] it seems sufficient to say simply that in examples like the one described, it is the *conscious* experiences and thoughts of the boy in question, as opposed to his behavior and dispositions to behave, that are overwhelmingly the main focus of a concerned onlooker. As regards the pain in particular, if there were no distinct and unobservable experience of a roughly familiar and quite awful sort that was believed to be present, if the observer really thought that no such feeling lay behind the observed behavior, then although there might still be a concern to staunch the bleeding and also one about possible damage to the boy's future physical capabilities, much of what makes such a situation seem urgent and terrible would simply be gone. (An alternative way to make essentially the same point is to alter the example by making yourself the injured party, making it abundantly clear that more than mere behavior would be involved.[6]) Thus logical behaviorism seems best regarded as one of those occasional manifestations of philosophical desperation that cannot be taken seriously.

The Argument from Analogy

Having dismissed the behaviorist view, the problem is then how to justify an inference from (a) observed facts about behavior to (b) conclusions about the conscious mental states (or conscious aspects of such states)[7] that are internal to the mind of the other person in question and thus not directly observable by the person whose beliefs about them are at issue. Here the obvious appeal, putting it as is natural in the first person, is to my own experience of the correlation between the behavior of *my* body and *my* mental states. Perhaps I was in the past injured in a way closely comparable to that pertaining to the boy, so that I can remember how behavioral manifestations of these or very similar sorts were correlated with inner experiences and thoughts. And even if I am fortunate enough not to have undergone a closely comparable incident, there will almost surely be in my history other cases that are sufficiently comparable to be relevant, cases of lesser injuries or injuries of a different though still broadly analogous sort.

The suggestion is then that the relation between (a) the observed behavior and behavioral circumstances of the other body (again construing this so as to include environmental circumstances of various kinds) and (b) the mental states of the other mind can reasonably be taken to be at least approximately parallel to that between (a) my own behavior and (b) my own mental states. This would include the idea that more extreme behavior and circumstances (for example, a harder fall, more serious observed injuries, or more desperate crying and moaning and pleading) would correlate with the comparably more severe pain; that an injury of a different sort (say, a burn) would correlate with a somewhat different sort of pain; and so on. Thus by being familiar with the correlations between my own behavior and my own mental states, I can seemingly infer, via a kind of analogy or proportion, to the existence and nature of the unobserved (by me) mental states of the boy. (Think of how this might work in various specific cases, using your imagination to fill in as many details as possible.)

This is what has come to be known as the *argument from analogy* for the existence and specific conscious states of other minds. Obviously its strength in a particular case will depend in part on the degree to which the believer's own personal history includes incidents that resemble reasonably closely the ones with which his beliefs about other minds are concerned: the beliefs of someone who has never experienced even moderately severe pain concerning such a case will be both less specific and less strongly justified than those of someone whose experience in this direction has been more extensive. But this seems intuitively to be exactly the right result, and thus does not constitute an objection.

What does seem to constitute a serious objection to the view that the main or exclusive justification for beliefs concerning other minds is the argument from analogy is that the *degree* of justification that this argument yields appears initially to be in general quite low, very much lower than we intuitively believe ourselves to have in cases like the one described. The problem is that I am able to observe the correlation between behavioral circumstances and mental states for only *one* person, myself, out of the potentially billions or more of possible cases to which the argument in principle would apply, thus seeming to generalize from a single example to all of these others. It is as if I attempted to reason to the characteristics of all oak trees or all lakes or all thunderstorms by examining a single example, and it has seemed obvious to many that the force of any such reasoning would be very weak. As we saw in discussing induction, the cogency of this sort of reasoning seems to depend on examining many different cases in which the circumstances not explicitly specified in the inductive conclusion vary as widely as possible, and finding regularities or apparent regularities that pertain to most or all of them, something that appears to be impossible in the case of other minds. Thus while the argument from analogy seems undeniably to provide at least *some* justification for our beliefs about other minds,[8] the result apparently falls far short of the degree of justification that common sense confidently ascribes.

Theoretical Reasoning Again?

Is it possible to do any better than this? For one familiar with the issues discussed in the previous chapter, the obvious suggestion is an appeal to *theoretical* reasoning of the sort discussed there, with our commonsense beliefs about the existence and characteristics of other minds being treated as components of a general theory that is justified because it best explains the behavioral evidence. The issues raised by this suggestion are complicated and difficult, and there is no space here for a full consideration of them. Instead, I will have to be content with raising some of the main problems and questions, leaving to you the job of thinking further about them.

The first question is whether (and, if so, how) this line of argument really does any better than the argument from analogy. It seems obvious that the account of the mental states of other people that I come to accept is still largely *suggested* by my experience of my own mental states and the way that they are correlated with my own behavior. But according to the view that we are now considering, the *justification* for the resulting "theory" is that it best explains the behavioral evidence, with the fact that it is apparently true of me, one example of the general sort of entity in question, playing only a very minor justificatory role.[9]

But this only points to the main question about the appeal to theoretical or explanatory reasoning in this area. It seems reasonably clear that the commonsense picture of mental states and their experiential connections provides *one* possible explanation of the behavioral evidence in question. But what reason, if any, is there for thinking that this explanation is the *best* explanation, once it is recognized that its applicability to my own case, though certainly of some relevance to this question, is in itself seemingly far from decisive?

There are three distinguishable subissues involved in this question, each of which will be briefly considered, though we will be unable to go very far here with any of them. The first is whether there is any good reason to think that the best explanation of the behavior in question will in fact invoke conscious mental states of any sort. Why couldn't there be, as some recent philosophers have suggested, an alternative explanation that did not appeal to conscious mental states at all, but instead invoked only nonconscious physiological processes of some sort? Part of what makes this question so difficult is the elusiveness of the very idea of consciousness itself. Is there something about behavior of the sorts that we are concerned with that is somehow better explained by inner processes involving consciousness, and what exactly might that be?

The second subissue is whether the best explanation of the behavior of others, even if it involves conscious states of some sort, might not involve quite a different set of such states from the ones that seem natural and obvious from a commonsense standpoint, perhaps having a totally different structure from those that I find in myself. Perhaps the most obvious difficulty that such a view would face would be in explaining *verbal* behavior, where the most straightforward alternative view would be that the utterance of a particular sentence is to be systematically explained as the expression of a corresponding conscious thought, but one that is different in each case from the one that is involved when I utter that same sentence (though it still in some way makes sense in the surrounding circumstances).[10]

A third subissue is whether even if the system of conscious states that best explains the behavior of others is broadly the same as the one that I find in my own case, there might not still be systematic differences in certain experienced properties. Here the most widely discussed possibility is that the spectrum of experienced colors might be systematically reversed or otherwise transposed, so that the colors that I experience in various circumstances are experienced by others in quite different circumstances: for example, such that the color that I experience when I look at fire engines and ripe apples is in fact the same as others experience when they look at newly mown grass and fresh leaves, and vice versa. (Think carefully about this specific possibility, remembering that if it were so, my use of color words would also presumably be "reversed," so that the word I would use to describe the color of ripe apples would be the same as that used by others, even though the property in question would vary in the way indicated.)

None of these essentially skeptical worries is easily dismissed, and the desire to somehow avoid them has led to a number of otherwise dubious views in the philosophy of mind and the philosophy of language, of which logical behaviorism is only the most conspicuously untenable.[11] In the end, however, the issue may well turn on whether the objection raised above to the argument from analogy is really as compelling as it at first seems, for it seems very hard to find a compelling argument for the superiority of the common-sense explanation of the behavior of others if the first-person evidence of the correctness of this explanation in one's own case has no serious weight for the overall issue. Think further about this on your own. What in your judgment is the best response to this overall problem?

The Problem of Testimony

What has come to be referred to as the problem of testimony has to do with the justified beliefs, knowledge, and information generally that we seemingly acquire, via communications of many different sorts, from other people. To appreciate the scope and significance of this problem, you should reflect on the immense number and variety of things that would be commonsensically classified as justified belief and knowledge, but that depend essentially on information supposedly received from others via personal communications (direct speech, letters, e-mail, etc.), books, newspapers and magazines, radio and television, the Internet and other computer sources, and so on—where "essentially" means that you in fact have no other, independent access to the alleged facts in question. Indeed, as we will see, there are many cases in which you could not imaginably have such independent access. (Here you should look again at the list of examples and categories of alleged knowledge in chapter 1, thinking about which ones seem to depend partially or wholly upon testimony.)

Examples of Reliance on Testimony
Here are examples of three of the more striking kinds of beliefs seemingly justified in this way, again stated, for reasons that should be obvious, in the first person: Consider first my belief that there is a city called "London," located in England on the river Thames, having certain general geographical features,

containing various buildings and sites that I could list, having a certain complicated history, serving as the seat of the British government, etc. As it happens, I have never been to London, so that I have no firsthand knowledge of any of this, but am justified in believing it (if indeed I am) entirely on the basis of information supplied in one way or another by other people, in books (including encyclopedias and atlases), newspapers and magazines, radio and television reports, and also in this case personal reports provided orally by those who have (they claim!) been there. But perhaps the most striking feature of this case is that even if I had been to London many times and had stayed there for long periods of time, there would still be many, many aspects of my comprehensive set of beliefs concerning London that would not be matters of firsthand knowledge for me: most of the history, obviously, but also a very large proportion of the claims about geography, specific buildings, and especially the political status of the city. Here it is important to bear in mind that such things as maps and labels on streets and buildings are merely more forms of information derived from others. (Think about this example carefully for yourselves: how much knowledge could I really have of London through my own unaided observation and reasoning?)

For a second example, consider a piece of supposed scientific knowledge: my belief that among the (fairly) fundamental constituents of the physical world are tiny particles (or at least seeming particles, since they sometimes behave like waves) called *electrons*, having a negative charge of a certain definite magnitude, constituting one of the ingredients of atoms of all kinds, and playing an important role in such phenomena as electric currents, the behavior of cathode-ray tubes, etc. Again, I have no firsthand knowledge of any of this. And here again, it is very hard to imagine how I or indeed anyone could come to have genuinely firsthand knowledge of the existence and nature of electrons[12]—though perhaps this could in principle be achieved by a very skilled scientist who set out to recreate all of the relevant evidence and theoretical reasoning from scratch on his own, something that it is doubtful that anyone has ever in fact actually attempted.

Third, at a more mundane level, consider my knowledge of various observable situations and events occurring more or less contemporaneously in my immediate vicinity: baseball games, concerts, traffic accidents and detours, governmental meetings, sales and other merchandising activity, bus and ferry operations, etc. All of these are things that at least in large part could be individually known by direct observation,[13] but it would obviously be impossible for me to directly observe all or even very many of them. Instead I rely on newspaper, radio, and television reports and advertisements, together in some cases with posted announcements and word of mouth.

Without such reliance, my (apparent) knowledge of what is going on even in the fairly nearby world would be drastically reduced.

The Issue of Justification

The central issue for present purposes is whether and how the beliefs that depend in this way on testimony of various kinds are *justified*. Though this has sometimes been questioned, it seems obvious that the mere fact that a belief has been acquired via reliance on testimony in itself confers no justification upon it. The other people from whom testimony is received may be lying or dissembling, and they may also be simply mistaken in what they sincerely say or otherwise report. Nor is there any very clear reason why one or the other or both of these possibilities might not be very widely realized. Thus some further reason or justification is apparently needed for thinking that beliefs acquired via testimony are likely to be true.

There are some preliminary issues here that should be noticed. It seems fairly clear that my justification for reliance on testimony depends in part on my having reasons (which may of course not be attended to very explicitly) for thinking that such testimony, in the sense of various sorts of linguistically formulated communications produced more or less deliberately by other people, has actually occurred; the issues raised by apparent "messages" whose status in this respect was seriously in doubt would be quite different.[14] In this way, the justification of testimonial belief depends in part on the prior issue just discussed of the justification for belief in the existence of other minds. It also depends on there being reasons for thinking that a particular series of events (a) constitutes a linguistic communication of some sort and (b) is to be interpreted in a particular way in terms of language and specific content.[15] We have already noticed briefly the difficulties that arise in connection with the other minds issue, and the problems raised by these latter issues are almost equally difficult. (Think about them for yourself.) For present purposes, however, I propose to set all of these issues aside by simply assuming that the existence and specific content of the particular pieces of testimony in question has *somehow* been established beyond any serious doubt.

In thinking about the main question that then arises, it will help to have two generic sorts of examples in mind: first, one in which someone says something to me directly; and, second, one in which the communication is transmitted via some sort of publication, as in a book or newspaper. Assuming that as a result of such testimony, I come to believe the claims thus transmitted, what reason or justification do I have or might I have for these beliefs? Even more fundamentally, what resources do I even have to draw on for such a justification?

It is clear enough what sort of answer Descartes (or someone in the general Cartesian tradition) would offer here: if I am to be justified in accepting beliefs on the basis of testimony, the Cartesian would hold, then I must be able, at least in principle, to construct an argument that such beliefs are likely to be true, one that relies only on the epistemological resources that are (the Cartesian assumes—is he right about this?) antecedently justified: on immediate experience, *a priori* and inductive reasoning,[16] and whatever else can be justified from those resources without relying on testimony itself, which I will here assume to include both beliefs about the material world and about other minds. How then might such an argument for the likely truth of testimony go? (Stop here and think carefully about this issue on your own before proceeding.)

Can Testimonial Beliefs Be Justified Inductively?

There is one fairly obvious line of argument that seems to work to some degree, but that unfortunately does not take us very far. In some cases, I may be able to independently check the reliability of a given person (or other source—for example, a map) fully enough to give me strong inductive grounds for thinking that the other things that he or she (or it) says are usually true. This possibility is most likely to be realized where the person in question is a close friend or family member, and in cases of very close association may not even require any very deliberate investigation. But the potential scope of this sort of justification is severely limited in ways that make it clear that it cannot even begin to provide a general justification for testimonial beliefs. There are far too many people (and other sources) whose testimony I rely on in various ways for all or even very many of them to be certified as reliable via this sort of argument. Moreover, I receive information via testimony on a very wide range of subjects: it would be practically impossible for me to check firsthand concerning very many of these, and quite a few involve matters that I am unable to check even in principle. And a further problem that arises at this point is whether someone whose reliability I am trying to check might in fact be much more or much less reliable about the specific claims or areas that I am able to independently check than about those that I am not.

Rather than attempting to certify the reliability of particular testimonial informants or sources in this way, I might instead attempt to construct an inductive argument for a general thesis to the effect, roughly, that testimony from others is, other things being equal, likely to be reliable. But the problems with this approach, though similar, are even more serious. The cases that I can investigate firsthand amount to only a vanishingly small proportion of either the persons and other sources that provide testimony or the subject matters to which such testimony pertains, seemingly making any such argument *extremely* weak. It is possible (a) that different people or sources might be reliable to very different degrees or (b) that the same person or source might be reliable to very different degrees about different subject matters, with either or both of these possibilities being realized in ways that are not reflected in my firsthand evidence.

Though there is obviously room for much more discussion, the indicated conclusion is that there is no way to construct an inductive argument that is very strong for the conclusion that beliefs resulting from testimony are likely to be true on the basis of the cases where the reliability of such beliefs can be determined firsthand. The evidence that we have in this way is simply too limited, both in size and in variety of subject matter, to adequately support such a conclusion.[17]

Coherence and Explanatory Reasoning

Is there a better line of argument to be found? Think again of the London example given above. Though this would not be true to the same degree for other people, in my case none of the large set of testimonially acquired beliefs that I have about London pertain to things that I have independently checked firsthand. Moreover, only a small proportion of the relevant class of testimonial informants (a few personal friends who report having been to London, some general reference works, and certain computer and media sources) are included in those for which I have any firsthand evidence of reliability—and even for those there is the problem, already noted, that the subject matter of the testimony that I have checked is for the most part quite different from that pertaining to London, calling into serious question whether and to what extent a generalization from the former to the latter is justified.

But though firsthand checking is of relatively little avail in this case (though not entirely worthless), there is nonetheless a striking fact about the testimony that I have pertaining to London that may well seem to be highly relevant to its reliability: the fact that the various alleged sources of information that I have about London, its history, its geography, etc., both agree with and consistently supplement each other to a very high degree. Think here of consulting maps of London in various atlases and other books and comparing the winding shape of the Thames, the locations given for various bridges and buildings, the layout of the main streets, and so on. Or think of examining several fairly detailed accounts of the history of the city, and comparing the descriptions and dates given for fires, plagues, sessions of Parliament, executions, constructions of new buildings, and so on. In addition to containing exactly the same information on various points, different sources can also overlap and complement each other in a complicated variety of ways: a historical map may agree with a contemporary one in broad features, while containing more specific details that differ in a way that fits with the account of the historical change and growth of the city given by other sources; different historical accounts may offer different details concerning a particular course of events, but in ways that fit together to make an intelligible picture that is more comprehensive than is provided by any one of them alone; geological or archaeological accounts may in similar ways fit with and complement more narrowly historical ones; and so on. The standard philosophical term for the way in which various accounts of London fit intelligibly together in these various ways is *coherence*: it is a striking fact that the (alleged) information presented by my various testimonial sources concerning London is, for the most part, highly coherent.

Moreover, a high degree of coherence is obviously a feature not only of testimony pertaining to London, but also of the testimony that I have in relation to an enormously wide and varied range of other subjects: various areas of science, a huge range of history, geography, and current affairs, and many, many other subjects as well. (Though it should also be noticed that there are areas in which the degree of coherence present is much less and some rare ones in which it is almost totally lacking. For example, information presented by various testimonial sources regarding nutrition is not very coherent, and I thereby conclude that such information is not in general very reliable.) Thus while the proportion of testimony that I can check firsthand is very small, I can, in a way, check the various sources of testimony against each other, with the result being in general, though not in every case, that they check out quite well.

But is this widespread coherence a reason for thinking that the testimony in question is *true*, so that I would be thereby justified in adopting beliefs on that basis? Here again the relevant sort of reasoning appears to be the explanatory or theoretical variety first noticed in chapter 4 and appealed to again in our discussions of both the external world and other minds. It seems utterly clear that *some* explanation is needed for the high degree of coherence in the testimony that I have pertaining to these various areas—which is just to say that the agreement and complementary fitting together of the different sources cannot plausibly be regarded as merely a matter of chance. Moreover, one main sort of explanation for such coherence is that the content of the testimony in question (a) was arrived at via accurate firsthand observation (together with relevant sorts of reasoning) on the part of people in a position to do this, and then (b) transmitted in reliable ways from person to person in what might be described as *chains of testimony*, and eventually to me. Call this the *accurate report and transmission explanation*. If it is the best explanation in a particular case, then it follows that the resulting piece of testimonial information is likely to be true.

But just how good is the accurate report and transmission explanation in different kinds of cases? What alternative explanations are available for coherent testimony? This again is a very complicated question, and, as with the analogous argument in the other minds case, I will have to content myself here with noting a few of the most important points and problems and then leaving the issue to your further consideration.

First, the explanatory argument invoking the accurate report and transmission explanation is clearly strongest where the alleged fact in question is one that is easy to observe accurately, was likely to be observed by many different people, and is easy to describe in a way that allows for reliable transmission from person to person, which means roughly that it can be easily, precisely, and concisely described in language (perhaps accompanied by supplements like photographs or charts or diagrams). Thus, for example, a set of coherent testimonial reports to the effect that a person was shot in a quite public place at some very recent time (setting aside any further issues such as who did the shooting or the identity of the victim) seems fairly strongly to demand this sort of explanation; whereas this would be much less obviously the case for a similarly coherent set of reports about a complicated religious movement in the fourteenth century.

Second, there seem to be three main sorts of possible alternatives to the accurate report and transmission explanation of a set of coherent testimonial statements, given that mere chance is in general not a plausible explanation. (a) There are cases where a certain sort of mistake is natural enough to make it likely that many people will independently make it, thus leading to many testimonial reports that agree with each other in this respect but are nonetheless all mistaken. This is most obviously true at the stage of the original firsthand observations, where, for example, a woman dressed like a man might well be described as a man by a large number of independent observers. But it could also take the form of a natural and tempting mistake in a chain of reasoning or (though this is probably the least likely version) of a way of misreporting earlier testimony in a testimonial chain that is so natural as to make it likely that many different people will fall prey to it. (b) Coherent but false testimony might also result from either collusion or shared biases of some sort. Here there are many different possible forms that these phenomena might take and motives that might produce them. (Try to imagine some of these.) (c) Perhaps the most frequently realized alternative is also one that people are often insufficiently attentive to: what seem to be coherent pieces of independent testimony may all result from the copying or repetition, whether deliberate or inadvertent, of one original source, which could well be itself mistaken.[18] Think here of the way in which a rumor may circulate so widely that it comes to be repeated in ways that may seem independent by many different people. Or the way in which an error in a work of history may appear, again seemingly independently, in other works that rely on that one as a source.[19]

From a broadly commonsense standpoint, these different alternatives will be more or less plausible in relation to each other and to the accurate report and transmission explanation, depending on the specific subject matter and circumstances that pertain to a particular piece of testimony. Some cases make the hypothesis of independently replicated error quite plausible, while others seem to rule it out more or less completely. Some cases offer plausible motives and opportunity for collusion or the operation of shared bias, while in others one or the other of these seems to be lacking. (Try to think of examples of your own of these different sorts of cases.) The most difficult alternative to assess is often the third one of copying or repetition of one source by others, since this is possible in relation to any subject matter and often can only be recognized by tracing the testimonial chains back to their source.[20]

Third, one clear though relatively unsurprising upshot of these considerations is that the justification that attaches to beliefs derived from testimony (where the reliability of the source cannot be independently checked to any serious degree) can vary widely from one instance to another, depending on the degree of coherence manifested in the testimonial reports, the number of (apparently) independent sources, and the various factors already noted that add to or detract from the plausibility of the various explanatory alternatives. One question that it is often important to ask and whose answer sometimes tells strongly against the accurate report and transmission explanation is whether there is any plausible way in which the alleged information in question could have been initially acquired by the original sources of the testimonial chains: no matter how great the degree of coherence may be, a negative answer to this question will point strongly toward one of the other alternative explanations, probably one or the other of the last two. (Consider, for example, a striking agreement between different books and other sources as to the significance of a certain set of astrological conditions.)

Fourth, none of the foregoing considerations speaks very directly to the justification of isolated pieces of testimony: a single statement made to me by some person or a single claim set forth by a source of some other kind, such as a book. Apart from inductive considerations of the sort discussed earlier, the justification of beliefs of this sort will depend for the most part on general principles concerning the reliability of different sorts of people and other sources with respect to different sorts of subject matter, with these principles being themselves largely justified on the basis of beliefs derived from testimony. The strength of the resulting justification will again vary widely from case to case, but it is unlikely to reach the level attained by beliefs accepted on the basis of a highly coherent set of testimonial reports in circumstances favorable to the accurate report and transmission explanation.

Fifth, the deepest concern in all this is a worry about *circularity*. At various points, the foregoing discussion has appealed to basically commonsense judgments about the plausibility of various possibilities, such as widely replicated mistakes, collusion, and so on. It is clear that those of my own beliefs that are justified independently of testimony can give me some basis for such assessments, but it is also clear that much of what common sense appeals to here itself depends in various ways on testimony. (Think carefully about the various ways in which this is so.) It should also be pointed out that the justification of testimony might work in stages, with testimony of some kinds or on some subjects being justified first and then providing a basis for the justification of further testimony.

But the fundamental issue, which I will pose but not attempt to resolve here, is whether the initial nontestimonial basis for such assessments is strong enough and extends widely enough to get this whole process adequately started; or whether, on the contrary, some or all of our apparent testimonial knowledge can only be justified by appeal to assessments of plausibility that themselves depend on testimony of the very kinds that those assessments are needed to justify. Thus, for example, it might turn out that ruling out the possibility of widespread collusion depends on an assessment of human motives and capacities in this area that can only be justified by appeal to testimony that might itself, until this possibility is ruled out, be a product of collusion or conspiracy.

Especially for this last reason, the justification of testimonial beliefs that can be arrived at via appeal to coherence (supplemented to some degree by firsthand checking) may turn out to be substantially weaker than our commonsense outlook would lead us to expect in this area. Thus you should consider carefully whether there are any further alternatives for the justification of such beliefs that have been overlooked here. (One other point that should be suggested by the foregoing discussion is that any very adequate assessment of the justification of testimonial beliefs will depend on distinguishing different kinds of cases in a much more fine-grained way than has been possible here. This is something that you should bear in mind in thinking further about this issue.)

The Problem of Memory

The third and most fundamental of the issues to be considered in this chapter has to do with knowledge and especially justification deriving from memory. It seems clear at a commonsense level that I am often justified in believing something because I remember or seem to remember it, but why exactly is this so and how does such justification work? One thing that makes this issue fundamental is the way in which all or virtually all of our justification depends in one way or another on memory. This point will be developed more fully at the end of the present discussion (but you should try right now to think of some of the ways in which it is so).

Some Examples of Apparently Justified Memory Beliefs

Here again, there are many different sorts of cases, and we may begin by considering a fairly representative sample of these. Consider first my present memory of having just within the last few minutes made myself a cup of tea. I have the propositional *belief* that I did this, along with further propositional beliefs about many of the details (that I did it downstairs in the kitchen, that I used a teabag, that I started with cold water, and so on). But I also in this case have many associated *images* that reflect various aspects of this process: images of holding the kettle under the water faucet, of watching the birds on the bird feeder as I waited for the water to boil, of the initial hissing followed by the shrill whistle of the tea kettle).[21] At least from a commonsense standpoint, it seems clear that both the belief that I have just made tea and many of the more specific beliefs about the details are strongly justified.

Second, suppose that I have just finished going through a complicated piece of reasoning, perhaps a logical or mathematical proof, one that is too complicated for me to hold all in mind at once. I believe that I went through the steps and that they were cogently connected with each other, even though I do not presently have all or perhaps even any of them explicitly in mind. In this case, it is rather less likely that there are images involved, at least any that capture any very significant part of the process. But again, in many such cases at least, the belief seems again to be strongly justified.[22]

Third, consider a more remote example of what might, like these other cases, be called *personal* memory, my belief, apparently deriving from memory, of having once lived for a substantial period of time in Austin, Texas. This example differs from the first one in that there is much less relevant imagery involved, and almost none or perhaps none at all that has any very clear bearing on the truth of the specific belief in question. (For example, though I have an image of the house in which I lived for a number of years, there is nothing about that image that indicates in any clear way that the house was in Austin.) There is also much less associated propositional memory of relevant details, though there is some (that I lived in the northern part of town, that I lived in a rented house on Shoalmont Drive, that there was a creek not far from the house that occasionally flooded, etc.).[23] And once more, the belief in question seems to be reasonably well justified, though not as strongly as in the first two cases.

Fourth, consider my memory of a fact that was learned in some way at an earlier time but was never a matter of my own direct experience (a case of what might be called *factual* memory, in contrast to personal memory). I believe, apparently on the basis of memory, that Descartes died in Sweden, where he had accepted a position as a kind of glorified tutor to a rather demanding and unappreciative queen. Obviously if this is a genuine case of memory (rather than something that I have in some way imaginatively dreamed up), then the fact in question was communicated to me at some point via some book or article or lecture or conversation, but I have no specific memory of how or when this occurred nor any relevant imagery connected with the event, such as an image of the cover of the book or of the lecturer. (In this case, it is in fact rather likely that I have encountered the fact in question more than once in a variety of sources.) I do remember some collateral details, such as that the death occurred during a cold winter and that Descartes had been forced by the queen to get up much earlier than he was accustomed to. And here again, the belief seems commonsensically to be fairly strongly justified, where here the justification depends ultimately on both memory and testimony.

The Varieties of Memory Beliefs and of Memory Mistakes

As these cases may suggest, the main dimensions along which cases of memory or apparent memory beliefs may resemble or differ are these: first, whether the belief in question was originally acquired by firsthand experience (perception or introspection) or in some other way, with various sorts of testimony being the main alternative;[24] second, the presence or absence of beliefs pertaining to further, related details; and, third, the presence or absence of relevant imagery (and the degree to which such imagery bears on the truth or falsity of the main claim in question or, in the case of nonpersonal memory, on the way in which the alleged information was originally acquired).[25]

What all of these cases have in common, on the other hand, is that the beliefs and accompanying images (if any) have a distinctive phenomenological character that makes them *seem* to derive from memory. Exactly what this character is and how it works has been a subject of lengthy and rather inconclusive philosophical discussion.[26] For present purposes, I propose to simply take it for granted that we are dealing with beliefs whose apparent memorial character is in this way immediately obvious.

In thinking about the question of justification, it will also be helpful to have clearly in mind the three rather different general sorts of mistakes that appeals to memory are susceptible to. (Try to think for yourself what these might be before proceeding.) (1) Most obviously, the memory process itself may introduce the mistake,[27] so that something that was originally perceived correctly (or accurately received from an informant, in the case of remembered testimony) is recalled incorrectly. (2) It may be that the memory process itself is working perfectly, but that the original perception or the information originally received was mistaken (where this last possibility could involve either a misunderstanding of the information received from the informant or an error or deception on the part of the informant). This second kind of mistake is not, strictly speaking, a mistake in memory, but it is still a way in which an apparent memory belief might be mistaken. (3) The memorial character of the belief in question may itself be spurious, a kind of mistake that is seemingly much rarer but still undeniably occurs. I will take this to include both (a) the case where something that presents itself as a personal memory, sometimes even with accompanying apparent memories of details and images, is really a factual memory of something learned from an informant that has in effect been dressed up with imagined details (for example, if I have been told many times that I fell down and then cried on a certain occasion as a small child, I may now seem to myself to remember the occurrence in question, even though the resulting details and images are imagined); and (b) the case where some belief apparently resulting from factual memory is in fact just involuntarily invented or conjured up or else is produced in some other way that does not involve genuine memory at all, such as by post-hypnotic suggestion (or perhaps even the action of a Cartesian evil genius). And it is possible to have cases that in effect combine both of these last sorts of mistakes: I might seem to remember something that is really just invented or imagined and then involuntarily add images that give the illusion of a personal memory.

Here the main difference between case (3b) and the relevant version of case (1) has to do with the *causation* of the belief: in case (1) the belief is still caused by the prior reception of the relevant piece of testimony, whereas in case (3b) this is not so. (Though there is obviously room here for difficult borderline cases.) As this suggests, an important feature of the concept of memory is that a memory belief must be caused in the right way by the experience of the event or piece of earlier testimony that is being remembered. Here the qualifier "in the right way" is essential, since there is also the possibility of "deviant" causal chains.[28]

The Justification of Particular Memory Beliefs

The issue we have now to consider is whether and how memory beliefs of these various kinds are *justified*, that is, what sorts of reasons, if any, we have for thinking them to be true, rather than mistaken in one of the ways indicated—where we are obviously interested in reasons that depend in some way on their status as apparent memories, not independent reasons that we might have for the propositions in question. Here there are again a number of different possibilities (which you should attempt to list for yourself before going further):

1. Where the belief in question is accompanied by other apparent memory beliefs about various details and surrounding circumstances, together with relevant images in the case of personal memory, it seems often possible to argue that the best *explanation* of the way in which all of these elements fit together or *cohere* with each other is (a) that the original firsthand experience or testimonial source was accurate and (b) that the information originally acquired in this way is being accurately recalled. Here you should ask yourself just how strong the case is for each of the two elements of this explanation in various sorts of cases, starting with examples like those considered above.

2. In addition to the memory images that are tightly related to the content of the belief and to each other, there are also in many cases other images that are too fragmentary and too distantly connected with the content of the belief to play a role in a coherence argument of the sort just indicated. Thus in the case of my apparent memory of having lived in Texas, there are many, many associated images that neither have any clear bearing on whether I was in fact in Texas nor are closely enough related to other images or more detailed beliefs to yield any very serious degree of coherence. It is clear, however, that we are generally more inclined to accept apparent memories that involve even this sort of imagery than those that do not, and here again the reason seems to be an appeal to the best explanation of this fact, where the idea would be that a memory that is not genuine would be less likely to bring with it even this sort of imagery. (Ask yourself whether this is so and how such a fact could itself be known.)

3. Another sort of justification for memory beliefs of both main kinds[29] is present perception (or, more rarely, introspection). Perhaps the most

familiar example of this is where a remembered past action is of the sort that would produce a relatively permanent result that can be independently checked via perception. Thus I remember having left my keys in the pocket of a certain garment, and when I look there, I find them just as expected. A somewhat different case is where the checking relies in part on testimony: fearing that I have lost my keys, I call my wife and ask her to check whether they are in the pocket in question. And the products of apparent factual memory can also be checked in both of these ways: my memory of an alleged historical fact can be checked by consulting other testimonial sources; and a remembered fact about the geography of a city that I am visiting might be checked via direct perception. Notice that in each of these cases, the resulting justification seems to again rely on an implicit argument that the best explanation of the agreement between the memory and the perception or testimony is that the former is in fact an accurate memory of an original perception or of a piece of testimony that was itself accurate.

4. In addition to these various ways in which a particular memory belief might be justified by appeal to specific features of these various sorts that obtain in that particular case, it is also possible if these other sorts of justification are successful to establish inductive generalizations to the effect that certain specific kinds of memory are highly reliable, either in general or for a particular person. (This *may* be what lies behind arguments of sort (2).) And these generalizations can then be used in turn either to argue that a particular apparent memory belief for which the basis for a justificatory argument of sorts (1), (2), or (3) is unavailable is nonetheless likely to be true or to strengthen the justification provided by such arguments.

Can Memory Be Justified without Circularity?

But though these various ways of justifying particular memory beliefs or even particular kinds of memory beliefs are fine as far as they go, they do not speak clearly to the deepest epistemological issue concerning memory, one that parallels the issue raised previously about testimony: can the general reliance on memory be given a *noncircular* justification by appeal to other sources of justification that can plausibly be taken to be independent of memory—immediate experience, *a priori* insights and reasoning, and whatever else, if anything, can be justified by appeal to those sources without relying on memory itself?

The answer to this question appears to be "no." The basic problem that afflicts all attempts at such a justificatory argument is that reliance on memory is essential to accumulate the elements required for the argument and preserve them in mind long enough to allow the needed reasoning to take place. This point can be best appreciated by thinking carefully about the four ways of justifying particular memory beliefs that were just suggested, seeing how each of them depends on other memories. It is clearest for (4), the appeal to induction, since the various cases that provide the evidence for the inductive conclusion do not somehow occur all at once, but must rather be remembered as they are accumulated.[30] The same general point also applies to mode of justification (1), where memory is required to retain enough claims or images in mind to achieve any serious degree of coherence. Similarly, any very strong justification along the lines of (2) will require more images than can occur at once, and so will depend on memory. A particular instance of mode of justification (3) need not depend on memory in quite these ways, since the content of the memory to be justified can be compared directly with a present perception. But any attempt to generalize from such particular justifications will require that they be remembered. Moreover, it is doubtful that the reasons, whatever exactly they may be, for regarding the explanatory hypotheses put forward by arguments of varieties (1), (2), or (3) as providing the *best* explanation can be arrived at without reliance on memory. (Think about how specific claims of this sort might be justified.)

This result is hardly surprising. It is a reflection of the more general point that memory must play an essential role in assembling and keeping track of the resources for a justification of any but the simplest, most immediate beliefs. Any argument of any complexity or even any very large collection of sensory or mental states cannot all be held in mind at once, but must be collected and juxtaposed and reviewed over a period of time, using memory—perhaps aided by more tangible sorts of record-keeping such as writing things down on paper.

But if this most fundamental sort of appeal to memory cannot be justified in a noncircular fashion, doesn't this mean that memory and all that depends on it isn't really justified at all—so that our justified beliefs would be restricted to those that are immediately justified, that is, to those pertaining to immediate experience and to simple self-evident truths that require no argument? Indeed, such an extremely skeptical conclusion has often been suggested. Is there any way to avoid it?

One possible solution would be the view that memory should be regarded as a basic or foundational source of justification, on a par with the apprehension of immediate experience and the *a priori* grasp of self-evidence. Such a view might be applied to memory in general or, perhaps more plausibly, restricted to certain sorts of memory, particularly the fundamental sort of memory that allows us to retain various cognitive resources in mind long enough to allow comparison and argument. But while a foundationalist view of memory is dialectically very appealing, it seems to me doubtful that it is really tenable. The problem, I would suggest, is that while each of the other foundational sources includes within itself reasons of a sort for the claims that are accepted on the basis of it, memory does not. For a claim about immediate experience, the reason is the conscious awareness of the experiential content itself (see chapter 9 for more about this); while for *a priori* insight, the reason is the apparent necessity of the claim in question. In the case of memory, however, there is only an awareness of something having occurred in the past without any sort of further reason for thinking that this claim is correct. Thus, I would suggest, memory fails to be, as it might be put, *justificationally self-sufficient* in the way that foundational status seems to require. (This is a *very* tricky and difficult point, one that you will have to think about very carefully in order to try to decide whether it is correct—perhaps after reading chapter 9.)

But if I am right that memory cannot in this way be treated as part of the foundation, are we not then left after all with skepticism? In a way, I think that we are. But it is important to get the skeptical result in question into clear focus and to see how it differs from other sorts of skeptical views. A skeptic about induction or about the external world or about other minds questions whether the specific sorts of evidence that we have for those kinds of claims is really enough to make it likely that they are true—with the implication being that we should perhaps stop accepting those claims on that sort of evidence. But skepticism about the most fundamental sort of memory does not really so much imply that there are certain sorts of claims that we should cease to accept, since to follow and know that we are following such a policy would itself depend on memory. (Think about how and why this is so.) Instead, it is better viewed as challenging whether we are indeed the sorts of ongoing cognitive agents, integrated over time, that could deliberately follow any such policy or have good or even bad reasons for most of their beliefs.

There is no way in which I can *argue* that I am such a temporally integrated cognitive agent without presupposing that I am, and thus no way to refute the skeptical hypothesis that I am in some unfathomable way merely the fragmentary and momentary appearance of a cognitive agent, one whose recollections of earlier experiences, earlier stages of argument, and prior consideration of various issues are largely or entirely delusive. Of course, this *seems* entirely preposterous, but this apparent preposterousness is not somehow a product of instantaneous reflection, but depends instead on just the sorts of recollections in question, so that it cannot be appealed to in order to defend them without begging the question.[31]

Thus while we can debate and hope to solve the more specific sorts of epistemological issues raised in previous chapters and earlier in this one, we have no choice but to *assume* the reliability of memories of this most fundamental sort. One way to put the point is to say that when we ask more specific epistemological questions, that is, ask what reasons we have for various kinds of beliefs, there is nothing about these questions that mandates or even really suggests that the answer can take account only of what is available or accessible at a moment and thus with no appeal to memory. In this way it is natural and, I believe, correct to regard this most fundamental and essential sort of memory, that which allows us to retain various cognitive resources in mind long enough to consider and reason from them, not as an additional cognitive resource on a par with immediate experience and *a priori* insight, thereby raising comparable issues of justification, but rather as the indispensable means whereby whatever cognitive resources are otherwise available are preserved and made available on an ongoing basis, as they must be if they are to be of any value to creatures like us.

This is not to deny, as we have seen, that skeptical questions can be raised about this sort of memory, as indeed they can about essentially anything. But such questions are best viewed, not as questioning or challenging the justification of particular beliefs, but rather as challenging our very existence as temporally integrated cognitive agents. It is the former, narrower sorts of epistemological issues with which epistemologists have primarily been concerned and on which we will continue to focus here.

Notes

1. It is important to construe the behavioral description so as not to beg the very question at issue, which means at least roughly that it should be taken to pertain only to matters that are unproblematically accessible to ordinary sensory observation. Thus, for example, *actual pleading* seems to presuppose an underlying mental state of a contentful and purposive sort, but *apparent pleading* can be understood as limited to the observable behavior: the uttering of certain words and the manner in which they are uttered, along with accompanying gestures, facial expressions, and the like.

2. Notice that this way of putting the issue in effect assumes that the problem discussed in the previous chapter, that of justifying beliefs in external physical objects and situations on the basis of sensory experience, has already been in some way solved. We thus have epistemological issues at two different levels, with the one at the higher level (the problem of other minds) depending for its very formulation on the presumption that the one at the lower level (the problem of the external world) has somehow been solved.

3. The more explicit labels are needed to distinguish the view in question from behaviorism as a thesis about the proper method of scientific psychology: the thesis that

psychological investigation and theorizing should appeal only to behavioral (as opposed mainly to introspective) evidence. Whatever its other merits or deficiencies may be, this *methodological behaviorism* has no direct implications for the issue with which we are presently concerned.

4. Logical behaviorism is thus a kind of analogue, at this higher epistemological level, of the phenomenalist view discussed in the previous chapter: faced with the problem of inferring from evidence of a certain sort to claims that apparently go beyond that evidence and are about facts of an entirely different sort, each of these views claims that the content of the latter claims really amounts to no more than a complicated and open-ended constellation of the evidential claims in question.

5. Perhaps the most influential is that offered by Hilary Putnam in "Brains and Behavior," reprinted in his *Mind, Language and Reality: Philosophical Papers, Volume 2* (Cambridge: Cambridge University Press, 1975), pp. 325–41.

6. As one opponent put it, proponents of behaviorism have to "feign anesthesia" with regard to their own mental states.

7. I will hereafter not bother with this qualification.

8. Though even this has sometimes been questioned, mainly by followers of the Austrian philosopher Ludwig Wittgenstein. For a helpful discussion of the Wittgensteinian objection, see Akeel Bilgrami, "Other Minds," in *A Companion to Epistemology*, ed. Jonathan Dancy and Ernest Sosa (Oxford: Blackwell, 1992), pp. 317–23.

9. It could also be questioned whether I am really strongly justified in believing that the explanatory account in question applies to me. Might not the appearance that this is so be an illusion, with the behavior with which my mental states seem to be correlated being caused by something quite different? The main historical position that advances such a claim is *epiphenomenalism*: the view that conscious mental states, though they genuinely exist and are distinct from bodily phenomena, are mere impotent side effects of the physical process, playing no role in the correct explanation of behavior.

10. The possibility of such a view is at least suggested by W. V. Quine's doctrine of the indeterminacy of radical translation, as developed in his book *Word and Object* (Cambridge, Mass.: MIT Press, 1960). Quine's own view is that there are *indefinitely many* interpretations of what is expressed by a given sentence that are *equally* compatible with all the behavioral evidence. Quine is a *verificationist*: that is, he holds the positivist view that only what can be verified is meaningful. Thus, in the present case, he holds that there is no fact of the matter about what the sentence really means that goes beyond what can be behaviorally verified, and thus concludes that its meaning or content is simply indeterminate. But one not wedded to verificationism could hold instead that one of these meanings is correct in my own case and one or more others in relation to other people.

11. There is, for example, also the cluster of views that has grown up around the so-called private language argument put forth by Wittgenstein. See, for example, Norman Malcolm, "Knowledge of Other Minds," in Malcolm, *Knowledge and Certainty* (Ithaca, N.Y.: Cornell University Press, 1963), pp. 130–40.

12. Sometimes it is claimed that an entity like an electron can be observed and thus experienced via a device like a cloud chamber, but this should not, I suggest, be taken se-

riously. What is experienced in such a case (indirectly, if perceptual subjectivism is correct) is the track of water droplets produced by the passage of the charged particle, not the particle itself.

13. Note, however, that my own unaided observation cannot in fact reveal to me things such as that it is the *Seattle City Council* that is meeting in a certain place or that it is the *Seattle Mariners* who are playing in a particular game—think carefully about each of these examples.

14. Imagine a rock formation that seemed to spell out an English message but where there were serious grounds for doubting that it could have been produced by an English-speaking person or even positive grounds for thinking that it resulted from various sorts of inanimate natural processes.

15. There are also occasional cases of testimony involving gestures or other non-linguistic means of conveying a certain content (such as by displaying photographs), but for the sake of simplicity, these will largely be ignored here.

16. Assuming, for the sake of the argument, that a justification of induction along the lines suggested in chapter 4 is successful.

17. By an "inductive argument," I mean here the sort of argument discussed at length in chapter 4, in which a regularity found in observed cases is generalized to all cases of the same kind. Some philosophers use the term "inductive argument" more broadly to include any argument that is not deductively conclusive, in which case the argument suggested in the next section would also count as "inductive."

18. Some cases of this sort might also count as cases of collusion, if the copying is deliberate and not motivated by a belief that the original source is correct.

19. This might be revealed or at least suggested by a citation in a footnote, but this degree of scholarly care is not always exercised, especially if the point is relatively unimportant. Another example of the same general kind is the way in which a large number of seemingly independent books on the operation of a particular computer program may contain the same mistaken claim concerning the result of a certain command because they are all derived from the software company's description of how the program is intended to work, with the discrepancy being due to a "bug" of some sort.

20. Too close a similarity in wording or formulation between different sources may provide a clue here, as in the detection of plagiarism.

21. In this case, it is also worth noting that my memory beliefs receive support from my present perception of a steaming cup of tea sitting on my computer table—though this does not seem to be essential for the justification of the memory belief.

22. Here too there may be some relevant perceptual support for the belief in the form of perceptions of notes or jottings that reflect some of the relevant steps—though this again seems inessential.

23. In this case, the memory belief is not supported by any present perceptual evidence, though with sufficient effort some could almost surely be found (in the form of the perception of records, letters, etc.—note the reliance on testimony).

24. Though one can, of course, also remember something that was arrived at in part via some sort of reasoning from premises acquired in either or both of these ways.

25. In addition, there is the degree to which supporting evidence deriving from current perception and introspection or possibly from testimony or general knowledge of various kinds is present or available—though justification that depends on this sort of evidence does not pertain in any specific way to memory.

26. Hume's pretty obviously inadequate suggestion was that memory always involves images that are "faded" in comparison with perception, though more "lively and vivacious" than those of imagination. (Consider this suggestion carefully and see if you can find clear examples that show why it doesn't work.)

27. "Mistake" in the sense of an inaccurate report. Both here and in some of the subsequent cases, the possibility exists that the resulting belief is still true, either by sheer chance or, as in case (3a) in the text, for some further reason. But I will largely ignore this possibility here.

28. Suppose that I experience something directly, relate it to some friend, forget about it entirely myself, am told about it in vivid detail by the friend in question, and then later seem to remember experiencing it entirely as a result of the vivid testimony. My eventual apparent memory belief is caused by my original experience, but not "in the right way."

29. Already noticed briefly in some of the endnotes.

30. They could, of course, be recorded in writing or in some other way. But it is difficult to see how information thus recorded could be retrieved in a justified form without relying at least on the memory of having made the record.

31. While the issues are not quite the same, I would suggest that much the same thing should be said about two other basic cognitive abilities: the ability to genuinely understand various claims and the ability to see in the simplest cases that one claim follows from another. With regard to each of these abilities also, there is a skeptical issue that can be raised and that cannot be answered in a non-question-begging way.

Contemporary Responses to the Cartesian Program

Introduction to Part Two

Part one of this book has presented an account of the central problems of traditional epistemology, reflecting in part the historical development of the subject in the time since Descartes. Many of these problems, as we have seen, grow out of Descartes's seminal epistemological discussion in the *Meditations*, and all of them have been approached here from a basically Cartesian perspective. Indeed, it is this perspective which arguably provides the original specification of the field of epistemology. It thus deserves to be regarded as something like the default perspective on epistemological issues and hence as the place for a student of the subject to begin.

But while this Cartesian outlook and the specific positions and arguments that it leads to are still, in my judgment, very much alive, a substantial portion of recent epistemological discussion has consisted of critical reactions against this perspective: various attempts to show that the Cartesian approach is in some important way mistaken or confused or wrongheaded, and hence that the issues and problems that it leads to can be more easily dealt with or perhaps even circumvented entirely by adopting a different approach.

My aim in part two is to explore the main anti-Cartesian arguments and positions, beginning with the least radical and proceeding to the most radical. In chapter 9, we will look at criticisms directed at the *foundationalist* character of the Cartesian view and consider the main proposed alternative to foundationalism: *coherentism*. In chapter 10, we will examine criticisms of the *internalist* character of the Cartesian approach and consider the alternative *externalist* approach. In chapter 11, we will consider the idea that traditional Cartesian epistemology should be replaced by a *naturalized* epistemology that treats epistemology as continuous with or perhaps even a department of natural science. Finally, in chapter 12, we will consider the nature and varieties of *skepticism* and the general issue of what sorts of responses to skepticism are possible. Included in the responses to skepticism will be several even more radical rejections of traditional Cartesian epistemology, even including a view that holds in effect that epistemology of any sort is fundamentally misconceived and should simply be abandoned.

Before we begin this discussion, one more preliminary remark may be helpful. It is a plausible conjecture that the most important underlying motive for these anti-Cartesian views is the belief that the Cartesian approach ultimately cannot solve the problems that it generates and hence will in the end lead inevitably to skepticism. If you think carefully about the issues and problems we have discussed already, especially those in the last two chapters, you will see that this pessimistic outlook, though by no means clearly correct, is not without a good deal of plausibility. But the question you should bear constantly in mind as we discuss these alternative views is whether they really do any better in this regard—or whether they are not really, as I will be repeatedly suggesting, themselves just thinly disguised versions of skepticism.

~

CHAPTER NINE

Foundationalism and Coherentism

As we have noticed in a few places, though without very much discussion or elaboration,[1] Descartes's basic epistemological approach is *foundationalist* in character: it views justification and knowledge as ultimately derivative from a set of basic or foundational elements whose justification does not depend in turn on that of anything else. For Descartes, as for many foundationalists, the foundation for knowledge and justification consists of (i) a person's immediate awarenesses of his or her own conscious states of mind, together with (ii) his or her *a priori* grasp of self-evidently true propositions. Beliefs deriving from these two sources require no further justification, whereas beliefs about most or all other matters, and especially beliefs concerning objects and occurrences in the material world, require justification or reasons that ultimately appeal, whether directly or indirectly, to immediate experience and *a priori* insight.[2] As the term "foundation" itself suggests, the underlying metaphor is an architectural one: think of a building or structure, perhaps a very tall one with many different levels, but all of them resting on a bottom level that does not rest in the same way on anything else.

Most historical epistemological views have been broadly foundationalist in character (though they have not always agreed with Descartes about the specific composition of the foundation). But in recent times a fairly wide-spread apparent consensus has developed to the effect that the whole foundationalist approach is deeply flawed and ultimately untenable.

In the present chapter, we explore this issue. We begin by considering a basic problem pertaining to the structure of justified belief or knowledge, one that is usually taken to provide the most telling argument in favor of foundationalism and that will also help to clarify the foundationalist view. Next we consider some of the main objections that have been advanced against foundationalism. This will lead to a consideration and assessment of the main contemporary alternative to foundationalism, namely *coherentism*.[3] Doubts about the tenability of this alternative will then motivate a reconsideration of foundationalism in the final part of the chapter.

The Epistemic Regress Problem and the Foundationalist Argument

I will formulate the general problem abstractly, since it is the structure and not the particular beliefs that matters. Suppose that there is a belief, which we will refer to as B_1, that is allegedly justified for a particular person at a particular time, and consider what specific form this justification might take. One obvious possibility is the following: B_1 might be justified because the person holds some other justified belief B_2 (which might of course be a conjunction of simpler beliefs) from which B_1 follows by some rationally acceptable kind of *inference*, whether deductive, inductive, abductive (inference to the best explanation), or whatever. I am not suggesting that the mere existence of this other belief and of the inferential relation is by itself sufficient for B_1 to be justified. Clearly if the person in question is not at all inclined to appeal to B_2 as a reason for B_1 or has no idea that any inferential relation holds between the two or has a mistaken conception of this inferential relation, B_1 will not be justified in this way for him or her. For the moment, however, I will simply assume that whatever further conditions are required for B_1 to be justified for this person by virtue of its inferential relation to B_2 are in fact satisfied.[4]

But whatever these further conditions may turn out to be, it is clear at least that, as already stipulated, B_2 must itself be somehow justified if it is to confer justification, via a suitable inferential relation, upon B_1. If the person in question has no good reason to think that B_2 is true, then the fact that B_1 follows from B_2 cannot constitute a good reason to think that B_1 is true. Thus we need to ask how B_2 might in turn be justified. Here again one possibility, the only one that we have identified so far, is that the justification of B_2 derives, via a suitable inferential or argumentative relation, from some further justified belief B_3. And now if the question regarding the justification of B_3 is answered in the same way by appeal to another justified belief B_4, and so on, we seem to be faced with a potential *infinite regress* in which each answer to an issue of justification simply raises a new issue of the same kind, thus seemingly never reaching any settled result and leaving it uncertain whether any of the beliefs in question is genuinely justified.

To think more carefully about this issue, we need to ask what the alternatives are as to the eventual outcome of this regress. What, that is, might eventually happen if we continue to ask for the justification of each new belief that is cited as a reason for an earlier belief in the sequence? (You should think about this issue carefully for yourself before reading further. For the moment try to consider all apparent possibilities, no matter how bizarre or implausible they may seem and no matter whether or not they seem initially to be compatible with the alleged justification of the original belief B_1.)

In fact, there seem to be only four possible outcomes of the regress.[5] First, we might eventually arrive at a belief, say B_6, upon which the justification of the previous belief in the series rests, but which is itself simply *unjustified*. This, however, would surely mean that the belief whose justification rests directly on B_6 is also not really justified, and so on up the line, so that the original belief B_1 turns out not to be justified either—contrary to our original supposition. There can be no doubt that some alleged justificatory chains do in fact end in this way, but if this were true in general, and if there were no other sort of justification available that does not rely in this way on inference from other beliefs, then we would have the skeptical result that no belief is ever justified, that we never have a good reason to think that anything is true. This would obviously be a very implausible result, at least from a commonsense standpoint. (Is this a good reason to think that it could not be correct? And if so, how strong a reason is it?—think carefully about this.)

Second, it *seems* to be at least logically possible that the regress might continue *infinitely*, with new beliefs being appealed to at each stage that are sufficient to justify the preceding belief but are themselves in need of justification from yet another new belief. This is perhaps the alternative that it is most difficult to get a clear focus on. Is it really even a logical possibility? And if it is logically possible, is there any serious chance that it might turn out to actually be realized, either in a particular case or in general? (Think about this before reading further. Can you think of any *arguments* against the actual occurrence of this sort of justificatory structure?)

It is tempting to argue that no finite person could have an infinite number of independent beliefs, but this does not seem to be strictly correct. As I gaze at my bare desk, can't I believe, all at once, that there is not an armadillo sitting on it, that there are not two armadillos sitting on it, that there are not three armadillos sitting on it, and so on for all of the infinitely many natural numbers (positive whole numbers), thus resulting in an infinite set of beliefs? Moreover, the members of such an infinite set of beliefs might even stand in the right inferential relations to yield a justificatory chain, as is indeed true with the present example: that there is not even one armadillo is a good, indeed conclusive reason for thinking that there are not two; that there are not even two is a conclusive reason for thinking that there are not three; and so on.

But though the actual infinite regress alternative is interesting to think about, it still seems clear that it could not play a role in an account of how beliefs are actually justified. One reason is that it is difficult or impossible to see how this picture could be applied to most actual cases of apparently justified belief, where no plausible infinite chain of this sort seems to be forthcoming. A deeper reason is that it is clear on reflection that merely having an infinite chain of beliefs related in the right way is not in fact sufficient for justification. Suppose that instead of believing that there are no armadillos on my desk, I am crazy enough to have the infinite set of beliefs to the effect that for each natural number n, there are at least n armadillos on my desk. You may doubt that I could really be this crazy (I hope you do!). If I were, however, then I could construct an infinite justificatory chain: that there are at least two armadillos is a conclusive reason for believing that there is at least one, that there are at least three is a conclusive reason for believing that there are at least two, and so on. But it still seems clear that none of these beliefs would really be justified. The reason is that in such a justificatory chain, the justification conferred at each step is only *provisional*, dependent on whether the beliefs further along in the chain are justified. But then if the regress continues infinitely, *all* of the alleged justification remains merely provisional: we never can say more than that the beliefs up to a particular stage *would* be justified *if* all of the others that come further back in the sequence are justified. And if this is all that we can ever say in such a case, and if all chains of inferential justification were infinite in this way, and if there were no other account of how beliefs are justified that does not rely on inference from other beliefs, then we again would have the unpalatable skeptical result that no belief is ever genuinely justified.

The third apparent possibility is that the chain of inferential justification, if pursued far enough, would eventually circle back upon itself: that is, that some belief that has already appeared in the sequence (or perhaps a conjunction of such beliefs) would be appealed to again. The belief that has this status might be the original belief B_1, or it might be some later belief in the sequence; suppose again that it is B_6 and that the belief for which it is supposed to provide the justification on this second occurrence is B_{10}. The obvious problem with a justificatory chain having this structure is that the overall reasoning that it reflects appears to be circular or question-begging in a way that deprives it of any justificatory force: Dropping out some of the intermediate stages (and assuming that the inferences are all correct), B_1 is justified if B_6 is, and B_6 is justified if B_{10} is, and B_{10} is justified if B_6 is. But then B_6 is justified just in case B_6 is justified, which is obviously true, but provides no reason at all to think that B_6 is in fact justified; and since the justification of B_1 depends on that of B_6, such a chain of justification also provides again no real justification for B_1. Once again we have an apparently skeptical result: if all inferential justification were ultimately circular in this way, and if there were no noninferential way in which beliefs are justified, then no belief would ever be genuinely justified.[6]

The fourth and final alternative is the one advocated by the foundationalist. It holds, first, that there is a way (or perhaps more than one way) in which beliefs can be justified that does not rely on inferential relations to other beliefs and so does not generate a regress of the sort we have been considering; and, second, that any chain of alleged inferential justifications that genuinely yields justification must terminate with beliefs that are justified in this other, noninferential way. These noninferentially justified or *basic* beliefs are thus the *foundation* upon which the justification of all other beliefs ultimately rests.

The main argument for foundationalism is that this last alternative must be the correct one, since all of the other alternatives lead, in the ways we have seen, to the implausible skeptical result that no belief is ever justified. This may not be a conclusive argument for foundationalism, since it is hard to see any very clear basis for asserting that total skepticism could not possibly be correct (think about whether you agree with this), but it is surely a very powerful one, both intuitively and dialectically. Moreover, the most standard version of foundationalism, which is at least approximately the one reflected in part one of this book, has also a good deal of independent plausibility from a commonsense or intuitive standpoint: it certainly seems as though we have many beliefs that are justified, not via inference from other beliefs, but rather by sensory or introspective *experience* (and also by *a priori* insight). Thus the case for foundationalism appears initially to be quite strong.

Objections to Foundationalism

Nonetheless, as already remarked, there are many recent philosophers who hold that foundationalism is in fact seriously and irredeemably mistaken,[7] and we must try to understand the objections to foundationalism that they advance in support of this claim. These objections fall into two main categories, the first pertaining to the alleged relation of justification between the supposed foundational beliefs and the other, nonbasic beliefs that are supposed be justified by appeal to them and the second pertaining to the nature and justification of the foundational beliefs themselves.

The first kind of objection has to do with whether it is in fact possible on the basis of the foundation specified by a particular foundationalist position to provide an adequate justification for the other beliefs that we ordinarily regard as justified (which might be referred to as "superstructure" beliefs), or at least for a reasonably high proportion of such beliefs. For the Cartesian version of foundationalism we have been considering, the core of this issue is essentially the problem discussed in chapter 7: is it possible to justify beliefs concerning the external world of material objects on the basis of beliefs about immediately experienced states of mind[8] (together with *a priori* justified beliefs in self-evident propositions)?

A foundationalist view that cannot justify giving an affirmative answer to this question, one for which a significant proportion of the beliefs that common sense regards as justified cannot be satisfactorily shown to be justifiable by appeal to its chosen foundation, will itself amount to a fairly severe version of skepticism, with the severity depending on just how thoroughgoing this failure turns out to be. Such a skeptical result obviously tends to seriously undercut the foundationalist argument from the regress problem, discussed above, which advocates foundationalism as the only way to *avoid* an implausible skepticism (though the skeptical consequences of any foundationalist view will never be as total as those that apparently result from the other possible outcomes of the regress, since at least the foundational beliefs themselves will still be justified).

In fact, the shape and seriousness of this first general sort of problem varies widely among foundationalist views, depending mainly on just how much is included in the specified set of basic or foundational beliefs.[9] There are versions of foundationalism according to which at least some perceptual beliefs about physical objects count as basic or foundational, and views of this sort have substantially less difficulty in giving a reasonably plausible account of the overall scope of nonfoundational knowledge than does the Cartesian view that restricts the empirical foundation to beliefs about subjective states of mind. In fact, however, as we will see toward the end of the present chapter, it is the Cartesian view that turns out to provide the most defensible response, indeed in my judgment the *only* defensible response, to the second main sort of objection to foundationalism, that concerning the justification of the foundational beliefs themselves. If this is right, then a defensible version of foundationalism will have to meet this first problem, not by expanding the foundation, but rather by arguing that the more restricted Cartesian foundation is indeed adequate to avoid unacceptably skeptical results. (Much of part one is relevant to this issue, especially chapters 4, 7, and 8, though much more discussion would be needed to come very close to resolving it.)

Here, however, we will focus mainly on the second and seemingly more fundamental kind of objection to foundationalism, that which challenges the foundationalist to explain how the supposedly foundational or basic beliefs themselves are justified. In considering this issue, we will focus primarily on the empirical part of the foundation: the part that is not justified *a priori* and that thus consists of contingent beliefs, beliefs that are true in some possible worlds and false in others.[10] Most foundationalists follow the general line taken by the Cartesian view and hold that foundational beliefs of this kind are justified by appeal to sensory and introspective *experience*. But despite the apparent obviousness of this answer, it turns out to be more difficult than might be thought to give a clear account of how it is supposed to work.

There are in fact at least two ways of developing the problem that arises here, though they are perhaps in the end just different ways of getting at the same underlying point. The first version questions whether the whole idea of *sensory experience* justifying *beliefs* really makes intelligible sense,[11] and the starting point of the argument is the view that the distinctive content of a sensory experience is itself *nonpropositional* and *nonconceptual* in character.

Think here of an actual sensory experience, such as the one that I am presently having as I look out my window. (You should supply your own first-hand example.) There are many trees of different kinds at least partially in my field of view, and what I experience is a variegated field of mostly green with small patches of brown and gray and other colors, with many, many different shades and shapes, all changing in complicated and subtle ways as the wind blows or clouds move by. Given some time and close attention, I could apparently make many, many propositional and conceptual judgments about what I am experiencing: that one patch is larger than another, that one shape is similar to or different from another, that a particular patch is brighter than the one that was there a moment earlier, that various specific colors for which I have learned names are present, etc.[12] But my most fundamental experience of the sensory content itself is not propositional or conceptual in this way. It is not general or classificatory in character, not a consciousness *that* the experiential content falls under certain general categories or universals. The experienced sensory content itself is what these general or classificatory judgments are about, what makes them true or false, but this content is different from and vastly more specific than the various conceptual classifications, in a way that makes it extremely doubtful that it could ever be *fully* described in such conceptual terms. (Think *very* carefully about this difficult point, considering lots of examples—which are fortunately very easy to come by. Imagine trying to describe such an experienced sensory content to someone else, perhaps over the phone. One problem is that our vocabulary in this area is obviously very inadequate. But even if you did have an adequate vocabulary, isn't it clear that it would be very, very difficult to actually give anything close to a complete description, and—the real point—that the sensory content of which you are conscious and which you are attempting to describe does not itself already involve or consist of such a conceptual or classificatory description.)

Remember that the issue we are presently concerned with is whether sensory experience can *justify* beliefs. But if sensory experience is in this way nonconceptual, and given that beliefs are obviously formulated in propositional and conceptual terms, it becomes hard to see how there can be an intelligible justificatory relation between the two. How can something that is not even formulated in conceptual terms be a reason for thinking that something that is thus formulated is true? The present argument concludes that there can be no such justificatory relation—and hence, as the only apparent alternative, that the relation between sensory experience and beliefs must be merely *causal*. As the contemporary American philosopher Donald Davidson puts it:

> The relation between a sensation and a belief cannot be logical, since sensations are not beliefs or other propositional attitudes [that is, are not formulated in conceptual terms]. What then is the relation? The answer is, I think, obvious: the relation is causal. Sensations cause some beliefs and in *this* sense are the basis or ground of those beliefs. But a causal explanation of a belief does not show how or why the belief is justified.[13]

And if this is correct, then we have the extremely surprising result that the nonconceptual content of sensory experience, even though it undeniably exists, is apparently incapable of playing any justificatory role, and thus cannot provide the justification for foundational beliefs. Sensory experience in itself would thus turn out to have no very important epistemological significance. (Can this possibly be right? And if you think it couldn't, then what is wrong with the argument just given?)

The second, closely related antifoundationalist argument focuses on the person's *awareness* or *apprehension* of the experiential content.[14] Clearly (setting the previous argument aside for a moment) the experience that supposedly justifies a particular basic belief must have a correlative specific character that *somehow* makes it likely that that specific belief is true. Moreover, the person must somehow apprehend or be aware of the specific character of this experience if it is to provide him or her with justification (of an internalist sort) for his or her belief. But what is the nature of this apprehension or awareness of the character of the experience? There seem to be two and only two possibilities here, neither of them apparently compatible with the foundationalist view. (Thus the argument takes the form standardly referred to by logicians as a *dilemma*.)

One possibility is that the specific character of the sensory experience is apprehended via a reflective *conceptual* awareness, that is, another *belief*: the belief that I have such-and-such a specific sort of experience. Here it is important to keep the whole picture in mind. We started with one supposedly foundational belief, which was presumably about some feature of the experience. In order to explain how that first belief is justified by the experience we needed to invoke an independent apprehension or awareness of the experience, and the suggestion is now that this apprehension or awareness takes the form of another belief. But now there are two problems. First, the original, supposedly basic belief that the experience was supposed to justify appears to have lost that status, since its justification now depends on this further belief, presumably via an inferential relation. Second and more importantly, there is now also a new issue as to how this further reflective belief is *itself* justified. Since this reflective belief is supposed to constitute the person's most basic apprehension or awareness of the experiential content (that was the whole point of introducing it), there is no apparent way for it to be justified by appeal to that content, since there is no further awareness of the content to appeal to.[15] And to invoke a further conceptual awareness of that same content, that is, yet another belief, only pushes this issue one step further back. In the process of trying to avoid the original regress, we seem to have generated a new one.

But the only apparent alternative is that the most fundamental apprehension or awareness of the specific character of the sensory content does not take the form of a conceptual belief *that* the experience is of a certain specific sort, but instead is not formulated in conceptual or classificatory terms at all. If so, then any further issue of justification is apparently avoided, since there is simply no further claim or assertion to be justified. But the problem now is that it becomes difficult to see how such an apprehension or awareness can provide a basis for the justification of the original, supposedly basic belief: If the apprehension of the experiential content is not in any way belief-like or propositional in character, then there is apparently no way to infer from that awareness to the truth (or likely truth) of the supposedly basic belief. And in the absence of such an inference, it is obscure how either the experience or the apprehension thereof constitutes any sort of reason for thinking that the supposedly basic belief is true.

These two objections are in effect two ways of getting at the fundamental issue of what the alleged justificatory relation between sensory experience and propositional, conceptual beliefs is supposed to amount to, how it is supposed to work. The relation cannot be logical or inferential, both because logical or inferential relations exist only between propositional or conceptual items, and sensory experience itself is not propositional or conceptual in character, and because an appeal to something that can stand in logical or inferential relations could not provide a genuine solution to the epistemic regress problem. But what then is the nature of this relation?

You may well think that these arguments must be somehow mistaken, that there must be some way in which the right sort of sensory experience can justify a belief. But then how exactly does this work? We will return to this issue at the end of the chapter, after we have had a look at the coherentist alternative.

In Search of Coherentism

The first problem we face in a discussion of coherentism is trying to get a clear idea of what a coherentist view really amounts to. The central idea is that epistemic justification depends on the *coherence* of a set of beliefs, rather than on inferential derivability from basic or foundational beliefs. But elaborating this initial idea into a developed position turns out to be extremely difficult. And while there are many specific positions, both historical and contemporary, that are fairly standardly identified as versions of coherentism,[16] it is unclear exactly what, if anything, they have in common beyond this central idea—or even that they all are entirely consistent in their adherence to it. Thus it is more than a little uncertain whether there is any clearly defined general view that can be identified as coherentism.

The best way to handle this problem is to consider some of the key issues that any coherentist view that is to be a genuine dialectical alternative to foundationalism must apparently face, attempting to figure out what a genuinely coherentist response might look like. Having done this, and having examined the problems and difficulties that arise along the way, we will then be in a position to attempt a further evaluation of coherentism.

The Nature of Coherence

The first and perhaps most obvious issue is the nature of coherence itself. It is clear that coherence is supposed to be primarily a property of a *group* or *sys-*

tem of beliefs (though presumably a sufficiently complicated individual belief could be incoherent within itself). Proponents of coherence[17] speak of beliefs agreeing with each other or fitting together or "dovetailing" with each other. Part of what is required here is logical consistency: beliefs that are inconsistent with each other, that could not all be true at the same time in any possible world (for example, the belief that the earth is spherical and the belief that the earth is flat), plainly do not fit together or agree to any extent at all. But contrary to what opponents and even a few proponents of coherence sometimes seem to suggest, mere consistency is not by itself enough for any serious degree of coherence. Consider a set of entirely unrelated beliefs: the belief that grass is green, the belief that today is Tuesday, the belief that Caesar crossed the Rubicon in 49 B.C., and the belief that Matisse was a great painter. The set of beliefs is obviously consistent, simply because its members make no contact with each other at all and so could not possibly conflict, but it would be odd and misleading to describe it as coherent and perhaps still odder to suggest that this mere lack of conflict provides any real *justification* for these beliefs, any positive reason for thinking that they are true. And the same thing could obviously be true for a much larger set of beliefs.

In fact, it is clear that most of those loosely identified as coherentists have had a much stronger and more demanding relation among beliefs in mind, a relation in virtue of which a coherent set of beliefs will be tightly unified and structured, not merely an assemblage of unrelated items. Here it seems likely that all of the aspects or ingredients of this relation can be viewed as *inferential* relations of one sort or another among the component beliefs—with any sort of relation between two beliefs (or sets of beliefs) in virtue of which one would, if accepted, provide a good reason for thinking that the other is true counting as an inferential relation. The idea is thus that the members of a coherent system of beliefs are so related as to provide inferential support for each other, with the degree of coherence depending on the degree to which this is so, that is, on the number and strength of these inferential connections.

Although it is impossible to give a very good example of a coherent system of beliefs in the space reasonably available here, the following may help you to get a little better hold on the idea. Suppose that you are watching four birds in your back yard and form a set of ten beliefs about them, consisting of the beliefs with regard to each of the four (a) that the bird in question is a crow and (b) that the bird in question is black, together with the general beliefs (1) all crows are black and (2) that all black birds are crows. This set of ten beliefs is too small to be highly coherent, but it is far more coherent than the set of unrelated beliefs described earlier. The eight specific beliefs provide inductive support (one sort of inferential relation) for each of the two general beliefs, each member of the four pairs of specific beliefs provides deductive support (another sort of inferential relation) for the other when taken together with one of the general beliefs, and there are also inferential relations of an inductive sort between any seven of the specific beliefs and the eighth.[18] Thus this set of beliefs is about as closely unified as a set this small could be (though some mathematical examples might be even better in this respect) and provides an initial model of what a coherent set of beliefs might look like.[19]

One general class of relations among beliefs that has received a great deal of emphasis in recent discussions of coherence is relations having to do with *explanation*. We have already seen in our earlier consideration of theoretical or explanatory reasoning[20] how the fact that a hypothesis provides the best explanation for a set of justified claims might provide a reason for thinking that the hypothesis is true. But it is equally true that an explanatory hypothesis can, if accepted, help to provide inferential support for some of the claims that it could explain, though other premises will also be required. (The example in the previous paragraph provides a rough example of this sort of situation, though it is debatable to what extent, if at all, an inductive generalization really explains its instances.) Thus explanatory relations provide a basis for inference and so constitute one ingredient of the general idea of coherence, one that goes beyond deductive and inductive relations.[21] It seems excessive, however, to hold, as is sometimes done, that explanatory relations are all there is to coherence.

But while the foregoing discussion may suffice to give you some initial grasp of the concept of coherence, it is very far from an adequate account, especially one that would provide the basis for *comparative* assessments of the relative degrees of coherence possessed by different and perhaps conflicting systems of beliefs. And it is comparative assessments of coherence that seem to be needed if coherence is to be the sole basis that determines which beliefs are justified or even to play a significant role in such issues. There are somewhat fuller accounts of coherence available in the recent literature,[22] but none that come at all close to achieving this goal. Thus practical assessments of coherence must be made on a rather ill-defined intuitive basis, making the whole idea of a coherentist epistemology more of a promissory note than a fully specified alternative.

A Response to the Epistemic Regress Problem: Nonlinear Justification

A second, equally urgent issue is how coherentism might respond to the epistemic regress problem. Of the four alternatives with regard to the outcome of the epistemic regress that were outlined above, the coherentist must apparently opt for the third, the idea that chains of inferential justification circle or loop back upon themselves, rather than ending in unjustified beliefs, going on infinitely, or terminating with foundational beliefs. Advocates of coherentism have occasionally claimed that such a view is acceptable as long as the circles and loops are large and complicated enough. But this response seems simply irrelevant to the objection discussed above: that such a picture involves circular reasoning and hence that the supposed chains of justification have in fact no genuine justificatory force. A large and complicated circle is still after all a circle. Is there anything better that the coherentist can say here?

Perhaps the best hope for a viable coherentist response to the regress problem is an idea offered originally by the nineteenth-century British idealist Bernard Bosanquet.[23] It amounts to the claim that the very formulation of this problem depends on a basic mistake concerning the structure of inferential justification: the mistaken idea that relations of inferential justification fundamentally involve a one-dimensional, asymmetrical, *linear* order of dependence among the beliefs in question. Once this linear picture is accepted, it is argued, the regress of justification is unavoidable and can be solved only in the (allegedly untenable) foundationalist way. Bosanquet's contrary suggestion is that inferential justification, when properly understood, is ultimately nonlinear or *holistic* in character, with all of the beliefs involved standing in relations of *mutual* support, but none being justificationally prior to the others. In this way, it is alleged, any objectionable circularity is avoided. (Think carefully about the plausibility of this claim, looking back at the discussion of the circularity alternative.)

Such a view seems to amount to making the *group* or *system* of beliefs, rather than its individual members, the primary unit of justification, with the component beliefs being justified only derivatively, by virtue of their membership in such an adequately interrelated system. And the general property of such a system, in virtue of which it is justified, is of course identified as coherence. (The contrast between the linear and nonlinear conceptions of inferential justification is drawn at a very high level of abstraction, and you will have to work to try to bring it down to earth by considering possible examples.)[24]

A further claim often made by proponents of nonlinear justification and by coherentist views generally is that the relevant "system" in relation to which issues of coherence and so of justification are to be decided is the entire set of beliefs held by the believer in question. Indeed, this is frequently taken completely for granted with little discussion. But such an extreme *holism* is in fact not required in any very clear way by the logic of the non-linear view, and it moreover poses serious problems that the coherentist might be better advised to avoid. The already rather fuzzy idea of coherence becomes even more so when applied to comprehensive systems of beliefs, which will inevitably contain many beliefs having no discernible connection with each other. Moreover, even the minimal requirement of consistency is in fact rather unlikely to be satisfied by such a system. Thus it seems to be a mistake for the coherentist to take his holism this far (though this admittedly raises the far from easy issue of just what the relevant group or system is in relation to a particular belief).

Coherentism and Sense Perception

A third crucial issue facing the would-be coherentist is what to say about the epistemic role of sensory perception or observation.[25] Here the coherentist seems to be faced with a stark choice. One alternative would be to simply deny that sensory perception plays any genuine justificatory role—deny, that is, that the fact that a belief is a result of perception contributes in any way to a reason for thinking that it is true. A coherentist who adopts this line need not deny the seemingly obvious fact that many of our beliefs are in fact *caused* by sensory experience. But he must insist that being produced in this way gives them no special justificatory status, so that their justification has to be assessed on the same basis as that of any other belief, namely by how well they fit into a coherent system of beliefs. Thus, according to this sort of view, a belief that is a mere hunch or is a product of wishful thinking or even is just arbitrarily made up but that coheres with a set of other beliefs (perhaps arrived at in the same ways!) will be justified, while a perceptual belief that is not related in this way to other beliefs will not be.

Such an extreme repudiation of the justificatory relevance of sensory perception or observation is both quite implausible from a commonsense standpoint and also greatly aggravates the issue, to be considered next, of why the fact that a belief satisfies the test of coherence is any reason for thinking that it is true. For these reasons, few coherentists have been willing to go this far.[26] But the alternative is to try to somehow accommodate an important justificatory role for sense perception or observation within the coherentist framework, something that it is not at all easy to see how to do, since at least the most straightforward ways of doing so seem to amount to a return to foundationalism.

Perhaps the best that the coherentist can do on this issue is to continue to insist that sensory experience in itself merely causes beliefs but cannot justify them, while adding that the fact that a belief was caused in this way rather than some other can play a crucial role in a special kind of coherentist justification. The idea is that the justification of these perceptual or observational beliefs, rather than merely appealing to the coherence of their propositional contents with the contents of other beliefs (so that the way that the belief was produced would be justificationally irrelevant), appeals instead to a general belief that beliefs caused in this specific way (and perhaps satisfying further conditions as well) are generally true, where this belief is in turn supported by inductive inference from many apparently true instances of beliefs of this kind, with the apparent truth of these instances being in turn justified by various inferences falling under the general heading of coherence. Such perceptual beliefs would obviously not be *arrived at* via inference, but they would still be inferentially *justified* in a way that allegedly depends ultimately on coherence: the coherence of the general belief about the reliability of beliefs caused in this way with the rest of the relevant system of beliefs.

In this way, it has been claimed, sense perception or observation can after all play a role in coherentist justification. Moreover, beliefs justified in this way, since their justification does not depend on their specific content but only on the way that they are caused, could either agree with or conflict with other beliefs that the person holds, thus providing the sort of independent check or test of one's beliefs that sensory observation is often claimed to provide. And a coherentist view could seemingly *require* (not merely allow) that beliefs justified in this way play a substantial justificatory role, while still retaining its coherentist character.[27]

Does the foregoing picture really succeed in accommodating the epistemic role of sense perception or observation within a coherentist framework? Like virtually everything about coherentism, the details are sketchy, and in fact there are very serious problems that lurk not far beneath the surface, some but not all of which will be addressed below.

Coherence and Truth

We come now to the most fundamental and obvious issue of all: Why should the fact that a belief satisfies the standards of a coherentist account be taken to show that it is justified in the sense of there being a good reason for thinking that it is *true*? What does coherence even have to do with truth or likelihood of truth (assuming, as we will here, that a coherence theory of truth is unacceptable[28]).

We may approach this issue by considering first how a coherentist might respond to two related, but more specific issues. The first of these is what is usually referred to as the *input* or *isolation* problem. If we assume, first, that there is much more to reality than a person's system of beliefs and, second, that most of those beliefs purport to describe that larger reality, then the obvious question is why the fact that those beliefs are coherent with each other constitutes any reason to think that what they say about the reality external to them is true or correct. Why couldn't a system of beliefs be perfectly coherent while nonetheless entirely impervious to any sort of influence or input from external reality, thus being completely isolated from it? But if this were so, it could seemingly be only an unlikely accident or coincidence if the beliefs in question happened to be true. Thus, it is argued, coherence is irrelevant to truth and so provides no basis for justification.

It is at this point that the defensibility of the coherentist account of sensory observation, briefly sketched above, becomes critical. For *if* that account can be fleshed out and defended, then (and, I would suggest, only then) the coherentist will have a response to this objection: that the observational beliefs justified in the way indicated are after all *caused* by external reality and so represent a kind of external input to the system of beliefs that can solve the isolation problem. Note that even the initial plausibility of this response depends on the fact that the way that observational beliefs are caused plays a role in their justification (and also on the admittedly vague requirement that beliefs justified in this way play a substantial justificatory role); if they were caused in this way but justified solely on the basis of the coherence of their contents with those of other beliefs, thus being on a par with hunches, products of wishful thinking, beliefs resulting from mere dogmatism, and so on (or if such observational beliefs were simply too rare to have much impact), then the influence of the world on the system of beliefs would be too minimal to make truth likely.

A second problem is raised by the apparent possibility of *alternative coherent systems*. Since coherence is a purely internal property of a group or system of beliefs, it seems possible to invent indefinitely many alternative systems of belief in a purely arbitrary way and yet make each of them entirely coherent, with *any* possible belief that is internally consistent and coherent being a member of some of these systems. But since the beliefs in one such system will conflict with those in others, they obviously cannot all be justified. Thus there must be some basis other than coherence for choosing among these systems and the beliefs they contain, so that coherence is not by itself an adequate basis for justification.

Here again the best response available to the coherentist seems to depend on the suggested coherentist account of observation. For *if* that account can be made to work, then the coherentist can seemingly require that any system whose coherence is to be a basis for genuine justification (i) must include such an observational ingredient and (ii) must *remain* coherent as new observational beliefs are added. There is no apparent reason to think that just any arbitrarily invented system of beliefs will satisfy these further requirements. Indeed, though the issues are very complicated, there is no very clear reason for thinking that more than one system will do so in the long run.

The responses to these two problems point toward a coherentist response to the general problem of truth. *If* (and this is still a very big if) the coherentist account of observational input can be successfully elaborated and defended, then the coherentist can attempt to argue that the best *explanation* for the long-run coherence of a system of beliefs in the face of continued observational input is that the beliefs in the system are being systematically caused by an external reality that they accurately depict, and hence that they are likely to be true.[29] Even apart from the worries about the account of observation itself, there is much more that would have to be done to spell out and elaborate this argument,[30] but for now, this initial outline of how an argument linking coherence with truth might go will have to do.

Further Objections to Coherentism

Coherentism emerges from the foregoing discussion as a shaky and problematic position at best, on the defensive from the beginning and afflicted with a multitude of problems and objections that are not answerable in any conclusive way. But there are many further objections as well. Here I will consider only two of them, both having to do in different ways with the general issue of the accessibility of coherentist justification to the believer.

First, if coherence is to be the basis for empirical justification,[31] then an *internalist* coherence theory must require that the believer have an adequate grasp or representation of the relevant system of beliefs, since it is in relation to this system that coherence and so justification are determined. Such a grasp would presumably take the form of a set of reflective beliefs (or one comprehensive reflective belief) specifying the contents of the relevant system. And the seemingly glaring difficulty is that the coherentist view also seemingly precludes there being any way in which such reflective beliefs are themselves justified. Such beliefs are obviously contingent and presumably empirical in character; and yet any appeal to coherence for their justification would seem to be plainly circular or question-begging, since what is at issue is in part the specification of the very system of beliefs in relation to which coherence is to be assessed. Until I have a *justified* grasp of the contents of the relevant system, I can't tell which reflective beliefs of this kind are justified; but a justified grasp of the contents of that system depends on a prior answer to just this question.

Here it is hard to avoid suspecting that would-be coherentists have failed to adequately purge themselves of an intuitive outlook that is really compatible only with foundationalism. From a traditional foundationalist standpoint, there is no real problem about one's grasp of one's own beliefs, since this is a matter of immediate experience for occurrent beliefs and can be made so for dispositional beliefs. But coherentists reject any such appeal to immediate experience, and so cannot legitimately appeal to this sort of access.

Second, a less obvious but equally serious objection pertains to the coherentist's attempted account of observational input and the accompanying answer to the alternative coherent systems objection and argument for the connection between coherence and truth. An essential component of all of this is the idea that the observational status of a belief can be recognized *in a justified way* from within the person's system of beliefs, for only then could this status be used as a partial basis for the justification of such a belief, which then in turn would allow such observational beliefs to be appealed to for these various further purposes. Here again, recognizing that a belief is a result of sensory observation rather than arbitrary invention is at least reasonably unproblematic from a foundationalist standpoint that can invoke immediate experience. But for a coherentist, the basis for such a recognition can only be the further *belief*, itself supposedly justified by coherence, that a given belief has this status. And then there is no apparent reason why the various alternative coherent systems cannot include within themselves beliefs about the occurrence of various allegedly observational beliefs that would support the other beliefs in such a system, with these supposed observations being justified within each system in the way indicated above. Of course, such beliefs will not in general *really* be observational in character, but the coherentist has no way to appeal to this fact that is compatible with his coherentist framework. Thus there is no way consistent with coherentism to distinguish genuine observational input from this counterfeit variety, nor any way on the basis of the only sort of "observation" that is internally recognizable to answer the isolation and alternative coherent systems objections or to argue from coherence to likelihood of truth. (This is a *very* difficult point and you will have to think about it at some length to be sure that you see it clearly.)

These last two objections appear in fact to be completely devastating to coherentism. I note in passing that it might be possible to avoid or at least mitigate them by adopting an *externalist* version of coherentism. But externalism, as we will see in the next chapter, faces serious problems of its own; and in any case, an externalist version of coherentism would have no dialectical point, since if externalism were otherwise acceptable, a foundationalist version would be much more straightforward and easier to defend.

Foundationalism Revisited

The sort of view that is often regarded as the main contemporary alternative to foundationalism has been examined and found wanting, but that is not enough, of course, to answer the antifoundationalist arguments, in particular the arguments purporting to show that sensory experience is incapable of justifying conceptual beliefs and thus incapable of providing a foundation of the sort that the foundationalist is seeking. We thus need to return to those arguments and see whether they are really as powerful as they have often been taken to be.

It will be useful to begin with the second of the two arguments that were presented earlier in this chapter. This argument, as we saw, takes the form of a *dilemma* concerning the apprehension of the character of the experience, mainly sensory experience, to which the foundationalist wants to appeal for the justification of foundational beliefs: if the character of such experience is apprehended in a conceptual or propositional state, a belief, then it seems capable of providing a reason for thinking that further beliefs are true, but is also itself in need of justification; whereas if the apprehension of the character of experience is not in conceptual or propositional terms, if it does not involve any apprehension *that* the experience in question has one sort of general or classificatory character rather than another, the need for justification is avoided, but at the cost of rendering the apprehension seemingly incapable of providing justification for any further belief.

The suggestion that I want to offer here will be at least a bit easier to see if we focus initially on a somewhat different case, the case where the (alleged) basic belief in question is the reflective belief that I have some other specific occurrent belief. The natural place to look for justification for such a reflective belief is to the *experience* of having the other belief in question. And here the crucial fact that, I will suggest, allows an escape between the horns of the dilemma just mentioned is that my most fundamental experience or awareness of one of my own occurrent beliefs is *neither* a separate reflective belief or belief-like state that would itself require justification *nor* a noncognitive awareness of some sort that fails to reflect the specific character of the apprehended state, that is, in this case, the propositional content of the belief. Instead, I suggest, to have a conscious occurrent belief just *is*, in part, to have a conscious awareness of the content of that belief (and also of one's accepting attitude toward that content), an awareness that is not reflective (or "second order") in nature, but is instead partly *constitutive* of the first-level occurrent belief state itself. My further suggestion is then that it is by appeal to this nonreflective, constitutive awareness that a reflective, second-order belief can be justified—

though we now see that it is this constituent, nonreflective awareness rather than the reflective belief that ultimately deserves to be called "basic."

The ideas in the previous paragraph are perhaps more difficult and philosophically sophisticated than anything that you have encountered so far in this book, so I want to pause a bit to make sure that you have them in clear focus. The main distinction is between (a) a belief that is about *another*, distinct belief (and thus reflective or "second-order") and (b) the conscious awareness of a belief's *own* content that is, I am claiming, a constitutive or intrinsic feature of any conscious, occurrent belief, without the need for a second, independent belief. To take a specific example, suppose that I have the first-order, conscious or occurrent belief that the sun is shining. Then the relevant second-order or reflective belief, which might or might not actually be present, would have the content *I (presently) believe that the sun is shining*; whereas the intrinsic or constitutive awareness of the content of the first-order belief, an awareness that *always* occurs when I have such a belief, would just be the conscious thought *the sun is shining*, with no reference to me as the thinker. The crucial point is simply that an occurrent belief is, after all, a *conscious* state, and that what one is primarily conscious of in having such a belief is precisely its propositional content (together with the fact that this content is being accepted rather than, say, doubted or wondered about).

If this is right, then this constitutive awareness of content can seemingly provide a justifying reason for the reflective belief that I have an occurrent belief with that very content. Indeed, in the normal case, it is precisely because I am aware in the constitutive way of the content of my belief that I am led, when and if I reflect, to form the reflective belief that I have such-and-such a first-order belief. But, at the same time, there is no apparent way in which the nonreflective, constituent awareness of content itself requires any sort of justification: an issue of justification can, of course, be raised about the belief as a whole (do I have any reason to think that the sun is shining?), but not about my non-reflective awareness of the content of the belief. Because of its non-reflective, constituent character, this "built-in" awareness, as it might be described, thus neither requires any justification, nor for that matter even admits of any. Indeed, this constituent awareness of content might be said to be strictly *infallible* in something like the way that many foundationalist views historically have claimed: because it is this constitutive or "built-in" awareness of content that *gives* the belief its specific content, that *makes* it the particular belief that it is with the content that it has (rather than some other belief or some nonbelief state), there is apparently no way in which this awareness could be mistaken, simply because there is no relevant fact independent of the awareness itself for it to be mistaken about.[32]

This infallibility does not, however, extend to a reflective, second-order belief: though such a belief can, I am claiming, be justified by appeal to the awareness that is a constitutive feature of the first-order belief that is its object, it would still apparently be possible to reflectively misapprehend the content of one's own belief, to have a reflective belief that does not accurately reflect the content contained in the constitutive or "built-in" awareness. Such a mistake might be due to mere inattention, or it might result from the complexity or obscurity of the belief content itself or from some further problem or disorder. But unless there is some reason in a particular case to think that the chance of such a misapprehension is large, this mere possibility of error does not seem enough to prevent the reflective belief from being justifiable by appeal to the constituent awareness.

The foregoing provides an outline of how a certain specific sort of belief, namely a reflective, second-order belief about the existence and content of one of my own conscious, occurrent beliefs, can be basic or foundational in the sense of there being an internally available reason why it is likely to be true without that reason depending on any further belief or other cognitive state that is itself in need of justification—though, as we have seen, it is really the constitutive awareness of content rather than the reflective belief that ultimately turns out to be foundational. But though my immediate awareness of my own occurrent beliefs is a part of my overall immediate experience and plays some role in justification, the most important part of that experience for issues of justification is my immediate awareness of sensory content. My suggestion is that an essentially parallel account can be given of how this awareness too can justify foundational beliefs.

Consider then a state of, for example, visual experience, such as the one that I am presently having as I look out of the window in my study (see the rough description offered earlier in this chapter). Like an occurrent belief, such an experience is of course a conscious state. This means, I suggest, that in a way that parallels the account of occurrent belief offered above, it automatically involves a constitutive or "built-in," nonreflective awareness of its own distinctive sort of content, in this case sensory or "phenomenal" content. And, again in parallel fashion, such an awareness is in no need of justification and is indeed in a sense infallible in that there is no sort of mistake that is even relevant to it. Thus this awareness of sensory content is also apparently able to justify reflective beliefs that are about that content. For example, the reflective belief that I am experiencing a patch of bright green in the middle of my visual field can be justified by appeal to the constitutive or built-in awareness that is what makes that experience the specific experience that it is. (If, that is, I am in fact having that experience—here, as with belief, mistakes are possible, even if unlikely.)

But does this really answer the antifoundationalist arguments offered above? Even if it is correct that the constitutive or built-in awareness raises no further issue of justification, is there really an intelligible justificatory relation between it and a basic belief about the character of the experience? Perhaps this relation of justification is plausible enough in the case considered earlier, where the constitutive awareness is an awareness of the content of an occurrent belief, for there the awareness of content is in conceptual terms that connect in an obvious way with the conceptual content of the reflective belief, even if the constitutive awareness involves no conceptual *judgment* about that content that could demand justification. (Think again about the example described earlier.) But does this really work in the present and ultimately more important case, in which the content of the constitutive awareness is, as we saw earlier, not at all in conceptual terms (so that some, indeed, would refuse even to describe it as "content")? Aren't the earlier arguments still correct that there can be no intelligible justificatory relationship between the constitutive awareness of content of *this* sort and a conceptual belief that purports to describe it? (Here is a good place to stop and think about the issue for yourself, before proceeding.)

In fact, we are now in a position to see that these arguments rest on too simple a view of the alternatives for the relation between a sensory experience and a conceptual belief. If we grant (and indeed insist) that the specific content of such an experience is itself nonpropositional and nonconceptual in character, then it is quite correct that there can be no strictly *logical* or *inferential* relation between (a) this content (or the constitutive awareness thereof) and (b) a reflective, conceptual belief about that content: since the awareness of nonconceptual content is neither true nor false (because it makes no conceptual claim), it cannot be the case (as an inference would require) that its truth guarantees the truth of the belief. But such an experience, like other kinds of nonconceptual phenomena, can of course still be conceptually *described* with various degrees of detail and precision. The relation between the nonconceptual content and such a conceptual description of it is not logical or inferential, but it is also obviously not merely causal. Rather it is a *descriptive* relation, one in which the thing described does or does not fit or conform to the description. And where such a relation of description exists, the actual character of the nonconceptual object can obviously constitute a kind of reason or basis for thinking that the description is true or correct (or equally, of course, untrue or incorrect).

Thus suppose that I have a specific conscious state of sensory experience (an experience that includes a round, green patch in the middle of my visual field), and am, as already argued, consciously but nonconceptually aware of the specific sensory content of that state simply by virtue of having that experience. Suppose that at the same time I entertain a reflective belief that purports to describe or conceptually characterize that perceptual content, albeit no doubt incompletely (the reflective belief that I have a round, green patch in the middle of my visual field). If I *understand* the descriptive content of that belief, that is, understand what sort of experience it would take to fit or satisfy the conceptual description, then I seem to be in a good, indeed an ideal, position to judge whether the conceptual description is accurate as far as it goes, whether it fits the nonconceptual experience I am actually having, and if so, to be thereby justified in accepting the belief. Here again there is no reason to think that mistake is impossible and thus no reason to think that such a reflective belief is infallible. But as long as there is no special reason for suspecting that a mistake has occurred, the fact that such a belief seems to me on the basis of direct comparison to accurately characterize the conscious experience that it purports to describe seems to be an entirely adequate reason for thinking that the description is correct and hence an adequate basis for justification.

Such a reason is, of course, only available to one who has some sort of independent cognitive access to the character of the nonconceptual item, that is, an access that does not depend on the conceptual description itself. In most other cases, such as where it is some physical object or situation that is being described, one could have an access that is independent of the description in question only by having a second conceptual state embodying a second, perhaps more specific description, and this second description would of course itself equally require justification, so that no genuinely foundational justification would result. But in the very special case we are concerned with, where the nonconceptual item being described is *itself* a conscious state, one can, I am suggesting, be aware of its character via the constitutive or "built-in" awareness that any conscious state involves, without the need for a further conceptual description—and thereby be in a position to recognize that a reflective belief about that state is (or is not) correct.

Here we seem indeed to be in a position to make a direct comparison between a conceptual description and the nonconceptual chunk of reality that it purports to describe—something that seems intuitively to be essential if our conceptual descriptions are ever to make contact with reality in a verifiable way.[33] Such a comparison is only possible, to be sure, where the reality in question is itself a conscious state and where the description in question pertains to the conscious content of that very state, but in that specific case it seems to be entirely unproblematic.[34]

Thus at least the most standard version of foundationalism seems to have an adequate response to the second general sort of objection to foundationalism distinguished earlier: the one that pertains to the nature and justification of the foundational beliefs themselves. As already suggested, however, this response seriously aggravates the first kind of objection, the one that challenges whether the rest of what common sense regards as knowledge can be justified on the basis of the foundation thus arrived at. Whether the foundationalist can meet this sort of objection depends mostly on the eventual resolution of the issues discussed in chapter 7 (and, to a lesser extent, in chapters 4 and 8), issues which we will not pursue further here.[35]

Notes

1. Most extensively at the end of chapter 2.

2. The formulation just given is probably more or less the way that Descartes would have put the point, if he had spoken explicitly in these terms. More recent versions of foundationalism have tended to say instead that the foundation consists of the *beliefs* about immediately experienced conscious states of mind together with the *beliefs* deriving from the *a priori* grasp of self-evident propositions, rather than the immediate awarenesses or *a priori* insights themselves. The significance of this difference will be considered further in the text.

3. The contextualist view to be discussed in chapter 12 is also, in a way, an alternative to foundationalism.

4. It turns out to be surprisingly difficult to say just what these conditions are. Having the argument explicitly in mind at the time in question is surely not necessary. Indeed it is doubtful if the person need *ever* have thought in a fully explicit way about the inferential relation in question. Our lives are very busy, and explicit formulation and consideration of arguments is something we do only rarely and usually where the need is in some way urgent. (See if you can think of examples, perhaps ones where you are the person involved, of a person apparently being justified in holding a belief by virtue of an inferential relation that he or she has never explicitly considered up to the time in question.) At the same time, it seems also clear that the availability of the justifying argument must be at least part of the reason that the person holds the belief if it is to be justified on that basis; merely the fact that the argument would have occurred to the person if the belief had been challenged is not enough.

5. Though a given case might realize more than one of these on different branches of the justificatory chain. In the text, I ignore for simplicity the possibility and indeed likelihood that the chain would branch over and over as two or more beliefs are appealed to in justifying a previous one.

6. The coherentist alternative to foundationalism is sometimes characterized as a realization of this third alternative. But while there is some point to saying this, it is also, as we will see, rather seriously misleading. Whatever the merits of coherentism may turn out

to be, it will in fact give us no reason to question the objection to the third possibility just formulated.

7. Including an earlier incarnation of the present author. See my book *The Structure of Empirical Knowledge* (Cambridge, Mass.: Harvard University Press, 1985) (hereafter referred to as *SEK*).

8. In fact, as you may recall, the issue explicitly considered in chapter 7 was whether beliefs concerning material objects could be justified by appeal to the immediate experiences themselves, rather than by appeal to *beliefs* about those immediate experiences and their objects. (See note 2, above.) The significance of this difference and the problem that it poses for the foundationalist will be considered further in the text.

9. Which will depend in turn on the specific account given of how those beliefs are justified—see below. As the discussion in the text suggests, the main divergences in this area pertain to the empirical part of the foundation.

10. This assumes, of course, that an adequate foundation could not consist entirely of beliefs justified *a priori*, and you should think about whether this is correct and how it might be argued for. You should also ask yourself to what extent there are problems with the *a priori* part of the foundation that parallel those that pertain to the contingent, empirical part—and indeed whether an *a priori* part is really required at all. Some of these issues will be dealt with, at least by implication, in chapter 11.

11. See for example Donald Davidson, "A Coherence Theory of Truth and Knowledge," in *Kant oder Hegel,* ed. Dieter Henrich (Stuttgart: Klett-Cotta, 1983), pp. 423–38.

12. According to the view considered and tentatively adopted in chapter 6, these judgments are either about my sense-data or about my adverbial contents.

13. Davidson, "A Coherence Theory of Truth and Knowledge," p. 428.

14. This objection was first advanced by Wilfrid Sellars. See Sellars, "Empiricism and the Philosophy of Mind," reprinted in his *Science, Perception and Reality* (London: Routledge & Kegan Paul, 1963); and "The Structure of Knowledge," his Matchette lectures at the University of Texas, in *Action, Knowledge, and Reality,* ed. Hector-Neri Castañeda (Indianapolis, Ind.: Bobbs-Merrill, 1975), pp. 295–347, especially Lecture III. For a somewhat fuller development of it, see *SEK*, chapter 4.

15. Might such a belief be *self-evident*? Not at least in the sense that applies to *a priori* claims (see chapter 5): the contingent content of such a belief is not in itself a reason for thinking that it is true, since that content is true in some possible worlds or situations and not in others, and there is seemingly nothing else about the belief to appeal to.

16. Some of the main ones are the absolute idealist views of F. H. Bradley, Bernard Bosanquet, and Brand Blanshard; the views of some of the logical positivists, mainly Otto Neurath and a relatively early incarnation of Carl Hempel; the epistemological views of the contemporary philosophers Wilfrid Sellars, Keith Lehrer, Nicholas Rescher, and Donald Davidson; and the view held by the present author in *SEK*. The epistemological position of W. V. O. Quine, discussed in chapter 11, is also sometimes regarded as a version of coherentism, though this is much more debatable. For some discussion of some of these views and specific references, see *SEK*.

17. Who are not always coherentists, since coherence can play less central but still important roles in foundationalist views. See, for example, C. I. Lewis, *An Analysis of Knowledge and Valuation*, chapter 11 (who appeals to what he calls "congruence"); and Roderick M. Chisholm, *Theory of Knowledge*, 2nd ed. (Englewood Cliffs, N.J.: Prentice-Hall, 1977), chapter 4 (who appeals to what he calls "concurrence").

18. In thinking about this example, it is important to put aside your background knowledge that there are other black birds besides crows, as well as any justification that might be thought to result from your perception of the birds. We are concerned only with the *internal* coherence of the set of beliefs, and for that purpose anything outside that set of beliefs is irrelevant. (Thinking about this point may, however, suggest one of the main problems with the idea that coherence is the sole basis for justification.)

19. See also the discussion of coherence as it applies to the issue of testimony, in chapter 8.

20. Mainly in chapters 4 and 7.

21. In this way, the justification for induction offered in chapter 4 and the justification for belief in the external world offered in chapter 7 might each be viewed as involving an appeal to coherence.

22. See *SEK*, chapter 5 and appendix B.

23. See Bernard Bosanquet, *Implication and Linear Inference* (London: Macmillan, 1920).

24. For more development of this idea, see *SEK*, pp. 89–93.

25. There are also closely related issues concerned with introspection, which is often regarded as a kind of inner, nonsensory perception or observation, but I will not consider these explicitly here.

26. Two that at least seem to do so are Donald Davidson and Keith Lehrer. See the paper by Davidson referred to in note 11; and Keith Lehrer, *Knowledge* (Oxford: Oxford University Press, 1974).

27. Or at least its nonfoundationalist character. Such a view would not be a *pure* coherentist view, since the rationale for this further requirement is not in any clear way a product of coherence. But since the main dialectical rationale for coherentism is just the avoidance of foundationalism, this impurity does not seem to matter. For further discussion of all these matters, see *SEK*, chapters 6 and 7. (Though I should make clear that I no longer regard the view defended in that book as tenable.)

28. See the discussion in chapter 3. In fact, the adoption of coherentist views of justification constitutes the main historical motive for coherence theories of truth (though often enough the two were not very clearly distinguished).

29. This is an argument of the same general kind as the explanatory or abductive justificatory arguments that were discussed in chapters 4 and 7.

30. For a somewhat fuller but still pretty schematic version, see *SEK*, chapter 8.

31. I will assume (and indeed have been assuming all along) that the coherentist view attempts to account only for empirical justification: the justification of contingent, non-*a priori* beliefs. Since an *a priori* appeal is needed to establish some or all of the very ingredients of the concept of coherence (at least deductive inference relations and logical

consistency, but arguably inductive and abductive inference relations as well), a coheren-tist account of *a priori* justification appears to be viciously circular in a way that the sug-gested coherentist response to the general concern about circularity cannot overcome.

32. Of course, this also means that there is no independent fact that it is correct about either, which is an important qualification on the sort of infallibility in question.

33. Doubts about the possibility of such a confrontation have sometimes been ad-vanced as an additional argument against the correspondence theory of truth.

34. It is plausible to suppose that it is this sort of nonsxreflective, constituent aware-ness of the content of a conscious state that earlier epistemologists and some more recent ones have had at least primarily in mind in their use of the notions of "immediate aware-ness" or "direct acquaintance." (See the discussion in chapter 6.) But if this is right, then many discussions of immediate experience or direct acquaintance have been needlessly obscure, suggesting as they do some sort of mysteriously authoritative or infallible appre-hension of an *independent* cognitive object, rather than an awareness that is simply con-stitutive of the conscious state itself. And the occasional suggestions that one might pos-sibly be immediately aware of or directly acquainted with material objects simply make no sense on the present account of what immediate awareness amounts to. This is the fun-damental reason why, in my judgment, a defensible version of foundationalism cannot avoid the problem of the external world by including perceptual beliefs about physical ob-jects in the foundation (as the most straightforward version of direct realism in effect tries to do).

35. There is, however, one additional problem that should be mentioned. Even if the account of the foundation offered in this chapter is correct, and even if the argument from such a foundation to the justification of beliefs about the material world that was sug-gested at the end of chapter 7 can be adequately elaborated and defended, it might still be objected that at least most people in most situations fail to have access to the result-ing justification for beliefs about the material world simply because they do not in fact have the sorts of beliefs about their immediate sensory experience that are needed to pro-vide its starting point. Instead, people normally "leap" directly to beliefs about material objects and situations, without any intervening consideration of the nature of sensory ex-perience as such. Though the sensory experiences do of course still occur and indeed are causally responsible for perceptual beliefs about the material world, they are not normally themselves apprehended in conceptual terms. Think carefully about this problem, and see if you can figure out what possible responses to it there might be.

CHAPTER TEN

~

Internalism and Externalism

A second conspicuous feature of the Cartesian approach to epistemology, one that has also been the object of serious challenge in recent times, is its *internalist* character. For Descartes and those who follow his lead, as we have seen, epistemic justification or reasonableness can depend only on matters which are within the cognitive grasp of the believer in question, that is, of which he or she is or at least can be in some way justifiably aware: matters that are, as it might be put, accessible from within his or her first-person cognitive perspective. (This is a vague formulation that will need to be amplified and clarified.) Indeed, though this has sometimes been disputed, it seems plausible to say that until very recently an internalist approach was assumed without question by virtually all philosophers who paid any serious attention to epistemological issues.

But in spite of this historical consensus, many recent epistemologists have argued that the internalist requirement is fundamentally mistaken, that epistemic justification can depend in part or perhaps even entirely on matters to which the believer in question has no cognitive access at all, matters that are entirely *external* to his or her cognitive viewpoint. Thus, to take the most important externalist view, it has been held that a belief might be justified for a particular believer simply because the causal process that led to its adoption is cognitively *reliable*, that is, is a process of a general kind that in fact produces true beliefs in a high proportion of the cases in which it occurs—even if both the nature of the process and its reliability are entirely unknown and cognitively inaccessible to the believer in question.

Think very carefully about this externalist conception of justification. Having read this far in the present book, you might consider the idea that justification may result in this way from things that are external to the believer's cognitive perspective puzzling and even perhaps bizarre. How, you may want to ask, can a belief be justified for someone in virtue of a feature that he or she is entirely unaware that it possesses? Indeed, if features of a belief that are in this way external to the believer's cognitive perspective can yield justification, why not truth itself? Surely the fact that a belief is true is, in a way, the best possible reason for holding it, so that if access to the justifying feature by the believer is not required, why doesn't it simply follow that any true belief is justified simply by virtue of being true, no matter how or why it was arrived at or how irrational or careless or even crazy the person in question may have been. In fact, no externalist is willing to go this far, but in a way that merely heightens the puzzling character of the externalist view: why should some external facts and not others be relevant to justification?

The aim of the present chapter is to explore this recent controversy between internalist and externalist views of epistemic justification.[1] We will start by elaborating and clarifying the basic idea of internalism, and then proceed to consider, first, externalist objections to internalism, second, a leading example of an externalist view (the *reliabilist* view just briefly adumbrated), and, third, some major objections to externalism. This will put us in a better position to understand what is really at stake between the opposing views and to attempt on that basis to arrive at a tentative resolution of the issue.

What Is Internalism?

The fundamental claim of internalism, as already noticed several times above, is that epistemological issues arise and must be dealt with from within the individual person's first-person cognitive perspective, appealing only to things that are accessible to that individual from that standpoint. The basic rationale is that what justifies a person's beliefs must be something that is available or accessible to him or her, that something to which I have no access cannot give *me* a reason for thinking that one of my beliefs is true (though it might conceivably provide such a reason for another person viewing me from the outside). But there are some possible misunderstandings of this basic idea that need to be guarded against.

First, although the general Cartesian point of view that we have largely followed in this book holds that what is available in a person's first-person cognitive perspective is initially limited to (i) facts about the contents of his or her conscious mental states, together with (ii) facts or truths that are self-evident on an *a priori* basis, this rather severe limitation is not mandated by internalism as such. Thus, to take the most important alternative possibility, *if* it were possible to defend a version of direct realism[2] according to which perceptual beliefs about material objects are directly justified without the need for any inference from the content of sensory experience, then the facts about the physical world apprehended in this way would also be directly accessible from the first-person cognitive perspective and would thereby constitute part of the basis for internalist justifications. I am doubtful, for reasons indicated briefly in the earlier discussion, that any view yielding this result can in fact be successfully defended, but that is a separate issue.

Second, the basic internalist requirement is sometimes misconstrued as saying that justification must depend only on the believer's *internal* states, that is, on states that are, from a metaphysical standpoint, properties or features of that individual person. This would make it easy to understand why facts about the contents of conscious mental states can contribute to internalist justification, but would make it puzzling why facts pertaining to other sorts of internal states, such as dispositional or unconscious mental states or even states that are purely physical or physiological in nature, cannot do so as well. And it would be even more puzzling why self-evident truths that have nothing specifically to do with the individual person and his or her internal states (for example, truths of logic and mathematics) are also supposed to be acceptable as part of the basis for internalist justification.[3] But in fact this understanding of the internalist requirement is simply mistaken. As already briefly indicated, the "internal" of internalism refers to what is internal to the person's first-person cognitive perspective in the sense of being accessible from that perspective, *not* necessarily to what is internal in the sense of being metaphysically a state or feature of that person. Thus the contents of conscious mental states satisfy the internalist requirement, not simply because they are features of internal states of the person, but rather because those contents are arguably (see chapter 9) accessible in the right way. And if self-evident *a priori* knowable truths are also accessible from the first-person cognitive perspective (as both moderate empiricists and rationalists hold), then those truths are equally acceptable as part of the basis for internalist justification.

Third, the internalist need not deny that facts of other sorts can also come to be accessible in the required way from the first-person cognitive perspective. Thus, for example, if the reliability of certain sorts of testimony can be cogently established by reasoning that begins from what is initially available there, perhaps along the lines discussed in chapter 8, then the supposed facts reflected in such testimony become *indirectly* available as a basis for internalist justification. The internalist's insistence is only that such indirect availability must be grounded in reasons or arguments that begin from what is directly available—that is, available initially, before such further reasons or arguments are invoked.

Fourth, and most fundamentally of all, what is available from the first-person cognitive perspective must provide a complete *reason* for thinking that the belief in question is *true*, and whatever is needed to fully grasp this reason must be included in what is accessible. Thus, for example, to have internal access to some fact that could provide the basis for a justifying reason without also having access to whatever logical or inferential connection that reason also depends on is not to have full internal access to the reason in question.

Arguments against Internalism

But, as already noted, there are many recent epistemologists who reject internalism in favor of externalism. What reasons or arguments do they give? Though others have sometimes been suggested, by far the most important and widely advocated objections to internalism are the following two.

First, there is the claim that the internalist cannot give an intuitively acceptable account of the cognitive or epistemic condition of *unsophisticated epistemic subjects*: higher animals, young children, and even relatively unsophisticated adults. Take higher animals first, as perhaps the clearest case.[4] I own a five-year-old German shepherd dog named Emma. Emma is, judging from her behavior, a remarkably intelligent dog. She understands a wide range of commands, seems to exhibit an excellent memory for people and places (even those that she has not encountered for a long time), and can be amazingly subtle and persistent in communicating her desires and preferences and in responding to novel situations. Anyone who observed her very closely would, I think, find it impossible to deny that Emma has conscious beliefs and desires, together with other conscious mental states such as excitement or fear. But does Emma have any *reasons* or *justification* for her beliefs? Does she have any *knowledge*?

No one viewing Emma from the outside can, I would suggest, be entirely sure of the answer to this question. But despite her intelligence, it is hard to believe that Emma engages in very much or indeed any *reasoning*, and still harder to believe that she is capable of understanding complicated arguments. Indeed, it is doubtful whether Emma can even understand the basic idea of having a reason for a belief, an understanding that seems to be required for her to have fully explicit access to any reasons at all. Thus it is hard to avoid the conclusion that Emma has no justified beliefs and hence no knowledge, a result that is alleged by the proponent of this first objection to be highly implausible. Surely, it is argued, Emma is justified in believing and, perhaps even more clearly, knows such things as that there is a squirrel on the other side of the quad (as she skulks carefully toward it, freezing if it should happen to look in her direction) or that the person at the front door is her good friend Marc (as her initial hostile barking at the person's approach gives way to yelping and jumping with excitement and joy). (Think about this issue for yourself, using whatever dogs or cats or other higher animals you have known as examples. Is the objection right about *both* of the points in question: (a) that animals like Emma have no access to internalist reasons or justification; and (b) that they undeniably do have justified beliefs and knowledge?)

This objection to internalism, already at least reasonably compelling in relation to creatures like Emma, seems perhaps even more forceful when applied to relatively young children and to unsophisticated or cognitively limited adults. Surely, it is argued, no one in either of these categories is really able to understand complicated arguments of the sort, for example, that we have seen to be apparently required to arrive at a good reason for accepting an inductive conclusion or one about the external material world (assuming that direct realism doesn't work). (Indeed, most fully mature and capable adults have not in fact encountered such arguments or formulated them for themselves, making it hard to see how an internalist can consistently say that even the beliefs of these individuals about such matters are justified or constitute knowledge.) But surely, it is alleged, it is much more obvious that some or all of these various kinds of relatively unsophisticated individuals (and surely the mature and capable adults) do have justified beliefs and do have knowledge of the sorts in question than it is that internalism is true. And thus if internalism yields such implausible results, it should be rejected.

Second, while the first objection in effect concedes, for the sake of the argument, that successful internalist justifications for inductive beliefs or beliefs about the external world or other beliefs that common sense regards as justified can be in fact found, denying only that these are accessible to unsophisticated subjects (and possibly even to most mature and capable ones), the second objection argues that is it is in fact far from obvious that *any* acceptable internalist justification, whether generally accessible or not, can be found for many of these beliefs. This is a point that any reflective reader of this book should be able to appreciate. From an internalist perspective, it is at least possible—and perhaps even, as many would argue, likely—that no adequate justification for many or perhaps even most of our beliefs can be found, in which case no one would have justification or knowledge concerning the matters in question if internalism is correct. But this is again, it is alleged, an extremely implausible and intuitively unacceptable result, making the internalist view that leads to it equally unacceptable.

It is obvious that these two arguments are closely related and similar in their basic thrust. One way to put them together would be to argue that if internalism is correct, only at best a few epistemologists and students of epistemology will have access to good reasons for the vast majority of the beliefs that common sense regards as justified and as constituting knowledge (see again the list in chapter 1). But this once again seems extremely implausible, and so, it is claimed, internalism must be mistaken.

The problems that these arguments point to are real, and there is no very simple and straightforward reply available to them from an internalist perspective. Here, as so often in philosophy, we will have to see what the alternative view looks like before we will be in a position to decide how the two views really stack up against each other. But there is one issue worth raising at this point for you to think about as we proceed, and that is what the commonsense intuitions with which internalism is allegedly in conflict really amount to. Is the commonsense view merely that ordinary people or children or beings like Emma have *knowledge* and *justification* in some sense or other in relation to the beliefs in question—in which case, the accounts of justification or knowledge offered by the externalist (which we have so far indicated in only the sketchiest way) might prove to satisfy those intuitions? Or is the content of the relevant intuitions not rather that the beings in question do have knowledge and justification in just the specific sense that the internalist advocates: that they have true beliefs which they have good reasons for thinking to be true?—in which case showing that the beliefs in question are justified in an externalist sense wouldn't really help to avoid a conflict with those intuitions.[5]

A Leading Version of Externalism: Reliabilism

It is time to look more closely at a specific externalist view. Though many different such views have been proposed, we will focus here on the one that has been perhaps the most widely discussed and advocated, namely *reliabilism*.[6] Reliabilism has been mainly advocated as a view concerning the nature of epistemic justification, and it is in that form that we will consider it here.[7]

The central idea of reliabilism, as already briefly noted earlier, is that what makes a belief justified is the cognitive *reliability* of the causal process via which it was produced,[8] that is, the fact that the process in question leads to a high proportion of true beliefs, with the *degree* of justification depending on the degree of reliability. If the belief-producing process is reliable in this way, then (other things being equal) it will be objectively likely or probable to the same degree that the particular belief in question, having been produced in that way, is itself true. But what makes the view a version of externalism is that, as we have seen, reliabilism does *not* require that the believer in question have any sort of cognitive access to the fact that the belief-producing process is in this way reliable in order for his or her belief to be justified. All that matters for justification is that the process in question in fact be reliable, whether or not the person believes or has even the slightest inkling that this is so or the slightest understanding of what specific sort of process is involved.

The clearest and most plausible illustrations of reliabilism involve belief-producing processes like sensory perception. Thus suppose that a particular individual is so constituted, as a result of natural endowment and various sorts of previous training and experience, that a very high proportion of his or her visually induced beliefs about large-scale material objects (tables, trees, buildings, automobiles, etc.) and processes in his or her immediate vicinity under favorable conditions of perception are true. If this is so, then, according to the most straightforward version of reliabilism, those beliefs are justified.[9] The individual in question need have no belief or any other sort of awareness that the visual process in question is reliable, nor indeed any very specific conception of what it involves. Neither he nor she nor for that matter anyone else need have any very direct or easy access to the fact of reliability should the issue somehow be explicitly raised. All that matters is that the actual causal process via which such beliefs are generated is in fact, under those conditions about that sort of subject matter, highly reliable, whether or not *anyone* is aware of this at the time in question or indeed ever. And this is obviously a condition that might be satisfied by any of the unsophisticated cognitive subjects considered earlier: by unsophisticated adults, by young children, or by animals like Emma. When Emma comes to believe that there is a squirrel across the quad, then if her eyes are functioning in such a way that this reliability condition is satisfied (under the relevant conditions of lighting, etc.), then her belief is, according to the reliabilist, justified.[10]

The reliabilist's reliable belief-producing processes are not limited, however, to processes like sensory perception in which no prior beliefs or other cognitive states are involved in any very obvious way. For example, if the process of logical or probabilistic inference from other justified beliefs is also a reliable belief-producing process, then the beliefs that are produced by this process will also count as justified according to the reliabilist account. Here too, however, what matters is reliability itself and not any awareness on the part of the subject that the process is reliable nor any understanding of why a belief arrived at in this way genuinely follows from the relevant premises. Thus if Emma makes reliable transitions of this sort with no clear or explicit awareness of why or how she is doing so, her resulting beliefs would still count as justified. Of course, it *might* turn out that a more specific process that involves explicit and critical reflection on the logical relations and principles involved is even more reliable, in which case beliefs that result from a process of this more specific sort would be even more highly justified.

For the simplest versions of reliabilism, the account given so far is essentially the entire story. But it is also possible to have a more complicated versions of reliabilism, still fundamentally externalist in character, that add further qualifications of various sorts to ward off potential objections. The rationale for these will emerge as we consider the objections that have been raised against reliabilist views.

Objections to Reliabilism

Does reliabilism provide an acceptable account of epistemic justification, one that can replace the internalist view and thereby avoid the objections to internalism discussed earlier? In this section, I will consider three main sorts of objection that have been offered in relation to reliabilist views specifically. With only minor modification, at least the first two of these also apply to the other leading versions of externalism, but only the versions that apply to reliabilism will be explicitly considered. The first two objections question, on broadly intuitive grounds, whether the satisfaction of the reliabilist condition is (i) necessary or (ii) sufficient for the justification of a belief, while the third pertains to a difficult problem that arises within the reliabilist position.

The first objection challenges whether the satisfaction of the reliabilist condition is *necessary* for beliefs to be justified, that is, whether *only* beliefs that satisfy that condition are justified—as would have to be the case if reliabilism was successful in providing a complete account of epistemic justification.[11] Imagine a group of people who live in a world controlled by a Cartesian evil genius of the sort discussed earlier in chapter 2. The evil genius carefully controls their sensory and introspective experience, producing in them just the experiences they would have if they inhabited a particular material world, perhaps one exactly like our own, containing various specific sorts of objects and processes that interact and influence each other in a lawful way. The people in this position are, we may suppose, careful and thorough investigators. They accumulate large quantities of sensory evidence, formulate hypotheses and theories, subject their beliefs to careful experimental and observational tests, etc. Perhaps they even formulate philosophical arguments of the sorts considered earlier in this book for the likely truth of their resulting beliefs.

Are the beliefs about their apparent world that the people in such a Cartesian demon world arrive at in these ways *justified*? (Stop here and think about this issue.) From an intuitive standpoint, it seems hard (doesn't it?) to deny that they are. After all, their epistemic situation may, from their standpoint, well be entirely indiscernible from or even superior to our own. But in fact, because of the pervasive influence of the evil genius, the cognitive processes that produce their beliefs are in fact at least mostly unreliable: their perceptions and observations produce beliefs that are mostly or entirely false, and even if their further reasoning is impeccable, it begins with these false premises and so does not lead to reliable results. Thus the reliabilist apparently must say that his or her beliefs are in fact largely or entirely unjustified, a result that seems intuitively quite implausible.[12]

How do reliabilists respond to this objection? Some simply dig in their heels, "bite the bullet," and insist that this is the correct result and that the intuitive impression to the contrary is somehow confused or misleading. Others, however, have found this too much to accept and have instead proposed modifications to the reliabilist view that are aimed at avoiding it. Perhaps the most interesting of these is the suggestion that the reliability of a cognitive process, in the sense relevant to justification, should be assessed, not necessarily in the world that the believer whose beliefs are being considered in fact inhabits, but rather in "normal" possible worlds—that is, in possible worlds that *actually* have the features that our world is commonsensically believed to have. Thus if the cognitive processes employed by the victims of the evil genius would be reliable in a world of the sort that we believe ourselves to inhabit (one that thus, among other things, contains no evil genius), then those processes count as reliable in the relevant sense. And if reliability is understood in this way, then the reliabilist can agree that the beliefs of the people in the evil genius world are justified.[13] (This is a tricky view, and you will have to think about it carefully.)

How successful is this response? It avoids the objection in question, but only, it might be thought, at the price of rendering the reliabilist position seriously *ad hoc*. It is clear enough why *genuine* reliability should be thought to be cognitively valuable, whether or not it is the right basis for justification: beliefs that are arrived at in a genuinely reliable way are thereby objectively likely to be true. But why should we value what might be referred to as "normal reliability," whether or not it is correlated with genuine reliability? After all, beliefs that result from processes that possess normal reliability are not, on that basis alone, to any degree likely to be true.

The second objection is in a way the complement of the first. Instead of imagining a situation in which the cognitive processes that we take to be reliable are in fact unreliable, it imagines one in which there is a cognitive process that is in fact highly reliable, but which we have no reason to regard as reliable and perhaps good reasons to regard as unreliable. Thus suppose that *clairvoyance*, the alleged cognitive ability to have knowledge of distant occurrences in a way that does not depend on sensory perception or other commonsensical cognitive processes, does in fact genuinely occur and involves a process of some unknown sort that is in fact highly reliable for certain specific people under certain specific conditions (which might include a limitation to a certain range of subject matter). And suppose that some person who in fact has this ability arrives at a belief on this basis and that the requisite conditions for reliability, whatever they may be, are satisfied. Such a belief seems to satisfy the reliabilist requirement for justification, but is it in fact genuinely justified?[14]

There are several different possible cases here, depending on what else is true of the person in question. Such a person might (a) have no belief or opinion at all about the cognitive process involved or its reliability, or (b) believe, though without justification, that the belief results from a reliable process, of which he or she may or may not have any very specific conception, or (c) possess good reasons or evidence of an internalist sort that the belief in question is false, or (d) possess good reasons or evidence of an internalist sort that the process in question is *not* reliable, again with or without a specific conception of its character.[15] (If he or she possesses good reasons of an internalist sort that the process *is* reliable, that would of course provide a basis for an *internalist* justification.) All of these possibilities are worth thinking about (and you should try to imagine specific examples of each of them); but it is the first that seems most favorable to the externalist. It is hard to see how a further belief about the process that is itself unjustified can contribute to the justification of the initial belief; and it seems obvious that a belief that is held in the face of contrary reasons pertaining either to its subject matter or in the way in which it was arrived at is more suspect as regards its justification.

Imagine, then, a specific case of sort (a). Suppose that a certain person, Norman, is in fact a reliable clairvoyant with respect to the geographical whereabouts of the president of the United States.[16] He frequently has spontaneous beliefs or hunches, which he accepts without question, concerning the location of the president on a particular day, and in fact these are always correct. But Norman pays very little attention to news reports and other sorts of information about the president and his or her whereabouts and has never made any effort to check his hunches independently. Nor does he have any real conception of how such hunches might work or any general views about the reliability of such a process. Clearly (or at least pretty clearly—see the next objection) Norman's beliefs resulting from his spontaneous clairvoyant hunches satisfy the reliabilist's requirements for justification, but are they really justified? Or, or the contrary, doesn't it seem as though Norman is being thoroughly irrational and so is not justified in confidently accepting beliefs on this sort of basis? (Think about this question on your own. One way to develop the issue further is to ask whether Norman would be justified in *acting* on one of these beliefs if an urgent occasion should arise: perhaps someone is trying to contact the president on an urgent matter and asks Norman if he knows where to find him.)

Here again some externalists simply dig in their heels and insist that Norman's clairvoyant beliefs are justified, dismissing intuitions to the contrary as misguided. But others respond to this sort of case (and to other cases of the sorts enumerated earlier) by imposing a further requirement that amounts to a significant qualification on the reliabilist position: roughly that the believer not have immediate access to good reasons of an internalist sort for questioning either the specific belief in question or his or her own general ability to arrive at such beliefs in the way in question.[17] The way that this applies to Norman is that arguably he should have been suspicious of his beliefs about the president's whereabouts, given that he has no reason to think that he has any sort of reliable cognitive access to such information and given that people in general do not apparently possess the ability to arrive at reliable beliefs in such a way.

There are two questions that need to be asked about this response. One is whether it is possible to interpret it in such a way as to handle the Norman case without also creating an analogous problem for the reliably caused beliefs, for example those resulting from visual perception, that the reliabilist does want to say are justified on that basis alone. *If* our only justification for visual beliefs is of the externalist sort (something that the internalist will of course deny), shouldn't we be equally suspicious of them? If not, why not? The second question is whether it is possible to find a clear rationale for such a further requirement that is compatible with externalism. Why should internalist reasons be relevant in this negative way if they are not required for justification in general? I cannot pursue these questions further here, but you should think about them for yourself.

The third objection, known as *the generality problem*, pertains to the very formulation of the reliabilist position. What the reliabilist says, as we have seen, is that a belief is justified if the *general* sort of cognitive process from which it results is reliable in the way indicated. But at what *level of generality* should the relevant process be characterized? Consider my present visually induced belief that there is a white cup sitting on my computer table, and consider some of the different ways in which the cognitive process from which it results might be described (assuming as a part of all of these that my eyes are functioning normally): as the visual perception of a cup under good lighting at close range, as the visual perception of a cup (allowing for varied conditions and distances), as the visual perception of a "medium-sized physical object," as visual perception in general (including the perception of much larger and smaller objects), or just as sense perception in general (and this is only a small sampling of a much larger range of possibilities). Which of these descriptions of the cognitive process in question is the relevant one for applying the reliabilist's principle of justification?

What makes this question into a serious problem for the reliabilist is the fact that the proportion of true beliefs that is produced by the processes specified in these various ways seems to vary widely: I am much less likely to make a mistake about a cup that is perceived at close range under good conditions than I am about objects of visual perception or sense perception in general. Indeed, it seems, on the one hand, possible to specify the process in such fine detail as to make the description fit only this single case, so that the process thus described would be either 100 percent reliable (if the belief is true) or 100 percent unreliable (if the belief is false). And it also seems possible, on the other hand, to specify the process so broadly, including perceptions of objects that are much harder to identify and perceptions under very poor conditions, so as to result in a very low degree of reliability. But which of these widely varying characterizations of the process and corresponding degrees of reliability is the right one, according to the reliabilist view, for assessing the justification of this particular belief?

Without some way of answering this question in a specific and nonarbitrary way, the reliabilist has not offered a definite position at all, but only a general schema that there is apparently no way to make more definite. Certainly some ways of specifying the relevant process are more natural than others; but the epistemological relevance of such naturalness is questionable, and even these more natural specifications are numerous enough to have significantly differing degrees of reliability. Though reliabilists have struggled with this problem, no clearly satisfactory solution has yet been found.[18]

Of these three objections, it is the third objection that is the most immediately serious, since it in effect challenges the very existence of a definite reliabilist position. One externalist response to this problem has been the development of other externalist positions, positions that on the surface at least seem to avoid this issue—though it is open to question whether it does not still lurk beneath the surface. An adequate consideration of these other externalist views cannot be attempted here, but you may want to investigate some of them on your own.[19]

Internalism versus Externalism: A Tentative Assessment

The issue between internalism and externalism is very much alive in current epistemological discussion. One thing that makes it difficult to resolve is that if we set aside the generality problem (on the grounds that it may perhaps be solved or avoided by adopting a different version of externalism), the arguments and objections on both sides are fundamentally intuitive in character, and reasonable people may differ with regard to both the genuineness and especially the weight of the intuitions involved. In this concluding section, I will try to sort through the competing considerations and suggest a resolution of sorts. But I want to emphasize in advance that it is presented here *only* as a suggestion, one that would at best take a lot more reflection and argument to defend and that you will thus have to evaluate for yourselves by thinking carefully about all of the strands of this complicated issue.

We may begin by asking whether it is really as clear as we have in effect been assuming (and as those on opposite sides of this issue typically assume as well) that the internalist and the externalist views of justification are incompatible in a way that means that one must be right and the other wrong. Some philosophers have in fact suggested that perhaps there are instead two (or perhaps even more) different conceptions of knowledge or justification, one (or more) of them internalist and one (or more) of them externalist: conceptions that simply address different issues and serve different purposes, and that are thus not in any meaningful sense competitors between which a choice must be made.[20]

This is a possibility that it is not easy to assess, but that surely has at least some initial plausibility. We have already seen (in chapter 3) how difficult it is to arrive at a clear and univocal account of the concept of knowledge (or of the uses of the terms "know" and "knowledge"). Thus the idea that there might simply be different conceptions, varying among each other in several different dimensions of which the internal-external distinction might turn out to be one, cannot be easily dismissed. The situation as regards the concept of justification is somewhat different, in that justification is to some extent a technical concept within epistemology, albeit one that connects with more ordinary concepts such as reasons and rationality. But this makes it if anything even more plausible to suppose that there might simply be different concepts of justification, or at least of something that plays the same general role, which do not compete with each other in any very direct way.

Moreover, it seems clear on reflection that there are genuine epistemological issues for which an externalist approach is entirely reasonable and appropriate. For example, it might be important to ask whether one or another of a range of alternative methods of organizing and structuring scientific research is more likely to succeed in finding the truth in a given area, and it would be reasonable to investigate this issue by studying many cases of research organized in the various ways in question and seeing how frequently and how readily cognitive success is attained. Such an investigation would be naturally conducted from a *third-person* perspective, looking at the people employing the various methods from the outside and assessing their success from that perspective.[21] And if someone should choose to formulate the results of such an investigation by saying that the more successful methods and the beliefs that they lead to are more *justified* in what would be essentially a reliabilist sense, it is hard to see why anyone would want to object. Thus there is room in epistemology for the sorts of investigations whose results could be formulated (though this hardly seems essential) by using an externalist conception of justification (or perhaps instead of knowledge).

None of this has, however, any tendency to show that the internalist conception of justification and its correlative conception of knowledge are not equally legitimate in their own way. As we have already noticed above, the internalist approach pertains to epistemological issues that are raised from what is essentially a *first-person* rather than a third-person perspective, that is, to the situation where I ask what reasons I have for thinking that my own beliefs, rather than someone else's, are true.

It is worth noticing that even first-person questions can sometimes be usefully dealt with in a partially third-person way. If the epistemic issue I am concerned with pertains only to a narrow range of my beliefs, for example, to my memory beliefs concerning previous alleged episodes of sensory perception, then it might be appropriate to take advantage of third-person psychological studies of the ways in which various identifiable features of such beliefs are correlated with their accuracy or inaccuracy.[22] The point is that if only the beliefs in that limited range are under scrutiny, then I am free to appeal to other beliefs that I may have about such things as the reliability of such studies, the very existence of the studies (given the written reports), the existence of other people and of the written reports themselves, and so on, without worrying about whether and how these beliefs can themselves be justified.

But if the scope of the first-person inquiry is expanded, and I ask the global question of whether I have good reasons for thinking that *any* of my beliefs are true, such an appeal to third-person investigations is no longer available without begging the essential question. In this situation, as we have seen, I can only appeal initially to things that are directly or immediately known or justified for me, justified in a way that does not rely on other beliefs that are themselves in question—which is, of course, precisely the situation in which Descartes found himself. As noticed above, this in no way precludes my justifying the use of further cognitive resources by arguments that begin from what is immediately available: thus, for example, if the existence of other minds and the reliability of testimony apparently emanating from them can be established in a non-question-begging way on the basis of the more my foundational beliefs, then justification that relies on testimony would become available from the first-person cognitive perspective. But the merely external fact that, for example, testimony of a particular sort is reliable is simply not relevant by itself to the global first-person epistemological issue and can play no role in resolving it.

It has sometimes been argued that there is something misconceived or illegitimate about the global first-person epistemological issue that in this way seems to clearly demand an internalist conception of justification, but it is hard to find any very compelling argument for such a claim. Perhaps it is true, as the externalist alleges, that in the internalist sense of justification, the beliefs of animals, young children, and unsophisticated adults turn out not to be justified—though it could still perhaps be argued that some or all of these epistemic subjects have a tacit or implicit grasp of the relevant reasons and thus are justified in a weaker but still significant sense in at least many of their beliefs.[23] But supposing that the externalist is right about this conclusion, it is then simply a philosophical result to be respected, like any other, and not one that is altered in any real way by pointing out that such subjects may at the same time be justified in a quite different, externalist sense. Similarly, if it should turn out that, as alleged by many externalists, the internalist epistemological project leads finally to a largely skeptical result, this would again be a philosophical result that would have to be accepted, and that would not in any significant way be altered by adding that many of the beliefs in question are still justified— or rather, as we shall see shortly, *may* be justified—in a different, externalist sense.

Such a skeptical conclusion is admittedly very hard to accept from an intuitive, commonsense perspective. But this, I believe, is a reason (whose strength is not easy to assess) for thinking that the externalist must be wrong about the skeptical implications of internalism, not a reason for adopting a quite different conception of justification and knowledge. My suggestion would be that the commonsense intuition in question is not to be understood as holding merely that our beliefs are justified and constitute knowledge in some largely unspecified senses (which might then turn out to be the externalist ones)—or, still less, that it is an intuition about specifically externalist justification and knowledge (of which common sense seems to have little or no inkling). Instead, I submit, the commonsense intuition in question is precisely that we do after all have *good reasons* in our possession for thinking that our various beliefs are true, that is, that those beliefs are justified in precisely the sense upon which the internalist insists—even if we have a surprising amount of difficulty articulating explicitly just how this is so. And if this is what the relevant intuition really says, then an appeal to externalist senses of justification and knowledge are simply irrelevant and can do nothing at all, possible obfuscation aside, to accommodate that intuition or to avoid unpalatable skeptical results. (But whether I am right about this is a very difficult issue, one which you should consider carefully for yourselves. What do the intuitions in question really amount to?)

Finally, even if it is the case that the internalist and externalist conceptions of justification and knowledge are each legitimate and valuable in their own spheres, as defined by the rather different epistemological issues toward which they are aimed, it remains true that the internalist approach possesses a fundamental kind of priority. No matter how much work may be done in delineating externalist conceptions of knowledge or justification or reliability and in investigating how those apply to various kinds of beliefs or areas of investigation, there is a way in which all such results are merely hypothetical and insecure as long as they cannot be arrived at from the resources available within a first-person epistemic perspective. If, for example, an epistemologist claims that a certain belief or set of beliefs, whether his or her own or someone else's, has been arrived at in a reliable way, but says this on the basis of cognitive processes of his or her own whose reliability is at best an external fact to which he or she has no first-person access, then the proper conclusion is merely that the belief or beliefs originally in question are reliably arrived at (and perhaps thereby are justified or constitute knowledge in externalist senses) *if* the epistemologist's own cognitive processes are in fact reliable in the way that he or she no doubt believes them to be. But the only apparent way to arrive at a result that is not ultimately hypothetical in this way is for the reliability of at least some cognitive processes to be establish-able on the basis of what the epistemologist can know directly or immedi-ately from his or her first-person epistemic perspective. If this cannot be done (as the externalist in effect claims that it cannot), then the proper result is only that our beliefs *may* be justified (in the externalist sense) *if* in fact they are reliably arrived at, but that we have no reason at all to think that this is so. And this is itself, I suggest, a very powerful and commonsensically un-palatable version of skepticism—one that is quite unavoidable from an ex-clusively externalist standpoint. In this way, I suggest, the claim that exter-nalism makes it possible to avoid skepticism, on which the main arguments for externalism are based, turns out to be largely empty; and internalism re-mains the only viable approach to the deepest and most important episte-mological issues.

Notes

1. There are also externalist accounts of *knowledge* that simply replace the justification condition with their chosen externalist condition, making no claim to be giving an ac-count of justification. These views face at least some of the same problems, but they will not be explicitly considered here.

2. See chapter 7 and the brief discussion in endnote 34 of chapter 9.

3. For one expression of this puzzlement, see Alvin Goldman, "Internalism Exposed," *Journal of Philosophy*, vol. 96 (1999), pp. 282–83.

4. How much of this would also apply to lower animals, to such creatures as crabs, bee-tles, starfish, or earthworms, is a more difficult issue, one that I will leave to your consid-eration.

5. There is also one other moderately important argument that we are not yet in a po-sition to consider very adequately: the argument that externalism is to be preferred be-cause it fits better with a *naturalistic* approach to epistemology: very roughly, an approach that views epistemology (and philosophy generally) as continuous with and similar in na-ture to natural science. The whole idea of naturalistic epistemology will be the subject of chapter 11.

6. The leading advocate of reliabilism is Alvin Goldman. See especially his book *Epis-temology and Cognition* (Cambridge, Mass.: Harvard University Press, 1986), part one. Other leading externalist views are those of Robert Nozick and Alvin Plantinga. See Noz-ick, *Philosophical Explanations* (Cambridge, Mass.: Harvard University Press, 1981), chap-ter 3; and Plantinga, *Warrant: and Proper Function* (New York: Oxford University Press, 1993). These books are only a small sampling from a much larger literature.

7. The alternative, also sometimes advocated, would be the view that reliability, in the sense indicated in the text, is the correct requirement for knowledge in addition to belief and truth and perhaps an anti-Gettier condition, so that reliability would replace justifi-cation rather than providing an account of what justification amounts to.

8. Or perhaps the process responsible for its currently being held, since a belief might be arrived at via one process and continue to be held later because it is causally supported by a different process. But I will not bother with this refinement in the text.

9. We will look at more qualified versions later.

10. And if the degree of reliability is high enough, and the belief is true, and there are no Gettier-type problems, then Emma has knowledge.

11. This is a claim that reliabilists typically make, though it would be possible to have a quasi-reliabilist view that held that reliability was sufficient but not necessary for justification, perhaps conceding that an internalist justification could also be sufficient.

12. I am assuming here, in order to make the issue clearer, that the evil genius cannot deceive them about the contents of their own mental states or about genuinely self-evident truths.

13. See Goldman, *Epistemology and Cognition*, pp. 107, 113, for this response to the evil genius case. Goldman has since abandoned this attempted response. See his papers "Strong and Weak Justification," reprinted in Goldman, *Liaisons* (Cambridge, Mass.: MIT Press, 1992), pp. 135–37, and "Epistemic Folkways and Scientific Epistemology," reprinted in Goldman, *Liaisons*, pp. 155–75.

14. For a more extended discussion of this kind of objection to externalism, see *SEK*, chapter 3.

15. See *SEK*, chapter. 3, for more extended discussion of these possibilities.

16. The Norman case was originally presented in *SEK*, ch. 3.

17. For an example of what seems to me to amount to such a requirement, albeit not formulated in quite this way, see Alvin Goldman, "What Is Justified Belief?" reprinted in *Liaisons*, pp. 121–23.

18. The generality problem was originally formulated by Richard Feldman in his paper "Reliability and Justification," *Monist*, vol. 68 (1985), pp. 235–56. For a thorough exploration of the various solutions that have been proposed, see Earl Conee and Richard Feldman, "The Generality Problem for Reliabilism," *Philosophical Studies*, vol. 89 (1998), pp. 1–29.

19. See especially the views of Alvin Plantinga and Robert Nozick, in the works cited in note 6, above.

20. For versions of such a view with regard to knowledge, see J. L. Mackie, *Problems from Locke* (Oxford: Oxford University Press, 1976), pp. 217–20; and Ernest Sosa, *Knowledge in Perspective* (Cambridge: Cambridge University Press, 1991), p. 240 (and elsewhere in that book).

21. Such an investigation would be a contribution to what Philip Kitcher has described as "the meliorative epistemological project." See his paper "The Naturalists Return," *Philosophical Review*, vol. 101 (1992), pp. 53–114, and the discussion in the next chapter.

22. For a discussion of a study of this kind and of its epistemological relevance, see Goldman, "Internalism Exposed," pp. 290–92.

23. See *SEK*, chapter 3, for some discussion of this response.

CHAPTER ELEVEN

~

Quine and Naturalized Epistemology

A third and even more radical challenge to the Cartesian conception of epistemology is provided by the view that epistemology should be *naturalized*: that is, very roughly, should be transformed into or replaced by a discipline that is continuous with or perhaps even a subdiscipline of the natural science of psychology. In the most extreme versions at least, this would mean that the *normative* or *evaluative* issue of whether we have good reasons or justification for our beliefs would be simply replaced by the *empirical* issue of how those beliefs are causally generated, though others who still regard themselves as naturalized epistemologists have been unwilling to go this far.[1]

In this chapter, we will examine the idea of naturalized epistemology and some of the central arguments that have been advanced in support of it, together of course with problems and objections. Since the basic conception turns out to be rather elusive, I will begin with a close look at the account offered by the philosopher who was the earliest advocate of the view (and who first used and popularlized the term), the American logician and epistemologist Willard van Orman Quine. Next we will consider two central elements of naturalized epistemology, as identified by one of its leading recent proponents. In light of all this, I will suggest that while the idea of naturalized epistemology reflects some genuine insights and concerns, albeit fairly modest ones, there is no clear and defensible sense in which epistemology either can or needs to be naturalized. Indeed, as I will try to show, a thoroughgoing naturalized epistemology is ultimately self-destructive.

Quine on Naturalized Epistemology

What then is naturalized epistemology? In his paper "Epistemology Natural-ized,"[2] Quine argues that epistemology ("or something like it") should be transformed into "a chapter of psychology," more specifically into an empir-ical study of the relation between scientifically described sensory input ("a certain experimentally controlled input—certain patterns of irradiation in assorted frequencies, for instance") and the resulting cognitive output (con-sisting of "a description of the three-dimensional external world and its his-tory") [EN 83]. The result of this study would presumably be a set of empiri-cal generalizations specifying what sorts of claims or beliefs about the world result from various kinds of sensory input and how variations in that input produce variations in this result. But in Quine's view, apparently, the issue of whether and in what way the resulting claims or beliefs are *justified* would simply not be raised. His claim, in first approximation, is that while such a naturalized epistemology admittedly falls short of achieving the goals of tra-ditional epistemology, it goes as far in that direction as turns out to be possi-ble, and far enough to constitute a reasonable, albeit less ambitious substi-tute. (Stop and think right now about the nature and plausibility of this proposal. Can you see what sort of study Quine has in mind and what some of its results might be? More importantly, can you see any reason for regard-ing such a study as a version of or a reasonable replacement for more tradi-tional sorts of epistemological investigation like those reflected in the previ-ous chapters of this book? Is there any real continuity between the two studies, or is Quine simply proposing to change the subject in a radical and arbitrary way?)

The rationale offered by Quine for transforming epistemology in this way is basically that the more traditional approach to epistemology has failed more or less irredeemably and hence must be replaced by a more viable sub-stitute. As Quine develops it, however, the rationale for this conclusion turns out to depend on a rather narrow conception of traditional epistemology, roughly that put forward by the versions of empiricism that began with Hume and culminated in logical positivism.[3] According to this conception, episte-mology, at least insofar as it is concerned with knowledge of the physical world, involves two correlative goals: first, to explain the relevant concepts, for example, the concept of a physical body, in sensory terms (what Quine refers to as "the conceptual side of epistemology"); and, second, on the basis of this explanation, to arrive at a justification of claims about the physical world on the basis of sense experience (what Quine refers to as "the doctri-nal side of epistemology") [EN 71]. (In fact, as you should recognize, these are essentially the goals of the version of phenomenalism that attempts to translate physical object claims into sensory or phenomenal terms [see chapter 7].)

According to Quine, it has become clear, after a long struggle, that neither of these goals can be achieved. The attempt to define physical or material concepts in phenomenal terms fails to yield genuine translations, though Quine's reasons for this conclusion are rather different from and more technical than those considered earlier in this book. And since the attempt to justify physical statements conclusively on the basis of sensory evidence would require at least justified generalizations in sensory terms, the goal of "the doctrinal side of epistemology" is in any case rendered impossible by the problem of induction (which Quine views as unsolvable). All that is left, in his view, once these goals are abandoned as hopeless, is the attempt "simply to understand the link between observation and science," and there is no reason not to appeal to natural science in general and empirical psychology in particular to achieve this end. From the Cartesian standpoint, such an approach would be question-begging, since such scientific claims are among those whose justification is in question; but Quine argues that this is no longer a problem once the goal of justification has been abandoned [EN 75–76]. (Consider for yourself just how plausible this argument is before reading further.)

There are many difficulties with this line of argument. A relatively minor one is that Quine's picture of "the conceptual side" and "the doctrinal side" of traditional epistemology as more or less equally important vastly exaggerates the importance of the former. Construed in the phenomenalistic way in which Quine construes it, "the conceptual side" of epistemology is a feature only of the narrowest versions of empiricism, and even there is motivated primarily by the attempt to satisfy "the doctrinal side." Thus the failure to achieve the aim of "the conceptual side," to which Quine in fact devotes most of his attention in "Epistemology Naturalized," does very little to show that traditional epistemology as a whole has failed and hence needs to be replaced by the suggested naturalized surrogate.

More importantly, Quine's discussion seriously muddies the waters by failing to distinguish a stronger and a weaker conception of the goal of "the doctrinal side" of traditional epistemology. According to the stronger conception, deriving originally (as we have seen) from Descartes, the goal is to achieve *certainty* in our beliefs about the world, to establish that they are infallibly and indubitably true. For the weaker conception, on the other hand, the goal is the more modest one of showing that there are good reasons for thinking that our beliefs are at least likely to be true; complete certainty, while of course still desirable, is not at all essential. Though his discussion of "the doctrinal side" is too sketchy to allow full confidence on this point, Quine seems to slide illegitimately from the relatively uncontroversial claim that the stronger, Cartesian goal cannot be attained for beliefs about the external material world to the much less obvious claim that the more modest goal is not achievable either. Thus we are told that statements about bodies cannot be "proved" from observation sentences, that "the Cartesian quest for certainty" is a "lost cause," that claims about the external world cannot be "strictly derived" "from sensory evidence" [EN 74–75]; and on this basis it is apparently concluded that the entire "doctrinal side" of traditional epistemology, which Quine characterizes in one place as concerned with "the justification of our knowledge of truths about nature" [EN 71], must be abandoned. But this, of course, simply does not follow.[4]

What might cast some doubt on this interpretation of Quine's argument is the fact that he uses the term "evidence" to characterize even the project of naturalistic epistemology. Thus he claims that despite the failure of traditional epistemology, it remains undeniable that "whatever evidence there is for science is sensory evidence" [EN 75]. And further on we are told that the goal of naturalistic epistemology is "to see how evidence relates to theory, and in what ways one's theory of nature transcends any available evidence" [EN 83]; and also that "observation sentences are the repository of evidence for scientific hypotheses" [EN 88]. But what does Quine mean here by "evidence"? There is no apparent way to make sense of these remarks in terms of the ordinary normative or evaluative concept of evidence, according to which having *evidence* for a claim means having something that provides the basis for a *good reason* for thinking that the claim is true, since the concept of a good reason (or indeed a reason of any sort) is not a concept of empirical psychology. Psychology can describe ways in which beliefs of various sorts are *caused* by sensory experience (or, as Quine prefers to say, by "sensory stimulations"), but it is not within the province of psychology to offer any assessment of the rational acceptability of those beliefs on that basis. (Getting clear on this point will require thinking about just what the empirical science of psychology properly includes, something that you may not have previously thought very much about. The key question to focus on here is whether there is any apparent way in which the results of empirical study could have a bearing, not just on whether certain sorts of sensory observation or stimulation in fact causally result in the adoption of a particular belief, but on whether those experiences or stimulations constitute *good* evidence or *good* reasons for that belief—how could mere empirical investigation determine when this was so and when it wasn't?)

It thus seems reasonably clear that at least Quine's version of naturalized epistemology has nothing whatsoever to say about whether we have any good reasons to think that our beliefs about the world are true. And hence, if Quine is right that this sort of naturalized epistemology is the best we can do, the result is apparently tantamount to a thoroughgoing version of *skepticism*: we have a set of beliefs that describe the external world; part of that very set of beliefs describes how the beliefs in question are caused by sensory observation or "stimulation"; but we have no cogent reason of any sort for thinking that *any* of these beliefs (*including the psychological ones*) are true. And if knowledge necessarily involves the possession of such reasons, then we also have no knowledge.[5] Quine suggests at one place that this result simply describes "the human predicament" [EN 72]. But it is surely extremely implausible from an intuitive standpoint. Moreover, if this is the best that naturalized epistemology can do, then it is hard to see why it should be regarded as an adequate replacement for the more traditional variety.[6]

To see how Quine would respond to this sort of objection, we need to look at his conception of skepticism. In another work, he describes skepticism as "an offshoot of science," resulting from the scientific discovery of perceptual illusions in which our experience of the material world does not agree with what we really believe to be there.[7] Thus skepticism, in Quine's view, arises only from *within* empirical science, and hence can best be answered by empirical science itself:

> Retaining our present beliefs about nature, we can still ask how we can have arrived at them. Science tells us that our only source of information about the external world is through the impact of light rays and molecules upon our sensory surfaces. Stimulated in these ways, we somehow evolve an elaborate and useful science. How do we do this, and why does the resulting science work so well? These are . . . scientific questions about a species of primates, and they are open to investigation in natural science, the very science whose acquisition is being investigated.[8]

Thus, Quine claims, naturalized epistemology is in principle quite adequate to deal with skepticism.

But this view of the skeptical challenge is seriously inadequate in two distinct ways. In the first place, while it is quite true that skeptics have often appealed to various sorts of illusions to motivate their doubts (as reflected to some extent in the argument from illusion, as discussed in chapter 6), such an appeal is in no way essential to the basic thrust of skepticism. The fundamental skeptical move is to challenge the adequacy of our reasons for accepting our beliefs, and such a challenge can be mounted without any appeal to illusion. A prominent example of such a challenge is Hume's skepticism about induction (see chapter 4), mentioned in passing by Quine himself [EN 71–72], but there are many, many others. Such a challenge can in principle be raised against any alleged piece of knowledge: is the reason or justification that is available for the belief in question adequate to show that it is true or at least likely to be true? And to this general skeptical challenge, Quine's version of naturalized epistemology apparently has nothing at all to say.

Moreover, even if we restrict our attention to the more limited versions of skepticism that essentially involve an appeal to illusions, the sort of response that is offered by naturalized epistemology totally misses the main issue—which is, of course, reasons or justification. What the skeptic questions is whether, once the possibility of illusion is appreciated, our sensory experiences can any longer be regarded as providing good reasons for our various beliefs about the world. Such a skeptic need not doubt that our beliefs are caused in *some* way, nor that an account of how they are caused (one that may or may not be correct) can be given from within our body of beliefs about how the world operates. What he doubts is whether we have any good reasons for thinking that *any* of these beliefs about the world, including those that are involved in the causal account, are true, and to this issue of justification, the Quinean version of naturalized epistemology once again has nothing to say.

A different and perhaps even more obvious way to appreciate the irrelevance of this conception of naturalized epistemology to more standard epistemological issues is to consider its application to kinds of belief where a substantial degree of skepticism seems genuinely warranted, for example, to beliefs about alleged occult phenomena of various sorts, such as astrological or phrenological beliefs. For just as naturalized epistemology can say nothing positive about the justification of either science or common sense, and is thus impotent in the face of skepticism, so also it can say nothing distinctively negative about the justification of these less reputable sorts of belief. There is, after all, no reason to doubt that occult beliefs are also caused in *some* way, and thus no reason to doubt that psychology can offer an empirical account of how they are produced.[9] Such an account would no doubt differ in major ways from that which would be given for more properly scientific beliefs, but the differences would not, within psychology or empirical science generally, have any justificatory or normative significance. Thus the only epistemology that is possible on Quine's view apparently cannot distinguish between science and occult belief in any way that would constitute a reason for preferring the former to the latter. (This is in effect the reverse side of skepticism.)

Thus Quine's original version of naturalized epistemology seems to be both inadequately defended and also intuitively unsatisfactory because of its radically skeptical implications. In fact, relatively few of those who have adopted this label have gone as far as Quine in repudiating the normative or evaluative idea of justification as a central concern of epistemology. But what then does naturalized epistemology amount to when understood in a less extreme sense? Different philosophers would give different answers to this question, and we cannot investigate all of them here. But in the following two sections of this chapter, we will look at the two ingredients that one major proponent of naturalized epistemology has identified as central to the view: (1) the rejection of "apsychologistic epistemology," and (2) the rejection of any sort of *a priori* justification.[10]

Psychologism in Epistemology

In the strongest sense, an "apsychologistic" epistemology would be one that entirely ignored or excluded psychological considerations. Thus to reject "apsychologistic epistemology" is to claim that psychological facts should play a role, and presumably an important one, in epistemological discussion. In order to assess this claim, we will obviously have to consider the various specific ways in which psychological claims might have epistemological relevance. It will turn out, I will suggest, that while there are a number of perfectly reasonable ways in which such claims are indeed epistemologically relevant, none of them are even close to being central enough for their recognition to constitute a significant psychologization or naturalization of epistemology.

Perhaps the most widely discussed recent argument for some degree of psychologism in epistemology appeals to a possible situation in which a person has a belief B_1 for which he or she (a) has available the ingredients of a cogent justifying argument, but (b) fails to realize that the argument in question is available and holds the belief on some other basis. Suppose, to take an extreme case, that the person has some other justified belief B_2 and also believes justifiably that if B_2 is true then B_1 must be true, but somehow fails put all of this together into a justifying argument, and instead accepts B_1 on the basis of wishful thinking or astrological prediction or some equally dubious cognitive process. It seems obvious (doesn't it?) that in such a situation, B_1 is *not* justifiedly held by the person in question, and that this is so in part because of the correct psychological account of why B_1 is held: it is held for a bad reason or no reason rather than for the good reason that is available but unrecognized.[11]

This sort of example supports the conclusion that there is a *psychological* requirement for justification: in order for a belief to be justifiedly held by a particular person for a given reason, the person's recognition of that reason must be part of the psychological explanation of why the belief is held.[12] But while this result is of some importance (suggesting, among other things, that a defensible version of internalism must require, not merely that a justifying reason be internally accessible or available, but instead that it actually be internally accessed), it is hard to believe that there has ever been a serious epistemologist who would have denied it (though there have certainly been some who inadvertently failed to mention it). Thus the sort of psychologism that follows from this argument, which I will refer to as *minimal psychologism*, is entirely uncontroversial and involves at most a quite minor departure from traditional epistemology.

There is a second kind of psychologism that is equally undeniable, but also, I believe, equally innocuous from the standpoint of traditional epistemology. Various philosophers have made the logical or conceptual point that sensory perception necessarily depends on causal relations. The idea here is that I could not be correctly said to perceive a certain object unless that object played the right sort of role[13] in the causation of my perceptual experience. Analogous points could also be made about introspection and memory and, in a somewhat different way, about logical inference itself. It follows that the epistemological consideration of these concepts and, especially, the application of the epistemological results to actual cases will have to make reference to psychological facts about the causation of the beliefs involved. But this does nothing to show that the distinctively epistemological theses and arguments concerning such topics are themselves psychological in any interesting way. Thus, this second kind of psychologism, which we may label *conceptual psychologism*, again represents no significant advance toward the naturalist's main claim in this area, namely that empirical psychological results should play a central role in epistemology.[14]

There is yet a third kind of psychologism that must, I think, be acknowledged, one which, while in a way more substantive than those discussed so far, still poses no real threat to traditional epistemology. We have already taken brief notice in the previous chapter of the *meliorative* epistemological project,[15] that is, the project of improving the reliability and success of actual human cognitive functioning by doing such things as identifying ways of organizing research, methods of investigation, and even perhaps modes of reasoning that lead to cognitive success when employed by typical human investigators and distinguishing them from others that are less conductive to success. It is once more obvious and something that it is again hard to imagine anyone denying that serious attempts in this direction must take note of the psychological facts about the human cognitive efforts in question and especially of various sorts of human psychological limitations. Thus, for example, it does no good *for this purpose* to describe a complicated rule or schema for, say, inductive or explanatory inference, however logically impeccable it may be in itself, if it is one that human beings are for some psychological reason incapable of conforming to or at least reasonably approximating. And, to take the other side of the coin, it is presumably an important part of this general meliorative effort to provide critical assessments of inferential patterns and other modes of cognitive behavior that are actually exemplified in normal human practice, which clearly will require some knowledge of the relevant facts, psychological and otherwise, about that practice, for example, about the kinds of reasoning that people actually employ. All of these points, however, have at least mainly to do with *applying* epistemological assessments to actual practice, not with the basis upon which those assessments are themselves arrived at and justified. And thus there seems to be nothing about what we may call *meliorative psychologism*, understood in the way just indicated, that has any serious bearing on the nature of epistemological criticism and argument when considered in itself—and thus once again, nothing that supports any significant degree of naturalization.

Thus while there are indeed good reasons for a modest degree of psychologism in epistemology, none of the specific kinds of psychologism that we have identified, namely minimal, conceptual, and meliorative psychologism, seems to be in any way incompatible with the main thrust of the traditional Cartesian approach to epistemology or to support any very serious degree of naturalization. Thus if there is a good case to be made for naturalized epistemology, it must apparently rest on the other main ingredient of naturalism: the rejection of *a priori* justification.

Quine's Arguments against the A *Priori*

The way in which the rejection of *a priori* justification supports the idea that epistemology should be naturalized is a bit indirect. But it should be obvious to anyone who has read this far in the present book how vital the possibility of genuine *a priori* justification is to the traditional program of Cartesian epistemology or anything very close to it. The role of the *a priori* was perhaps most conspicuous in the arguments offered in defense of inductive reasoning and of beliefs concerning the material world, but in fact there is almost no part of our discussion to this point in which *a priori* reasons and arguments have not played an essential part. Descartes's own position relies heavily on *a priori* considerations, and the same is true of the arguments concerning the nature of immediate experience, the accounts of other minds, induction, and memory, the arguments for and against foundationalism and coherentism, the arguments for and against internalism and externalism, and of course the discussion of the *a priori* itself. It seems clear that no part of this discussion relied solely or even mainly on empirical considerations, whether psychological or otherwise, nor is it at all apparent how it could have done so while still dealing with the same basic issues. (Think carefully about this last point: What would an empirical, psychological approach to, say, the problem of induction or the problem of other minds even look like?) Thus if the objections to the very idea of *a priori* justification should turn out to be correct, this traditional approach to epistemology would apparently be doomed (though notice in passing that the argument just given is itself an *a priori* one!). Whether this result would also support naturalized epistemology in any serious way depends on whether the naturalistic approach is, as its proponents tend to assume, the only remaining alternative.

Though he does not raise them in the context of his main discussions of naturalized epistemology, the arguments for what I will refer to as *radical empiricism*, the view that there is no genuine *a priori* justification of any sort, are again mainly due to Quine.[16] Unfortunately, however, these arguments are, on the surface at least, aimed less at the general idea of *a priori* justification than at the specific form that this idea took in the general confines of twentieth-century "analytic" epistemology: the view referred to in chapter 5 as *moderate empiricism*. As we saw earlier, the moderate empiricist holds that while *a priori* justification genuinely exists, it extends only to propositions that are *analytic*. Quine himself tends to assume what might be described as a hypothetical version of moderate empiricism: the view that *if* there *were* any *a priori* justified claims, they would have to be analytic—or, equivalently, that moderate empiricism is the only account of *a priori* justification that is even possibly viable. If this were correct, it would be possible to argue against *a priori* justification, as Quine does in fact attempt to argue, simply by attacking the concept of analyticity. (But if rationalism is even a serious possibility, then such an argument would be incomplete at best.)

Quine's main thesis is in fact that the concept of analyticity is ultimately *unintelligible*. His main argument to this effect is what has become known as "the circle of terms" argument.[17] He claims that "analytic" is one member of a set of interdefinable terms (or concepts), the other members of which are such terms as "synonymous," "necessary," "definition," "contradiction," and "semantic rule." His argument is then basically that while these terms are indeed interdefinable, so that, for example, an *analytic* truth can be defined in the Fregean way as one that is transformable into a truth of logic by replacing one or more terms with terms that are *synonymous*, none of the terms in the circle can be adequately defined or explicated in a way that is independent of the others. Thus for someone who, like Quine, claims not to understand any of these terms or concepts, there is no way into the circle, no place where understanding can start. His conclusion is that none of these terms (or the correlative concepts) is really intelligible. (Here again you should try to evaluate this argument on your own before proceeding. Are the terms in question really interdefinable in the way that Quine claims? And is there really no way into the alleged circle?)

In fact, there are several different problems with this argument. One is that Quine's account of the supposed circle is at least partly mistaken, in that some of the terms included, "necessary" in particular, are not in fact correctly definable in terms of the others.[18] A second problem is that Quine appears to set aside for no good reason the most obvious way into the alleged circle: the idea of *meaning*. If we accept the idea that words have meaning, something that it appears to be impossible to rationally deny (even though Quine and his followers sometimes attempt to do so), then we can define synonymy as sameness of meaning, and then proceed to define analyticity in accord with the Fregean conception.[19]

The deepest problem, however, is that even if Quine's argument for the unintelligibility of the concept of analyticity were correct, it would fail to constitute a serious objection to the idea of *a priori* justification.[20] Think back to our earlier discussion of moderate empiricism and rationalism.[21] As we saw there, the basic argument for moderate empiricism relies on the idea that the appeal to analyticity provides an explanation of how *a priori* justification works that is clearer and less mysterious than that offered by the rationalist, so that only the moderate empiricist view can make clear sense of how *a priori* justification is possible. But this claim could hardly be correct if the very idea of analyticity were, as Quine claims, *unintelligible*, since a concept that is unintelligible can provide no real explanation of anything. Thus if Quine's argument against the concept of analyticity were correct, it would have the effect of destroying the case for moderate empiricism—including the case for the hypothetical version of moderate empiricism upon which Quine himself is relying. Quine and the naturalists who follow him are thus in the dialectically embarrassing position of concentrating their attack mostly on a view that, if Quine's most widely discussed and best-developed argument were cogent, would not in fact be the main alternative for an account of *a priori* justification. Quine cannot justify the rejection of *a priori* justification by arguing solely against moderate empiricism, for the claim that moderate empiricism is the preferred account of such justification, superior to that of the rationalist, will not survive such arguments, if they otherwise have any force.

What Quine and the other naturalists need, then, is a direct objection to rationalism—or, more or less equivalently, an argument that the idea of *a priori* justification is untenable even if not construed in a moderate empiricist way. Does Quine in fact have any such argument? Once the argument against analyticity is set aside as essentially irrelevant to the main issue, only one very clear possibility remains within Quine's own writings: an argument that begins with a celebrated thesis advanced by the French philosopher of science Pierre Duhem.[22]

Duhem was perhaps the first to notice that the empirical testing of a general claim or thesis by appeal to observation or experiment always depends on a variety of background claims or assumptions that are necessary to establish the very relevance of any particular observational or experimental result to the claim or thesis in question. Consider, for example, the theory which claims that among the fundamental constituents of matter are the extremely small, negatively charged particles (or particle-like entities) known as electrons. There is a massive amount of observational and experimental evidence that supports this theory, including such phenomena as the light emitted in cathode-ray tubes, tracks in cloud chambers, electrical currents, and many, many others. But none of these phenomena constitute direct observations of electrons in an unproblematic sense. Instead the relevance of the observations and experiments to the theory depends on a wide range of claims about the nature of the observational or experimental apparatus, the way that this would interact with electrons (if there were any), the sorts of observable effects that such interaction would produce, and the absence of any other plausible account of those various effects. Duhem focuses on a case in which one of the predicted observations derived in this way *fails* to occur. His thesis is that in any such case, the main claim or theory in question, in this case the claim that electrons exist, could in principle always be preserved in the face of the seemingly negative evidence by simply abandoning instead one or more of the relevant background claims or assumptions.[23]

Quine generalizes Duhem's view by arguing that in principle the modification or abandonment of *any* element of the overall system or "web" of belief, even a principle of logic or some other claim that is supposedly justified *a priori*, can serve in this way to resolve an apparent conflict with experience, and that it is always possible that such modification or abandonment might turn out to be the simplest solution and hence the overall most rational course. It follows, he claims, that any claim at all, or at least any that is not a matter of direct observation, can be rationally given up. The further argument is then apparently (on this Quine is not very explicit) that an *a priori* justified claim would have to be one which could *never* be rationally given up, so that if, as argued, no claim has this status, then nothing is justified *a priori*. (Here again, though the issues are quite difficult and complicated, you should try to evaluate this argument on your own before considering what I have to say about it. In trying to do so, I would recommend that you accept Duhem's thesis and Quine's extension thereof as provisionally correct, and look for other problems.)

In fact, whether or not Quine's extended (or perhaps exaggerated?) version of the Duhemian thesis is correct, the further argument just set out is clearly and utterly question-begging. For the most that Duhem's thesis, in however extreme a form, could show is that it might be rational to give up any claim in the web *if the only consideration relevant to rationality were how best to resolve conflicts with experience.* But to assume this is obviously tantamount to *assuming,* for no good reason, that rationality has only to do with accommodating experience and resolving such conflicts, which amounts to *assuming* that all justification is empirical and that *a priori* considerations have no independent rational force. But, putting the point the other way around, *if* there is genuine *a priori* justification, as the rationalist claims, then it would provide an *independent* reason why some claims should not be given up in spite of the fact that doing so would resolve a conflict with experience. Quine's argument begs the question by simply assuming that this is not so.[24]

Thus at least the main naturalist arguments against the possibility of *a priori* justification are unsuccessful, so that again no real defense of the supposed need to naturalize epistemology has emerged. In the final section of the chapter, I will argue that in addition to being undefended, the rejection of *a priori* justification (and so any version of naturalized epistemology that involves such a rejection) leads directly to epistemological disaster in the form of rampant skepticism.

Naturalized Epistemology and Skepticism

The argument to be offered was already considered briefly in chapter 5, but will be reiterated and further elaborated here. It depends on a distinction between two classes of beliefs: those which report the results of direct observation or experience and those whose content transcends the results of direct observation or experience. The latter class would include at least beliefs about the remote past, beliefs about the future, beliefs about present situations where no observer is present, beliefs about general laws, and the vast majority of the beliefs that result from theoretical science. (Any belief whose status in this respect is seriously uncertain may, for the sake of this argument, simply be consigned to the observational or experiential side of the ledger.)

I will assume here, without worrying about the details, that the fact that a belief is a report of direct observation or experience constitutes an adequate reason for thinking it to be true. (Rejecting this assumption would simply worsen the problem for the naturalistic views in question.) But what about the nonobservational or nonexperiential beliefs? If we are to have any reason for thinking these latter beliefs to be true, such a reason must apparently either (i) depend on an inference of some sort from some of the directly observational beliefs or (ii) be entirely independent of direct observation. A reason of sort (ii) is plainly *a priori*. And a reason of sort (i) can only be cogent if its *corresponding conditional*, a conditional statement having the conjunction of the directly observational premises as antecedent and the proposition that is the content of the nonobservational belief as consequent, is something that we have a good reason to believe to be true. But this latter reason can again only be *a priori*: if, as we may assume, all relevant observations are already included in the antecedent, they can offer no support for the claim that *if* that antecedent is true, then something further is true. Thus if, as the naturalist claims, there are no *a priori* reasons for thinking anything to be true (or, as Kitcher sometimes seems to suggest instead, none of any epistemological importance), the inevitable result is that we have no reason for thinking that any of our beliefs whose content transcends direct observation are true.[25]

This is already epistemological disaster, but a further consequence is that the vast majority of the claims about the nature of the world, the nature and reliability of human psychological processes, etc., to which naturalized epistemology appeals are things that we have no reason at all for thinking to be true—as, indeed, are the very theses that epistemology must be naturalized or that traditional epistemology is untenable (together with all normative claims of any sort). In this way, naturalized epistemology is *self-referentially inconsistent*: its own epistemological claims exclude the possibility of there being any cogent reason for thinking that those claims are true. Self-referential inconsistency is the deepest and most conclusive way in which a philosophical position can collapse upon itself.[26]

Summarizing, I have argued, first, that Quine's original argument for naturalizing epistemology fails either to show that this is necessary or to establish a viable alternative; second, that the reasons offered by others fail to show the need for psychologizing, and so naturalizing, epistemology in any important sense; third, that the main arguments of the naturalists fail to show that a traditional, rationalist conception of *a priori* justification is untenable; and, fourth, that the abandonment of any sort of *a priori* justification leads directly to epistemological disaster and also undercuts the very premises used to argue for it.

I will conclude this chapter with one further reflection. One thing that it is important to bear in mind about the issue of *a priori* justification is how easy it is to rely on *a priori* insights without explicitly acknowledging them, even to oneself. This is particularly easy where such insights pertain to fundamental patterns of reasoning and argument. Thus it becomes fatally easy for a proponent of naturalized epistemology or radical empiricism to continue to rely on the intuitively obvious rational credentials of logic, induction, and explanatory reasoning, while at the very same time denying the very possibility of the only sort of non-question-begging justification that such reasoning could have. The argument offered in this section can perhaps serve as a useful antidote to this kind of mistake.

Notes

1. As this might suggest, there is a certain affinity between naturalized epistemology and externalism, and indeed the two views have often been advocated by the same philosophers. Nonetheless they are not identical views, and it is quite possible to hold one of them while rejecting the other.

2. Reprinted in Quine, *Ontological Relativity and Other Essays* (New York: Columbia University Press, 1969), pp. 69–90. Further references in the present section to the pages of this article will use the abbreviation *EN* and will be placed in the text.

3. If you aren't familiar with this fairly famous (or notorious) school of philosophical thought, you might want to consult a dictionary or encyclopedia of philosophy. One thesis widely held among the positivists was moderate empiricism, as discussed in chapter 5; and others that were held, though not quite so widely or insistently, included phenomenalism, as discussed in chapter 7, and behaviorism, as discussed in chapter 8. The central positivist thesis, however, was *verificationism*: the view that any nonanalytic claim that is meaningful must be empirically verifiable, with positivists often tending to simply identify the meaning of a claim with the ways in which it can be verified.

4. It is possible that Quine would want to argue that even under the more modest construal, the goal of "the doctrinal side" is rendered unachievable by the complete intractability, according to him, of the problem of induction. But he offers no real argument to this effect.

5. It is important, however, to see that the main issue here does not turn on the term "knowledge." Even if, as some externalists believe, the ordinary meaning of "knowledge" does not require reasons or justification, but only something like reliable or truth-conducive causation of belief, it would remain true even for beliefs that constitute knowledge in this sense that we have no reason at all for thinking them to be true, and that result is enough in itself to constitute a very deep and intuitively implausible version of skepticism.

6. Notice also in passing that the belief that this is the best that we can do, that naturalized epistemology is all that is possible, is obviously not itself a psychological claim and thus cannot be part of the content of such an epistemology.

7. Quine, "The Nature of Natural Knowledge," in *Mind and Language*, ed. Samuel Guttenplan (Oxford: Oxford University Press, 1975), pp. 67–81; the quoted passage is from p. 67.

8. *Ibid.*, p. 68.

9. Of course, some sorts of occult beliefs may stand in conflict with the sort of scientific psychology that Quine has in mind. It is, however, not clear why such a conflict poses any problem once issues of justification are set aside; and in any case, there will be or could be other, occult versions of psychology that Quine can offer no reason for not taking just as seriously as the scientific brand.

10. See Philip Kitcher, "The Naturalists Return," *Philosophical Review*, vol. 101 (1992), pp. 53–114.

11. See *ibid.*, p. 60. Another presentation of essentially the same argument is to be found in Hilary Kornblith, "Beyond Foundationalism and the Coherence Theory," *Journal of Philosophy*, vol. 72 (1980), pp. 597–612, reprinted in Hilary Kornblith (ed.), *Naturalizing Epistemology* (Cambridge, Mass.: MIT Press, 1985), pp. 115–28, esp. pp. 118–19.

12. This is an approximate indication of a requirement whose exact formulation would require more discussion than there is room for here. One issue is the role that the recognition of the reason plays in the causal explanation of the belief: it is possible to imagine "deviant" causal chains in which the recognition of the reason helps to cause the belief, but not in the right way to yield justification. A second issue is what to say about cases of overdetermination, in which there are two or more causes for the belief in question, each of them sufficient to produce it, but only one of which involves the reason in question.

13. Again, "deviant" cases are possible.

14. See Kitcher, *op. cit.*, pp. 61–62, for a discussion of this point, though he would not approve of the label that I have used. Kitcher seems to concede that the acceptance of conceptual psychologism by itself fails to contribute very much to the overall case for naturalism.

15. The term is Kitcher's. See *ibid.*

16. The main source for these arguments is Quine's famous paper "Two Dogmas of Empiricism," reprinted in Quine, *From a Logical Point of View*, 2nd ed. (New York: Harper, 1963), pp. 20–46.

17. In "Two Dogmas," sections 1–4.

18. See the discussion of many of these concepts in chapter 5.

19. In other writings, Quine and his followers do offer more substantial objections to the concept of meaning, though still ones that are very hard to take seriously, especially from an intuitive, commonsense standpoint.

20. The term "*a priori*" is in fact not claimed to be part of the circle, nor could such a claim be plausibly defended.

21. In chapter 5.

22. See "Two Dogmas," section 6. There are two other possibilities for such an argument that are worth mentioning. One is Quine's famous argument for the indeterminacy of radical translation, which some have taken to be an argument against the *a priori*. Both this argument and its relevance to the *a priori* seem to me too uncertain and problematic

to be worth discussing here. (See my book *In Defense of Pure Reason* [Cambridge: Cambridge University Press, 1998], § 3.5 for more discussion.) The second argument is one that Kitcher rather tentatively attributes to Thomas Kuhn, which has to do with the conflict between alleged *a priori* knowledge of principles of reasoning and actual scientific practice. See Kitcher, *op. cit.*, p. 73, and my discussion in "Against Naturalized Epistemology," *Midwest Studies in Philosophy*, vol. 19 (1994), pp. 293–95.

23. The logical point here is that if we know that if P, Q, R, and S obtain, then T will obtain, the failure of T to obtain shows only that one of P, Q, R, and S is false, but does not by itself tell us which one is the mistaken one.

24. I also think that Quine is wrong that claims justified *a priori* would have to be impossible to ever rationally give up—see the discussion in chapter 5 and, for further elaboration, my book *In Defense of Pure Reason*, §§ 4.4–4.6.

25. I have formulated the argument in terms of a reason for thinking that the belief is true, rather than in terms of the belief's being (epistemically) justified, because I do not want to bring the controversy between externalist and internalist conceptions of justification, considered in the previous chapter, into the present discussion. My view is that the result arrived at in the text is enough to constitute epistemological disaster whether or not the beliefs in question may be said to be justified in some other sense of justification that does not involve our having a reason to think that they are true.

26. For a response to this argument, see Kitcher, *op. cit.*, p. 90. He argues there that the naturalist should simply reject the global skeptical challenge that gives rise to this problem as unanswerable and so, he seems to suggest, illegitimate. But it does not seem to me that this response will do. While this sort of answer may be appropriate for some skeptical problems, the issue of whether and why we ever have any reason to think that a conclusion that goes beyond observation is true is far too fundamental and inescapable to be dismissed as some clever dialectical trick. It is quite true, of course, that it is part of the naturalist's own position, or so immediate a consequence of it as to make no difference, that the skeptical problem posed above cannot be solved, but their explicit adoption of this consequence does nothing to make it less catastrophic or less self-defeating.

CHAPTER TWELVE

~

Skepticism

In this final chapter, we will look more explicitly at a number of issues relating to *skepticism*, including some further contemporary responses to skepticism (most of which amount in one way or another to further repudiations or dismissals of the traditional Cartesian approach to epistemology).

In fact, as you should realize, skepticism has been with us, though sometimes only in the background, almost from the beginning of this book: Skeptical hypotheses played a major role in Descartes's epistemological program, skeptical challenges of various kinds provided much of the focus for the subsequent discussion of particular epistemological issues in part one, and the threat of skepticism has loomed large in the arguments of the last three chapters. But despite this fairly pervasive presence, relatively little has been said so far about skepticism itself.

Most importantly, as we have seen in a number of places, especially but not only in part two, the threat of skepticism together with the commonsense or intuitive implausibility of skeptical results have often been employed as the basis for an *argument* for or against various specific epistemological views.[1] But while the intuitive appeal of such arguments is perhaps obvious enough, they cannot be fully evaluated without a more explicit examination of the dialectical issues surrounding skepticism, in particular the crucial question of whether and why the commonsense implausibility of skepticism constitutes a non-question-begging reason for thinking that skepticism is not correct.

The Varieties of Skepticism

The first thing we must take note of is that skepticism is not one specific view, but rather comprises a wide variety of views differing from each other in a number of different dimensions, which have to do with both the precise target of the skeptical attack and the specific claim or challenge concerning this target that the skeptic advances. Thus we will need to begin by sorting out these different varieties of skepticism, though a full discussion of all or even very many of them is clearly impossible within the confines of the present book.

The first issue that divides versions of skepticism is whether they are aimed at alleged *knowledge* or, more narrowly, at alleged *justification*. In fact, while it is knowledge that is more commonly the explicit target of the skeptic, I will suggest that the clearest and most perspicuous versions of skepticism are in fact aimed primarily at justification.

A skeptic who challenges whether someone has knowledge of some specified subject matter must presumably base that claim on a challenge to one or more of the elements that are required to constitute a state of knowledge, which I will assume here to be approximately specified by the general outline of the traditional conception of knowledge that was considered in chapter 3. Thus such a skeptical view must question either (i) the existence of a belief of the relevant sort or (ii) the truth of that belief or (iii) its justification or (iv) the satisfaction of the fourth, anti-Gettier condition (for those versions of the traditional conception that include such a condition).[2]

The first of these possibilities, a skeptical challenge to the very existence of the relevant belief, is both uncommon (because the main thrust of skepticism has been concerned with whether or not people's actual beliefs on various subjects, whose existence is thus taken for granted, satisfy some further standard) and also, I would argue, adequately answered by the account of the foundational status of beliefs about conscious states of mind that was offered at the end of chapter 9. A challenge directed at truth is certainly possible, but if such a challenge is argued for on grounds independent of issues about the justification of the belief, it will be metaphysical rather than epistemological in character and will in fact amount more to a positive claim of knowledge, albeit with a negative content, than to a version of skepticism. And it is difficult to see how there could be a general argument against the satisfaction of the standard anti-Gettier conditions: in particular, to take the specific such condition that was tentatively opted for in our earlier discussion, while it can occasionally be an accident (in relation to its justification) that a belief is true, it is hard to see on what basis this might be claimed to be likely to be true in general.

Thus, I suggest, the only very clear basis on which to challenge a claim of knowledge is to question the justification of the belief in question, or, what I will assume for the purposes of this chapter to be equivalent, to question whether the believer in question has a sufficiently good reason for thinking that the belief is true. A focus on knowledge might still be thought to be relevant if the specific issue raised by the skeptic is whether the belief is justified to the specific degree that is required for knowledge; but this specific sort of challenge would be clear enough to be worth discussing only if the requisite degree of justification was itself specified with reasonable clarity—which, as we saw in the earlier discussion, is not the case. For this reason, the most perspicuous versions of skepticism will be those that focus on justification directly, and it is on versions of skepticism that take this form that I will primarily focus here (though formulations in terms of knowledge will also work, as long as it is kept clearly in mind that justification is the real issue).

A second issue is what may be referred to as the *strength* of the skeptical claim or challenge. Here there is a spectrum of possible skeptical positions. On one end of the spectrum are versions of skepticism that make only the relatively weak claim that the belief or beliefs in question are not *conclusively* justified, not so strongly justified as to rule out any possibility of error;[3] while on the other end are versions of skepticism that advance the very strong claim that the belief or beliefs in question are not justified to any degree at all, that there is no reason that is at all cogent for thinking them to be true. For versions of skepticism that focus on claims about the external world (with which we will be mainly concerned here—see below), the former sort of claim is more or less trivially obvious and relatively unthreatening, while the latter is very difficult to defend. Thus the skeptical views that are both challenging enough to be interesting and reasonably plausible will fall toward the middle of the spectrum and will, as I will put it, challenge whether the beliefs in question are *strongly* justified, that is, justified enough to have a reasonably high likelihood of truth; and it is upon these versions of skepticism that we will mainly focus here.

A third issue dividing different versions of skepticism is the *scope* of the skeptical challenge: does it challenge the justification (or the status as knowledge) of all, or almost all, beliefs, or does it focus on beliefs in some narrower, perhaps very narrow, category? Views of the former sort will again be very difficult to make plausible (though they may nonetheless be dialectically defensible in a way that will be indicated later); whereas views of the latter sort will be less threatening, even though easier to defend.[4] Here too the most interesting versions of skepticism, those that are both intellectually threatening and reasonably defensible, will fall somewhere between these extremes, though still more toward the more global one. Here we will simplify the issue by focusing largely on the specific version of skepticism that concedes the justification of those beliefs that make up the Cartesian foundation, beliefs about the contents of conscious states of mind and about self-evident *a priori* truths, but challenges whether it is possible on that basis to arrive at a strong justification for beliefs about the external world, where this is understood broadly enough so as to include beliefs about ordinary material objects, about people other than the believer in question, about laws of nature and unobservable scientific entities, about history, and about the future.

A fourth, rather more subtle and tricky issue has to do with the character of the skeptical challenge itself. Sometimes skepticism is put forth as a thesis that is supposed to be established by positive arguments (which must obviously rely on premises that the skeptic himself or herself claims to be justified in accepting); while at other times it is put forth in a more negative way, challenging the positive arguments offered in support of claims of justification or knowledge, but not attempting to make a positive case to the contrary. One point that is obvious at once is that a truly global version of skepticism can only be defended in the negative way, since any positive argument relying on allegedly justified premises would be in conflict with the skeptical thesis itself. A second point, almost as obvious, is what I will refer to as negative versions of skepticism will be in one obvious way easier to defend, since they make no positive claim: the negative skeptic practices in effect the intellectual equivalent of guerrilla warfare, burning and pillaging, but not attempting to build anything positive that could itself be the object of attack.

Indeed, it is clear that there are some relatively global versions of negative skepticism that are completely impervious to any direct attack or refutation. Thus, to take the most extreme example, a skeptical view that challenges whether *any* belief is ever justified to *any* degree will be impossible to answer in a non-question-begging way, since any premise that might be employed in giving such an answer will be subject to the same challenge. Essentially the same thing will be true of versions of skepticism that reject the Cartesian foundation by either (a) challenging the justification of all allegedly self-evident truths or (b) challenging the justification of beliefs about the content of conscious states (without conceding the justification of some other class of contingent, empirical beliefs), since in either case the opponent of skepticism is left with too little to make the construction of an antiskeptical argument possible: it seems obviously impossible to *argue* that any a priori claim is justified without employing reasoning that could only be justified *a priori*; and equally impossible to argue for the justification of contingent, empirical claims without appealing to any contingent, empirical premise.

But while these purely negative versions of skepticism are in this way impervious to direct attack, this does not mean either (a) that they are correct or even (b) that this dialectical imperviousness constitutes a substantial reason in favor of their correctness. What is lurking here is the question of the correct allocation of the burden of proof as between the skeptic and his or her opponents: if the burden of proof were entirely on the antiskeptic, then negative versions of skepticism like the ones just described would triumph automatically. But it is far from clear that this is so, that the burden of proof is not at least partially on the skeptic (see further below).

Thus the most threatening versions of skepticism will not be purely negative in the way indicated, but also obviously will not rely on substantial positive premises that are themselves difficult to defend. The natural form for such a version of skepticism to take is for it to rely on *skeptical hypotheses* of various sorts, hypotheses such as Descartes's dreaming and evil genius hypotheses (see chapter 2) or the brain-in-a-vat hypothesis (see chapter 7). Another, rather narrower example of a skeptical hypothesis (suggested by Bertrand Russell[5]) is the hypothesis that the world was in fact created five minutes ago, with all of the memories about events that allegedly occurred earlier together with all evidence of other kinds that seems to reflect an earlier history (documents, photographs and movies, apparently older buildings and artifacts, fossils, etc.) being created at that same moment. If this were so, we would still have all of the same apparent evidence or reasons that we in fact seem to have concerning the occurrence of past events, but none of out beliefs about such events (except those pertaining to the last five minutes) would be true.

Such skeptical hypotheses thus describe allegedly possible ways in which (a) a believer could still have the same evidence or reasons in favor of a certain class of beliefs that we seem to have, even though (b) the beliefs in question are in fact false, thereby apparently showing, unless such hypotheses can be somehow ruled out or at least shown to be less likely than the nonskeptical alternative, that such evidence or such reasons do not genuinely constitute *good* reasons for thinking that the beliefs in question are true and so do not genuinely justify them. In the case of the dreaming, evil genius, and brain-in-a-vat hypotheses, the relevant class of beliefs comprises all of our beliefs about the external world and the evidence in question is all of our experiential evidence; for Russell's hypothesis about the creation of the world, the relevant class of beliefs is the narrower class of beliefs pertaining to the past prior to five minutes ago and the relevant evidence in question is the memories and other evidence of various kinds that seem to reflect such a past. The versions of skepticism in question are committed to the positive claims (a) that the hypotheses in question are genuinely possible, and (b) that all of the various relevant sorts of evidence could have existed in the same way even if the skeptical hypotheses were true, with both of these claims presumably being alleged to be established on an *a priori* basis. But beyond these two relatively minimal claims, the positions in question are able to adopt the negative stance of challenging their opponents to show how and why the beliefs in question are justified in spite of these skeptical possibilities, with no need to make any further positive argument.

Thus the specific version of skepticism that will be our main focus here concedes the justification of the two main parts of the Cartesian foundation, but challenges whether any beliefs about the external world are strongly justified and does so on the basis of some skeptical hypothesis like one of the more general ones just mentioned, which we will stipulate for the sake of variety and definiteness to be the brain-in-a-vat hypothesis.[6]

The Problem of the Criterion

Another issue that arises in the general vicinity of skepticism and that helps to shed some light on the issue of the allocation of the burden of proof between the skeptic and the antiskeptic is what has become known as "the problem of the criterion." This problem is standardly formulated[7] in terms of two questions about knowledge: "What is the *extent* of our knowledge?" (that is, which specific things do we know?); and "What are the *criteria* of knowing?" (that is, what standards or conditions must be satisfied in order to know something?). The problem arises because of the dialectical interplay between these questions. If we had a secure answer to one of them, we would be able, perhaps, to figure out the answer to the other: thus if we were sure of the criteria of knowledge, we would be able in principle at least to figure out which specific things satisfied those criteria and thereby determine the extent of our knowledge; while if we were sure of the extent of our knowledge, we might, though somewhat less straightforwardly, be able, by scrutinizing the various instances, to generalize to the required criteria. But if we are not sure of the answer to either of the two questions, then it becomes difficult to see on what basis the answer to either of them could be justifiably arrived at.

A version of this issue could be raised about how the general requirements for knowledge (belief, truth, justification, and an anti-Gettier condition, according to the traditional conception) are determined: Are these requirements determined by generalizing from instances of knowledge that are somehow identified in advance in a way that is independent of those requirements, or are they somehow arrived at first and then used to determine which specific things are known?[8] But the version that is more relevant to issues about skepticism has rather to do with determining when those general requirements are satisfied in particular cases, and here again, for essentially the same reasons offered earlier with respect to the issue raised by skepticism, the main focus is justification. For the specific issue of justification, there are again two questions: (1) which specific beliefs are justified? and (2) what are the criteria that must be satisfied for a belief to be justified? And there is again the same problem about which of these questions is to be answered first and how either of them can be justifiably answered without a prior answer to the other.

In his discussion of the issue, Roderick Chisholm distinguishes two main possible responses to this sort of problem[9]: a *generalist* begins with intuitively determined criteria of knowledge or justification and seeks to determine on that basis which specific beliefs are cases of knowledge or are justified, while a *particularist* begins with particular, intuitively determined instances of beliefs that (allegedly) constitute knowledge or are justified, and then seeks to generalize from them to the correct general criteria of knowledge or justification. (This is a good place to pause and try to think about this issue for yourself. What is the right response to the problem of the criterion? Does one of Chisholm's alternatives seem more plausible than the other to you, and, if so, why? For whichever one you favor (if either), you should think carefully about the underlying problem, which is explaining on what basis one of the two answers can be determined without a prior determination of the other— saying, as I have, that it is done "intuitively" doesn't really answer this question, since one can still ask what shapes or grounds the intuition in question. Another possibility, of course, is that there is some further alternative or alternatives that Chisholm is missing.)

Chisholm in fact opts for particularism. His own version of particularism is both too complicated and too elusive to be discussed here, but a reasonably straightforward and accessible version is provided by G. E. Moore's appeal to and defense of common sense in such papers as "Proof of an External World" and "A Defence of Common Sense."[10] In "Proof of an External World," Moore offers the following "proof" that external things, things existing outside of us in space, genuinely exist:

> I can prove now, for instance, that two human hands exist. How? By holding up my two hands, and saying, as I make a certain gesture with my right hand, "Here is one hand," and adding, as I make a certain gesture with the left, "and here is another." [144]

Moore's claim in relation to this performance is that he "certainly did know" at the moment in question that each of the existence claims about the hands was true, and accordingly that two hands and so at least those external things existed at the time in question [144–45]. And he also makes clear there is nothing very special about the two hands, and in particular that their being parts of his own body makes no difference to his knowledge that they exist; the same sort of argument, he suggests, could have been made about pieces of paper or rocks or shoes or books or many, many other objects. It is reasonably clear that Moore is claiming to be very strongly justified (and not in some externalist sense) in thinking that it is true that each of the hands exists.

Similarly, in "A Defence of Common Sense," Moore offers a long list of further claims that, in his view, he knows "with certainty" to be true: that his body exists, that it was born at a certain time in the past, that many other things having shape and size in three dimensions have existed at various distances from it, including many other human bodies, that he has perceived many such things, and so on [33–34]. It is again clear that he is claiming to be very strongly justified in holding these various beliefs and also that if these beliefs are indeed strongly justified, then Moore is again strongly justified in believing that there is an external world. Thus Moore seems to be claiming to be able on this basis to provide an answer to skeptical views like the one specified at the end of the previous section.[11]

It is obvious what response our envisioned skeptic would give to Moore: he or she would reject Moore's assertion that the initial claims about the hands were justified and similarly reject the analogous claims about the other things that Moore claims to know and to be justified in accepting. As Moore seems to himself to make the gestures with each of his hands, the skeptic will argue, he might nonetheless be merely a brain-in-a-vat that has no hands and only seems to itself to experience the hands and the gestures because of the stimulation being fed to it by the computer. Thus, the skeptic will argue, Moore's "proof of an external world" simply begs the question and has no real force. Moore (and Chisholm), on the other hand, will appeal to the enormous intuitive plausibility of Moore's perceptual beliefs about his hands and of the further claim that those beliefs are justified and constitute knowledge. (Think about this in relation to your own experience of your own hands— isn't it almost impossible to deny or even question that your hands exist or that your perceptual beliefs about them are justified?) The reason that this response is not simply question-begging, it might be argued, is that these antiskeptical claims are in fact far more initially plausible than any of the skeptic's claims and arguments, thereby making it more reasonable to conclude that *something* in the skeptic's position must be mistaken, even if we cannot say at the moment what it is, than to accept the skeptical conclusion.[12] This is the basic particularist response to skepticism.

Who is right here? (Once again, you will get more out of the subsequent discussion if you think about this issue and try to resolve it for yourself, even if only very tentatively, before proceeding.) On the one hand, the judgments of common sense are at least one central part of the basis for philosophical reflection about knowledge and justification, as about anything else; to reject them as having no weight would arguably leave not enough of a starting point to give us any real chance of getting anywhere in our epistemological inquiries. But to accept commonsense convictions as more or less beyond serious question, as Moore and other particularists seem in effect to do, does appear to rule out illegitimately even the possibility that skepticism might in fact be true, that common sense might in fact be mistaken. And, equally importantly, if this solution were accepted at face value, it would have the effect of stifling or short-circuiting epistemological inquiry at least as effectively as would simply acquiescing in skepticism.

The way out, I would suggest, is in effect to split the difference between these two alternatives, giving commonsense intuition more weight than the skeptic would allow but less than the particularist wants to claim. And the specific way to do this is perhaps to say something like the following: The commonsense conviction that beliefs about the external world are justified and do constitute knowledge creates a strong rational presumption that this view is correct and so that skepticism is wrong—rational because there is no rational alternative to a substantial reliance on common sense, no other starting point for philosophy that is extensive enough to allow our thought to get any real grip on the issues involved. This presumption is strong enough, I suggest further, to provide the basis for powerful objections to views like Quine's (see chapter 11) that seem to have the consequence that there is no such justification, and also to views like externalism (see chapter 10) that can account for it only by construing the justification in question in an intuitively unsatisfactory way. It is also strong enough to make it reasonable to suppose, as Moore indeed does, that reasons of some sort are available to rule out the skeptic's hypotheses and establish that our experience really does support the beliefs in question.

But though strong, this antiskeptical presumption is still only a presumption: to have a strong reason to think that there is a justification for beliefs about the external world is not the same thing as to actually be able to specify such a justification in detail—something that must ultimately be possible if it genuinely exists. Thus this presumption can at least in principle be defeated by the long-term failure of epistemologists to actually succeed in specifying the justification in question. Many epistemologists would no doubt want to say that this failure has already been long-term enough to warrant the conclusion that the presumption in favor of common sense is in fact mistaken. The opposing view—which I am inclined to opt for (albeit tentatively)—is that the failure so far is adequately explained by the extreme difficulty and complexity of the issues—

and also by the pronounced tendency of philosophers in the twentieth century especially to evade the main issues rather than even attempting to deal with them in a direct way. Here we have one of the deepest and most difficult issues pertaining to the possibility and nature of epistemology—one that you will obviously need to ponder further on your own.

Some Further Responses to Skepticism

Before proceeding further, it may be useful to list briefly the main responses to skepticism that we have discussed so far, taking them in the reverse of the order in which we have encountered them.

First, there is the particularism of Moore, Chisholm, and others. I have suggested that this view is unacceptable because it gives too absolute a weight to commonsense intuition and thereby illegitimately rules out the very possibility of skepticism. Because of this, the answer that it offers to skepticism will be unsatisfying to anyone who is at all inclined to take the issue posed by skepticism seriously in the first place.

Second, there is the program of naturalized epistemology. But if taken in its strong, Quinean form—or, I would suggest, in any form in which it constitutes a real alternative to traditional, Cartesian epistemology—naturalized epistemology seems at bottom to concede everything that the skeptic wants, while avoiding this appearance only by changing the subject.

Third, there are externalist views of justification and of knowledge. I have argued that while these may be unobjectionable as alternatives adopted for purposes in the direction of Kitcher's "meliorative epistemology," they provide at best only a hypothetical response to the skeptic. Given the externalist accounts, we will have justified beliefs and knowledge *if* the right external conditions are satisfied. But unless some further response to the skeptic is available, we will have no reason to think that this possibility is in fact realized and thus no reason to think that any of our beliefs, including those couched in terms of the externalist concepts of justification and knowledge, are true.

Finally, of course, there is traditional Cartesian epistemology itself, which attempts to answer the skeptic head-on by arguing that beliefs about the external world are justified. An initial account of how this response might go was offered in part one of this book, especially in chapters 4, 6, 7, and 8. It is obvious both that the account given there is only an outline and also that the problems it faces are serious enough to make it far from clear that it can be successfully filled in (though my own belief is that it is also much less clear than is sometimes thought that it cannot). The point for the moment, however, is that we seem to have found so far no alternative that has any real chance of doing any better, indeed none except particularism that does not simply surrender to skepticism without any real struggle—and particularism avoids this fate only by in effect begging the question.[13]

But, as already suggested, such direct engagement with the epistemological issues and with the skeptic has been the exception rather than the rule in recent epistemology. I will conclude this chapter and this book by taking a brief look at some further contemporary responses to skepticism, all of them intended in one way or another to avoid a direct confrontation with the issues that the traditional Cartesian approach attempts to address.

Contextualism I: The Rejection of Global Epistemological Questions

The first of the further views to be discussed is sometimes regarded as a further alternative to foundationalism and coherentism. According to one version of what is usually referred to as *contextualism*, both the foundationalist and the coherentist are guilty of making a fundamental mistake: they take seriously and attempt to answer the *global* issue of whether and how all our beliefs, taken together, are justified. It is this global question that gives rise to the regress problem and thus spawns the opposed foundationalist and coherentist ways of dealing with that problem. Contextualists endorse the objections to both of these positions and argue that neither can succeed.

The contextualist view, in contrast, is that all meaningful issues of justification are, as it might be put, *local* in character: they concern the justification of one or more specific beliefs within a limited *context* in which the justification of the vast majority of other beliefs is taken for granted by all the parties and is thus not in question. Such local issues of justification arise from specific disputes or concerns, which help to define the relevant context and background assumptions. They are commonly raised by ordinary people for various limited and practical purposes. Global epistemological issues, in contrast, are a philosopher's invention, never raised by ordinary people in natural contexts, and having no imaginable practical import. Thus neither those issues nor the various skeptical views that arise in relation to them need be taken seriously; as it is sometimes put, one should simply "refuse to entertain the skeptical question."[14]

There can be little doubt that *some* of what the contextualist says is correct. Global or even relatively large-scale epistemological issues (such as the problem of induction or the problem of the external world) are very unlikely to be raised in practical contexts by ordinary people, and their sheerly practical significance is far from obvious—though it is perhaps an exaggeration to say that they have none at all. (What do you think about this?) And the issues that do naturally arise in ordinary contexts are local in just the way that the contextualist indicates. But this only shows so far that the larger issues with which traditional epistemology has been mainly concerned are (hardly surprisingly!) theoretical, philosophical issues, not that they are somehow misconceived or meaningless. Apart from some undefended antiphilosophical or anti-intellectual bias (which is undeniably a feature of some contextualist positions), is there any further reason or argument to be found as to why the large-scale and global epistemological issues need not be taken seriously or can somehow be dismissed?

In fact, the only very clear reason that is offered by contextualists is the claim that such issues, once taken seriously, cannot be satisfactorily dealt with, so that those who do take them seriously are inevitably driven toward skepticism. Those who have read this far in the present book will realize that this claim possesses a significant degree of plausibility, even if it is by no means as obviously correct as the contextualist claims. The problem, however, is that our inability to satisfactorily deal with an issue is not in any clear way a reason for thinking that it must be misconceived or meaningless. In the present case, it is only if it is *assumed*, on no apparent basis, that skepticism could not possibly be correct that the alleged fact that taking large-scale and global epistemological issues seriously leads to skepticism would constitute any sort of reason for adopting the contextualist stance.

Indeed, if no further argument is forthcoming, contextualism, rather than being a way of avoiding skepticism, is once again more properly viewed as a thinly disguised *surrender* to skepticism. Convinced, rightly or wrongly, that the threat of skepticism cannot be met, the contextualist simply chooses to ignore or evade the issue entirely. But even if such pessimism should turn out in the end to be warranted, a more forthright and open endorsement of skepticism seems clearly preferable.

Contextualism II: Relevant Alternatives

From the standpoint of traditional epistemology, establishing that a belief is justified means finding some evidence or reason for thinking that it is likely to be true, which in turn means at least that the evidence or reason makes the belief in question more likely to be true than any of the alternative possible beliefs that might seem to fit with or account for that evidence. This is, of course, precisely why skeptical hypotheses such as the brain-in-a-vat hypothesis pose such a difficult challenge. For Moore to be justified in concluding that his two hands exist, it would seem, he must somehow find some reason for thinking that the sensory evidence that seems to point to their existence fits better with or is better accounted for by the actual existence of the hands than it is by the alternative hypothesis that he is merely a handless brain-in-a-vat who is receiving computer-generated stimulation that results in a mere experience of hands. And this, as we saw in effect in chapter 7, is far from easy to do.

According to a second version of contextualism, however, the justification of the belief about the hands does not in general require showing that this belief is more likely to be true in relation to Moore's experiential evidence than any alternative hypothesis that would fit with or account for that evidence. What is required instead is only that the belief in question be capable of being shown to be more likely to be true in relation to the evidence than any alternative hypothesis that is *relevant* in the context in question (with the degree of justification varying with the degree of relative likelihood). Here, as with the previous version of contextualism,[15] the underlying idea is that we do not normally raise epistemological questions in the fully general way that is presupposed by traditional epistemology and that lends force to skepticism. In many contexts, the relevant issue is only whether the belief in question is more likely to be true than any of a much more limited range of alternatives that are, for one reason or another, particularly salient.

An example will help to clarify this view: Suppose that I seem to experience a coniferous tree standing in front of me and come to believe on this basis that there is such a tree and (on the basis of its specific characteristics) that it is a redwood. Here the relevant alternatives will in many contexts be limited to the other possibilities with regard to the kind of tree I am looking at that are compatible with my experience, given my degree of expertise about trees: perhaps the tree is instead a Douglas fir, or a spruce, or a giant sequoia, or a yew. But the possibility that the tree might be a nonconifer whose branches and leaves have been carefully pruned and sliced and sculpted so as to present a coniferous appearance would not normally be relevant—unless perhaps I have some specific reason to think that someone who performs this sort of arboreal mutilation has been active in the area. And the hypothesis that I am a brain-in-a-vat and that what seems to be an experience of a tree is really just the result of the computer-generated stimulation would not be a relevant alternative in any ordinary context—though it might, according to at least some views of this sort, be relevant in some distinctively philosophical contexts. Something similar would be said about the case of the hands, except there it is hard to find *any* alternative hypothesis that is likely to be relevant in normal contexts; but perhaps we can imagine that Moore has been asleep and knows that there is a mad doctor going around amputating people's hands and replacing them with superficially similar rubber substitutes. Even given such a relatively unusual context, however, the brain-in-a-vat hypothesis would not normally be a relevant alternative.

Another way to put what is essentially the same view is in terms of what has come to be known as the denial of the thesis of *epistemic closure*. It is natural to suppose that if a person is justified in believing some proposition P (that there is a redwood tree), then he or she is also thereby justified in believing any other proposition Q that is known by him or her to be a necessary consequence of P (that the tree is not a sculpted deciduous tree or that it is not merely an element in the experience of a brain-in-a-vat), so that the class of propositions justified for a given person is, in logical jargon, *closed* under the relation of known necessary consequence.[16] One reason in favor of this thesis is that it is surely plausible to suppose that reasoning from a belief that is justified via a known relation of necessary consequence leads to further justified beliefs: if one has a good reason for thinking that P is true and also a good reason to think that if P is true, Q must be true, surely that is a good reason to think that Q is true. A second is that it is hard to see what having justified beliefs is worth if it is not possible to reason from them in this way and be justified in accepting the results. But of course the skeptic makes use of the same basic logic, arguing that if my seeming reason for P does not exclude the falsity of Q, then it is not a good reason for P after all: thus if my experience of the apparent tree is insufficient to show that there is a normal conifer (and so, given its specific features, a redwood), rather than a sculpted deciduous tree or an element in a brain-in-a-vat's experience, then it is also insufficient to show that there is a redwood.

A proponent of the relevant alternatives view will argue at this point, as we have seen, that I can be justified in believing that the tree is a redwood and that Moore can be justified in believing that his hands are real as long as the sensory experiences in question exclude all of the *relevant* alternatives (if there are any), even though they do not exclude the irrelevant sculpted deciduous tree or brain-in-a-vat hypotheses. This then amounts to the denial of epistemic closure: I am justified in thinking that the tree is a redwood; I know if it is a redwood, then it is neither a sculpted deciduous tree nor something that exists only in the experience of a brain-in-a-vat; but I am nonetheless not thereby justified in believing that that these last two alternatives are false.[17]

One thing that is deeply puzzling and seemingly unsatisfactory about such views, however, is that it becomes very unclear what the content of my belief about the redwood (or Moore's justified belief that his hands exist) really amounts to, if it does not exclude the skeptical possibilities in question: what exactly is it that I (or Moore) believe, such that these possibilities are still left open? Moreover, while it is surely correct that the epistemological issues raised in practical contexts often take the form that the relevant alternatives view indicates, one in which the question is only whether a particular belief is the correct choice from a limited range of alternatives, this in no way shows that the more general question of whether the belief is justified in relation to all possible alternatives cannot still be meaningfully and legitimately raised—with the only apparent reason for not raising it being again the conviction that it cannot be satisfactorily answered. Thus this version of contextualism, like the previous one, seems to amount to a thinly disguised surrender to skepticism, rather than a genuine response.

Pragmatic Views

Both of the versions of contextualism are views that have emerged explicitly only in very recent times. A much more venerable response to skepticism, or rather a large and complicated family of related responses, is offered by the philosophical movement known as *pragmatism* (sometimes claimed to represent the only distinctively American philosophical view). Though there are pragmatic views on many different philosophical issues and topics, the core of pragmatism, at least from a historical standpoint, is epistemological. Pragmatists have offered theories of both truth and justification. The pragmatic theory of truth was briefly considered in chapter 3 (though that was again only one of many versions). Here I want to briefly explore a relatively simplified version of a pragmatic theory of justification, one that is aimed more or less explicitly at skepticism about the external world. While it is doubtful that any historical pragmatist ever held a view quite this simple, it still seems to me to make clear enough both the appeal of pragmatism and the fundamental problem faced by any pragmatic epistemological theory.

The basic pragmatic response to issues of epistemic justification is that beliefs are justified just in case they lead or tend to lead to *success in practice* when adopted. Thus a pragmatic response to the general issue of whether our various beliefs in external physical objects, other people, and so on are justified would point out that there is no real doubt that acting on such beliefs leads generally to practical success, and would conclude on that basis that those beliefs are indeed justified. What could be more obvious than that beliefs about various sorts of physical objects are valuable and indeed quite essential in dealing with the complexities of everyday life and in choosing actions that will lead to satisfactory results? From this pragmatic standpoint, while there may perhaps be relatively localized epistemological issues that pose genuine problems, the classical problems discussed earlier in this book can be solved so easily as to be unworthy even of serious discussion. (Stop for a moment and think about this response to epistemological problems and to skepticism. At this point in the book—and in the course that you may be taking—it probably seems initially quite appealing, a wonderful release from grappling with problems and difficulties and arguments that no doubt seem often unnatural and foreign from the standpoint of ordinary life. But you should always be suspicious when what seemed to be a serious intellectual problem is solved or dismissed too easily. Is the pragmatic solution really as simple and unproblematic as it seems?)

In fact, there is a very serious difficulty with the view just described, one that in my judgment extends to the whole pragmatic approach, albeit one that pragmatists have mostly ignored. The pragmatic view that we are considering holds that a belief is justified if adopting and acting on it leads to success in practice. But that the belief *genuinely* leads to such success is of course *itself* a claim about what happens in the external world and not by any means a simple one. Thus the claim that practical success has indeed been achieved is from the standpoint of traditional epistemology just one more claim in need of justification, and moreover one whose justification almost certainly requires the prior justification of simpler claims about the existence of various kinds of material objects and external situations and, at least in most cases, other people. Of course we believe in a commonsensical way that the actions we take in light of our beliefs are generally, though not of course invariably, successful, and this belief (like many other beliefs about the external world) *seems* to accord with our experience. But whether such beliefs about success are actually justified by the experience in question is just one facet of the whole problem of the external world, one that is in no obvious way any easier to deal with than the rest. In this way, whatever basis there may be for skepticism about the external world in general will apply at least as much to skepticism about the actual occurrence of the success to which the pragmatist appeals. Thus our pragmatist, far from answering skepticism, seems merely to have missed the whole point of the problem.

It is hard to see any effective response that a pragmatist can make to this criticism. One possibility would be to retreat to the view that a belief is justified if it *seems* to succeed in practice, but it is hard to see why this amended view should be thought plausible. The mere appearance of practical success, understood in the only way in which it can be unproblematically available to the pragmatist, does not seem in any obvious way to constitute a better reason for thinking that a belief is true than does just the appearance of truth itself. Thus at least this simple version of pragmatism appears to be an utterly dead end. (Whether this is true—as I suspect—for all versions of epistemological pragmatism, even though they may be much more complicated in various ways than the view just considered, is something that you will have to investigate for yourself.)

Rory's Rejection of Epistemology

The final antiskeptical view that I want to briefly consider is also the most radical of all—indeed I put it forth more to give you some idea of how radical the rejection of traditional epistemology can become than in the expectation that you will find it plausible. The view in question is in some ways a kind of combination of contextualism and pragmatism, though it goes well beyond either of those views in its antiepistemological stance (and is antiskeptical only in the sense that if epistemology itself is rejected, there is no room left for skeptical challenges to arise and be taken seriously). It is advanced by the American philosopher Richard Rorty, most clearly in his book *Philosophy and the Mirror of Nature*.[18]

Rorty's fundamental view is that epistemology, by which he has mainly in mind the traditional Cartesian approach that has been the central focus of this book, rests on a set of "assumptions" that are, as he likes to put it, "optional" and should be abandoned. There are three supposed assumptions of this sort that he seems to have most centrally in mind. The first two are those that are reflected in the Cartesian view of the foundation for epistemic justification: first, the "assumption" that immediate or "given" awareness of the contents of one's own states of mind exists in a way that could provide a basis for justification; and, second, the "assumption" that the mind is capable of apprehending self-evident *a priori* truths (though Rorty follows Quine in failing to distinguish the idea of *a priori* justification in general from the moderate empiricist account of such justification). In support of the claim that these "assumptions" are fundamentally untenable and should be rejected, Rorty appeals in part to arguments offered by the American epistemologist Wilfrid Sellars and by Quine. What he seems to have in mind is at least approximately the second of the two arguments against empirical foundationalism that were considered in chapter 9, together with the Quinean "circle of terms" argument against analyticity that was considered in chapter 11.[19] I have suggested in those discussions that neither of these arguments is in the end very compelling—though, as has been discussed extensively in this book, Rorty is right that both of these elements of the Cartesian foundation are essential to traditional epistemology.

None of this matters very much, however, for the third of the "assumptions" that Rorty identifies and proposes to reject is even more fundamental, so much so indeed that it is quite clear that if he were right in rejecting it, nothing would be left of epistemology (or indeed of science, history, and much else). It is nothing less than the assumption that the mind indeed represents independent reality in any way that could then give rise to the issue of whether or not the representations are true and then to the further issue of whether or not we have good reasons to think that they are true. According to Rorty, the whole idea of beliefs or other mental states depicting or describing reality is simply a mistake, as is the correspondence theory of what it is for such depictions or descriptions to be true.[20] And it is of course even more abundantly clear that epistemology cannot survive, indeed that epistemological issues cannot be even meaningfully raised, once this "assumption" is discarded.

But what, you should be asking, could possibly constitute a good reason for thinking that the very idea that beliefs represent things outside or independent of them is mistaken? And what on earth would an alternative to this view even look like? In fact, surprisingly enough, these questions can be answered together, for Rorty's presentation of his alternative view is also to a very large extent his argument.[21] The view in question is what he calls "epistemological behaviorism": the view, roughly, that what it is correct or justified to say (or think?) is *entirely* a function of social practices and social conventions, of what other people in your "linguistic community" allow you to say. This is a radically relativistic view: a claim or argument is justified if it is accepted without challenge in the relevant community; and there is nothing more to truth than relatively stable acceptance of this sort. But what is thus accepted will vary from society to society and from period to period, and there is simply no intelligible issue as to which society or period is correct in what it accepts—nor about what the claims thus accepted really say about the world. All that matters is "continuing the conversation" according to the (evolving) standards of the community.

It goes without saying that there is no room in this picture for any serious form of skepticism—or for any meaningful idea of knowledge or justification or truth or objectivity or rationality. You may well feel, however, that this is too great a price to pay for the avoidance of skepticism. And of course the issue of self-referential inconsistency (see the end of chapter 11) rears its head once more, for there is clearly no way for Rorty to claim meaningfully that his own view is true or justified or that there are good reasons of any other sort to accept it. Is there any reason why a view that is in this way self-defeating should be taken seriously? I can think of none, but once again you should decide this question for yourself.

Notes

1. Here you might find it helpful to revisit those earlier passages, using the index as a guide.

2. An issue in the vicinity that is sometimes raised is whether it is possible to have knowledge without knowing that you have knowledge, or whether, on the contrary, that

if you know, you must also know that you know (a claim sometimes referred to as "the KK thesis"). Explore this issue for yourself by (a) figuring out what conditions are required to know that you know according to the traditional conception and then (b) trying to figure out whether it is plausible to suppose that these conditions must be satisfied whenever the conditions for knowledge simpliciter are satisfied. Part (a) of this task will involve applying each of the three main conditions for knowledge—it is easier to ignore for this purpose the anti-Gettier condition—to each one of those very same conditions, since to know that you know, according to the traditional conception, requires knowing separately that each of the three conditions is satisfied: knowing that you believe, knowing that the belief is true, and knowing that the belief is justified. As you will discover, it is not very clear whether the KK thesis is correct or not, but the specific issues that this question turns on turn out to be rather different than you might initially suppose.

3. Skeptical views of this sort are sometimes formulated by denying that the beliefs in question constitute knowledge, where the underlying assumption being made, sometimes not very explicitly, is that knowledge itself requires conclusive justification.

4. Some views of the latter sort, for example those that challenge occult beliefs of various sorts, seem to be not only plausible but clearly correct. It is important not to lose sight of the point that a general refutation of any sort of skepticism, in addition to being obviously extremely difficult to accomplish, would clash as strongly with commonsense intuition as do most versions of skepticism.

5. In his book *The Analysis of Mind* (New York: Macmillan, 1921), pp. 159–60.

6. Actually, of course, the brain-in-a-vat hypothesis is not quite one where the believer has all the evidence we have even though all of his beliefs about the external world are false, since the existence of the brain and the vat itself are enough to make some very general beliefs about the external world true. But it comes close enough for present purposes.

7. E.g., in Roderick M. Chisholm, *Theory of Knowledge*, 3rd ed. (Englewood Cliffs, N.J.: Prentice Hall, 1989), pp. 6–7.

8. Think about this version of the problem for yourselves, looking back at the discussion of those requirements in chapter 3 for help. Though the right solution is certainly not obvious, my suggestion is that it will be more or less parallel to that offered in the text for the more specific version of the issue that is discussed next.

9. See the work cited in note 7 (which is only one of Chisholm's many discussions of the problem of the criterion).

10. Both reprinted in Moore, *Philosophical Papers* (London: Allen & Unwin, 1959). References in the text are to the pages of the reprint of this volume published by Collier Books (New York) in 1962.

11. Though Moore admits (*ibid.*, p. 148) not to be able to give a proof that he is not dreaming, his reason is that while he no doubt has "conclusive reasons" for asserting that he is awake and so not dreaming, he is unable to say explicitly what those reasons are. The idea seems to be that he has an implicit grasp of those reasons that suffices for justification, even though he is not at present able to formulate them explicitly. Think for yourself about whether this is a tenable and plausible position.

12. The originator of this sort of argument was probably the British philosopher Thomas Reid. See Reid, *Essays on the Intellectual Powers of Man*, ed. Baruch Brody (Cambridge, Mass.: MIT Press, 1969) (first published in 1785).

13. I count Descartes's own views as simply an early and relatively inadequate version of the general program of traditional Cartesian epistemology. The other main view not mentioned explicitly in the listing above is coherentism. As construed in the discussion in chapter 9, coherentism is simply a version of traditional epistemology that attempts rather quixotically to get by with only the *a priori* part of the Cartesian foundation and, not surprisingly, does not succeed. But it is worth noting that Quine's view is sometimes regarded as a version of coherentism and that a particularist view could also take a coherentist form, as indeed could some of the other views yet to be considered. I would suggest that this adaptability is a weakness rather than a strength of coherentism, suggesting that the basic conception of coherentism is too sketchy to provide much of an epistemological view by itself and so needs to be supplemented by one of these other views in order to amount to anything very definite. A further possibility that this suggests, one that I am also inclined to accept, is that the widespread but seemingly rather superficial appeal of coherentism results from the fact that it has so little real content of its own as to allow it to be adapted or co-opted in these very different ways: this would explain why there has been so much rather vague sympathy with coherentism but so few developed coherentist views.

14. See David Annis, "A Contextualist Theory of Epistemic Justification," *American Philosophical Quarterly*, vol. 15 (1978), pp. 213–19; and Michael Williams, *Unnatural Doubts* (Oxford: Blackwell, 1992).

15. In fact, it would be relatively easy for someone to hold both of the versions of contextualism together. But it is easier to discuss then separately, and I will leave to you the job of thinking about both what the combined view would look like and whether it would be any more defensible than the two versions taken separately.

16 The thesis of epistemic closure is more standardly formulated in terms of knowledge rather than justification; but for essentially the same reason given in the earlier discussion of varieties of skepticism, the real issue is justification.

17. One of the most extensive discussions of epistemic closure and how it might be rejected, though one that is formulated in relation to an externalist account of knowledge, is that of Robert Nozick in his book *Philosophical Explanations* (Cambridge, Mass.: Harvard University Press, 1981), chapter 3.

18. Princeton: Princeton University Press, 1979.

19. Though it is hard to be very sure about this because Rorty's accounts of the two arguments (*ibid.*, chapter 4) are both extremely sketchy and pretty far from what either Sellars or Quine explicitly says.

20. Indeed, Rorty sometimes seems to repudiate the whole idea that conscious mental states exist at all, preferring to focus on what a more traditional philosopher would regard as their linguistic manifestations.

21. He also describes this view as the "crucial premise" of Sellars's and Quine's arguments (*ibid.*, p. 170), but this is an *extremely* questionable claim.

Conclusion

We have reached the end of the book, and it is time to briefly take stock. Part one of the book was devoted to the Cartesian epistemological approach and to the various specific problems and issues that grow out of it. We saw there that the resulting internalist, foundationalist view is confronted by a number of very serious problems. Tentative solutions were suggested for many of these, but even the most optimistic Cartesian would have to admit that it will take much more work to develop these fully and show that they really succeed, if indeed this can be done at all.

Part two has been devoted to the presentation and assessment of a number of different proposed alternatives to the Cartesian view, all of them at least largely motivated by the conviction that the Cartesian view cannot in the end be successfully developed and defended, that it leads ultimately only to skepticism. Thus we have looked at the coherentist alternative to foundationalism, at the externalist alternative to internalism, at the idea of naturalized epistemology, at two different versions of contextualism, at a pragmatist account of justification, and finally at Rorty's complete repudiation of epistemology. The conclusion that I would draw from these various discussions is that none of the other views we have considered offers any very satisfactory epistemological alternative to traditional Cartesian epistemology, any way of avoiding the difficulties that the Cartesian view supposedly leads to that is not ultimately self-defeating or worse.

Even this picture, it must be acknowledged, is not really complete, even in outline. Recent epistemology is in a state of incredible ferment, and there are yet further views and positions and proposals that I have had no space to consider here (but that you or your instructor may want to look at). There is the idea of *virtue epistemology*, which offers the rough suggestion that epistemological issues might be better dealt with via a consideration of epistemic virtues such as open-mindedness, carefulness, intellectual courage, and the like, and perhaps also further epistemic goals such as understanding. There are also views and issues falling under the rubric of *social epistemology*, which focuses on the ways in which knowledge is created and transmitted via various sorts of social structures and on what it is for a society, as opposed to an individual, to possess knowledge. There are various positions and suggestions falling under the general rubric of *feminist epistemology*, though these are very multifarious and do not lend themselves to any very simple general characterization. There is *Bayesian epistemology*, which attempts to use results in probability theory centering around Bayes's Theorem to shed light on epistemological issues.

None of these views and positions is very well developed at the present time, which is one reason, in addition to sheer considerations of space, for excluding them from detailed consideration in this book. Nor is it at all clear that any of them can offer an alternative to the traditional Cartesian approach that is better than those we have considered, though there are certainly some who would make such a claim. My own view is that what is defensible in these alternative views will turn out to be fundamentally *complementary* rather than antagonistic to the Cartesian view, raising new issues that are of interest in their own right (just as was suggested above to be the case with externalism), but neither doing better with the fundamental Cartesian issues nor offering any good reason why those issues should be abandoned. But this is a question about which only time will tell.

The other tentative conclusion that I would like to offer for your consideration, one which am inclined to believe but which you, of course, may decide not to accept, is that traditional Cartesian epistemology, despite its admitted difficulties, is by no means the hopeless project that its critics, from Hume and Kant to Quine and Rorty, have portrayed it as being. My own view is that much of the reason why epistemology is not further advanced at this fairly late date stems from the somewhat puzzling tendency of so many philosophers to evade or bypass the central issues, rather than confronting them directly and attempting to deal with them on that basis. No doubt this long-standing trend, which has in fact been rather more pronounced in very recent times, is unlikely to disappear very quickly. But it may perhaps be hoped that a new millennium will bring with it a less evasive approach to epistemological issues—and perhaps some readers of this book will play a part in that.

~

Bibliography

Introductory note: The epistemological literature, especially the recent epistemological literature, is vast, and any attempt at listing even the most important items would be unmanageably long and overwhelming to the introductory student. What follows is instead intended merely to suggest some of the works that students who have worked through the present book may find especially helpful as starting points for further reading in the field. (The endnotes in the rest of the book may also be helpful in relation to particular topics.) I have restricted myself here to books (in one case to a long section of a book), including some that are anthologies of articles or excerpts, and have not tried to include the literature pertaining to Descartes and other historical figures. Starting with these items and following up the references that they contain should enable any reasonably persistent student to effectively find his or her way into the larger literature. (Those items that contain especially valuable bibliographies are flagged with an asterisk.) The items listed are of widely varying degrees of difficulty, but none should be inaccessible to students who have mastered the present book. Most or all of them should be available in any reasonable collegiate library. The brief annotations include a specification of the chapter or chapters of the present book to which the item in question is especially relevant.

Alston, William P. *Epistemic Justification.* Ithaca, N.Y.: Cornell University Press, 1989. A collection of papers by a leading contemporary epistemologist. Leans toward foundationalism and externalism while also making an effort to accommodate internalist intuitions. Mainly relevant to chapters 9 and 10.

Alston, William P. *The Reliability of Sense Perception.* Ithaca, N.Y.: Cornell University Press, 1993. Argues that no noncircular argument that perceptual beliefs are likely to be true is possible. Mainly relevant to chapter 7.

Armstrong, D. M. *Perception and the Physical World*. London: Routledge & Kegan Paul, 1961. A defense of direct realism, combined with critiques of representationalism and phenomenalism. Mainly relevant to chapter 7.

*Audi, Robert. *Epistemology: A Contemporary Introduction to the Theory of Knowledge*. London: Routledge, 1998. Discusses most of the topics considered in the present book and a number of others as well. Audi's own views lean in the direction of foundationalism and rationalism. Relevant to every chapter, but especially to chapters 3, 5, 6, 7, 8, 9, and 12.

Audi, Robert. *The Structure of Justification*. Cambridge: Cambridge University Press, 1993. A collection of closely related articles offering a subtle version of internalist foundationalism that attempts to accommodate the insights of both coherentism and reliabilism. Mainly relevant to chapters 5, 9, 10, and 11.

Austin, J. L. *Sense and Sensibilia*. Oxford: Oxford University Press, 1962. A famous (or infamous?) attempt to "dissolve" the problems discussed in chapters 6 and 7 by appeal to the doctrines of "ordinary language philosophy." Relevant to those chapters.

Ayer, A. J. *Language, Truth and Logic*. 2nd ed. London: Gollancz, 1946. One of the major statements of logical positivism, containing discussions of *a priori* justification, perception, and other minds. Mainly relevant to chapters 5, 6, 7, and 8.

BonJour, Laurence. *In Defense of Pure Reason*. Cambridge: Cambridge University Press, 1997. A defense of a rationalist theory of *a priori* justification, including an *a priori* justification of induction. Mainly relevant to chapters 4 and 5.

BonJour, Laurence. *The Structure of Empirical Knowledge*. Cambridge, Mass.: Harvard University Press, 1985. A defense of a coherence theory of empirical justification. Mainly relevant to chapter 9.

Butchvarov, Panayot. *The Concept of Knowledge*. Evanston, Ill.: Northwestern University Press, 1970. A subtle and difficult defense of foundationalism (in relation especially to perceptual knowledge) and of rationalism. Mainly relevant to chapters 3, 5, 6, 7, and 9.

Coady, C. A. J. *Testimony*. Oxford: Oxford University Press, 1992. A study of the issue of testimony. Relevant to chapter 8.

Chisholm, Roderick M. *The Foundations of Knowing*. Minneapolis: University of Minnesota Press, 1982. A collection of papers by perhaps the most respected recent epistemologist. See especially the long paper entitled "Theory of Knowledge in America." Mainly relevant to chapters 5, 6, 7, 9, and 12.

Chisholm, Roderick M. *Theory of Knowledge*. Englewood Cliffs, N.J.: Prentice Hall, 1st ed., 1966; 2nd ed., 1977; 3rd ed., 1989. The successive editions present Chisholm's evolving views, including defenses of versions foundationalism and rationalism. Difficult, especially because of Chisholm's tendency to formulate his positions via a series of sometimes fairly cryptic definitions, but rewarding to careful study. Mainly relevant to chapters 3, 5, 6, 7, 9, and 12.

Chisholm, Roderick M., and Robert Swartz, eds. *Empirical Knowledge*. Englewood Cliffs, N.J.: Prentice Hall, 1973. A valuable though somewhat dated collection of twentieth-century papers and excerpts. Mainly relevant to chapters 6, 8, and 9.

Dancy, Jonathan, ed. *Perceptual Knowledge*. Oxford: Oxford University Press, 1988. A good anthology of recent work on perception and related topics. Relevant to chapters 6, 7, 9, and 10.

*Dancy, Jonathan, and Ernest Sosa. *A Companion to Epistemology*. Oxford: Blackwell, 1992. An encyclopedia of epistemology, containing short articles (with bibliographies) explaining and discussing a wide variety of epistemological topics, including brief discussions of the views of many important epistemologists, both historical and contemporary. Relevant to every chapter.

Dretske, Fred I. *Knowledge and the Flow of Information*. Cambridge, Mass.: MIT Press, 1981. A reliabilist view relying heavily on information theory. Relevant to chapters 3, 7, and 10.

Fales, Evan. *A Defense of the Given*. Lanham, Md.: Rowman & Littlefield, 1996. A defense of foundationalism, with special reference to sense-perception. Mainly relevant to chapters 6 and 9.

Goldman, Alvin. *Epistemology and Cognition*. Cambridge, Mass.: Harvard University Press, 1986. The most complete presentation and defense of Goldman's reliabilist view, combined with an extensive discussion of related material from cognitive psychology. Mainly relevant to chapter 10, though there are parts that are relevant to most of the other chapters.

*Greco, John, and Ernest Sosa, eds. *The Blackwell Guide to Epistemology*. Oxford: Blackwell, 1999. A collection of essays by major epistemologists, each of which expounds and develops one major epistemological topic. Relevant to chapters 3, 5, 6, 7, 9, 10, 11, and 12. Also contains essays on virtue epistemology, social epistemology, and feminist epistemology.

Haack, Susan. *Evidence and Inquiry*. Oxford: Blackwell, 1993. Critiques of coherentist and foundationalist views, together with a presentation of an alleged compromise between the two, "foundherentism." Also critiques of reliabilist and naturalist views and of Rorty. Mainly relevant to chapters 9, 10, 11, and 12.

Jackson, Frank. *Perception*. Cambridge: Cambridge University Press, 1977. A comprehensive exposition and defense of the sense-datum theory. Mainly relevant to chapters 7 and 8.

Kirkham, Richard L. *Theories of Truth*. Cambridge, Mass.: MIT Press, 1992. A good discussion of the various theories of truth. Mainly relevant to chapter 3.

*Kornblith, Hilary, ed. *Epistemology: Internalism and Externalism*. Oxford: Blackwell, 2001. A good collection of recent articles on the internalism-externalism issue. Mainly relevant to chapter 10.

*Kornblith, Hilary, ed. *Naturalizing Epistemology*. Cambridge, Mass.: MIT Press, 1985; 2nd ed., 1994. A collection of articles and excerpts defending the idea of naturalized epistemology. Mainly relevant to chapter 11.

Lehrer, Keith. *Theory of Knowledge*. Boulder, Colo.: Ridgeview, 1990. A defense of a version of coherentism, together with a critique of foundationalist and externalist views. Mainly relevant to chapters 3, 9, 10, 11, and 12.

*Levensky, Mark, ed. *Human Factual Knowledge*. Englewood Cliffs, N.J.: Prentice Hall, 1971. Contains sets of contrasting articles on memory, other minds, and perception. Relevant to chapters 7 and 8.

Lewis, C. I. *An Analysis of Knowledge and Valuation*. La Salle, Ill.: Open Court, 1946. A very detailed development of an internalist foundationalist view that includes a version of phenomenalism and a defense of moderate empiricism with regard to the *a priori*. Also includes a discussion of memory and an account of valuational knowledge. Mainly relevant to chapters 5, 6, 7, 8, and 9.

Moser, Paul K. *Knowledge and Evidence*. Cambridge: Cambridge University Press, 1989. A defense of foundationalism, especially with regard to perceptual knowledge, combined with an explanatory account of the inference to the external world and critiques of coherentist and externalist views. Mainly relevant to chapters 6, 7, 9, and 10.

*Moser, Paul K, ed. *A Priori Knowledge*. Oxford: Oxford University Press, 1987. A good collection of articles and excerpts pertaining to *a priori* justification and knowledge. Relevant to chapter 5.

Nozick, Robert. *Philosophical Explanations*. Cambridge, Mass.: Harvard University Press, 1981, chapter 3. A defense of an externalist view that differs from reliabilism. Also includes an argument against epistemic closure. Mainly relevant to chapters 3, 10, and 12.

Plantinga, Alvin. *Warrant: The Current Debate*. Oxford: Oxford University Press, 1993. An often incisive critique of many recent epistemological positions, including foundationalism, coherentism, and reliabilism. Mainly relevant to chapters 3, 9, and 10.

Plantinga, Alvin. *Warrant and Proper Function*. Oxford: Oxford University Press, 1993. An exposition and defense of Plantinga's own nonreliabilist version of externalism, together with applications to many specific epistemological problems. The central idea is that justified beliefs are those that result from "properly functioning" cognitive faculties. Relevant to chapters 4, 5, 7, 8, 10, and 11.

Price, H. H. *Perception*. 2nd ed. London: Methuen, 1950. Perhaps the most extensive study ever of the fine details of sensory experience and their relevance to beliefs about the material world, though Price's own attempt to split the difference between phenomenalism and representationalism is very idiosyncratic. Relevant to chapters 6 and 7.

Quine, W. V. *Word and Object*. Cambridge, Mass.: MIT Press, 1960. The most comprehensive statement of Quine's philosophical views, though the epistemological elements are often hard to discern clearly. Mainly relevant to chapters 5 and 11.

Robinson, Howard. *Perception*. London: Routledge, 1994. A defense of the sense-datum theory, together with a brief and somewhat tentative defense of phenomenalism. Mainly relevant to chapters 6 and 7.

*Roth, Michael D., and Leon Galis, eds. *Knowing: Essays in the Analysis of Knowledge*. New York: Random House, 1970. A collection of articles and excerpts centering around the Gettier problem (including Gettier's original paper). Relevant to chapter 3.

Russell, Bertrand. *The Problems of Philosophy*. Oxford: Oxford University Press, 1912. Russell's most accessible epistemological work and still one of the best introductions to the subject. Mainly relevant to chapters 3, 4, 5, 6, and 7.

Salmon, Wesley. *The Foundations of Scientific Inference*. Pittsburgh, Pa.: Pittsburgh University Press, 1967. A study of the various responses to the problem of induction and other related topics. Relevant to chapter 4.

Shope, Robert. *The Analysis of Knowing*. Princeton, N.J.: Princeton University Press, 1983. An exhaustive treatment of the concept of knowledge, focused mainly on the enormous variety of solutions that have been offered to the Gettier problem. Relevant to chapter 3.

Skyrms, Brian. *Choice and Chance*. 3rd ed. Belmont, Calif.: Wadsworth, 1986. A good introduction to induction and probability theory (though the possibility of an *a priori* defense of induction is not considered). Relevant to chapter 4.

*Sleigh, Robert. *Necessary Truth*. Englewood Cliffs, N.J.: Prentice Hall, 1972. Another good collection of articles and excerpts pertaining to *a priori* justification and knowledge. Relevant to chapter 5.

*Sumner, L. Wayne, and John Wood, eds. *Necessary Truth*. New York: Random House, 1969. Yet another good collection of articles and excerpts pertaining to *a priori* justification and knowledge. Relevant to chapter 5.

*Swartz, Robert J. *Perceiving, Sensing, and Knowing*. New York: Doubleday, 1965. An extensive collection of articles and excerpts on perception and related issues from the first two-thirds of the twentieth century. Now a bit dated, but still quite valuable. Relevant to chapters 6 and 7.

Williams, Michael. *Unnatural Doubts*. Princeton, N.J.: Princeton University Press, 1991. A defense of a contextualist approach to knowledge and skepticism, with criticisms of opposing views. Mainly relevant to chapters 9 and 12.

Index

~

About the Author

Laurence BonJour is professor of philosophy at the University of Washington.